"Crazy" Therapies

"Crazy" Therapies

What Are They?
Do They Work?

Margaret Thaler Singer
and
Janja Lalich

Cartoons by Jim Coughenour

Jossey-Bass Publishers
San Francisco

Substantial discounts on bulk quantities of Jossey-Bass books are available to corporations, professional associations, and other organizations. For details and discount information, contact the special sales department at Jossey-Bass Inc., Publishers (415) 433–1740; Fax (800) 605–2665.

For sales outside the United States, please contact your local Simon & Schuster International Office.

 Manufactured in the United States of America on Lyons Falls Pathfinder Tradebook. This paper is acid-free and 100 percent totally chlorine-free.

Library of Congress Cataloging-in-Publication Data

Singer, Margaret Thaler.
    "Crazy" therapies : what are they?, do they work? / Margaret
Thaler Singer, Janja Lalich. — 1st ed.
      p.   cm.
    Includes bibliographical references and index.
    ISBN 0-7879-0278-0 (alk. paper)
    1. Psychotherapy—Popular works.   2. Psychotherapy patients—Abuse
of. 3. Psychiatric errors. 4. Consumer education. I. Lalich,
Janja. II. Title.
RC480.515.S56   1996
616.89′14—dc20
                   96-16107
                   CIP

HB Printing 10 9 8 7 6 5 4 3 2 1   FIRST EDITION

Contents

To my parents, Margaret McDonough Thaler and Raymond Willard Thaler
To my husband, Jay
To my children, Sam and Martha
To my grandchildren, James and Nicholas
—Margaret Thaler Singer

To my mother, and to my Aunt Darlene,
both of whom always believed in me
—Janja Lalich

We also dedicate this book to all those who suffered a crazy therapy, and
especially to those who shared their experiences in the hope that others might not
fall prey to a similar fate.

Acknowledgments

Many thanks to the numerous friends and colleagues who helped us gather material and locate sources, especially R. Christopher Barden, J.D., Ph.D.; Priscilla Coates; Patricia Crossman, M.A.; Ford Greene, Esq.; Alan Jacobs; Jesse Miller, Ph.D.; Bernard Rimland, Ph.D.; Sidney L. Willens, Esq.; John D. Winer, Esq.; and Russell Worral, O.D.

Our enduring gratitude goes to various reference librarians at the University of California, Berkeley; the Oakland Public Library; the Alameda Library; and the Graduate Theological Union in Berkeley for their patience, perseverance, and helpfulness.

We appreciate the encouraging words and kind but necessary "fixings" of our editor extraordinaire, Alan Rinzler. His contribution to this book has been invaluable. And we heartily thank all the staff at our publisher, Jossey-Bass, who've been among our greatest fans, as well as a steadfast source of support and good cheer.

Most of all, we send barrels of thanks to Janja's partner, Kim, for all those sensational home-cooked meals, which helped get us through these many months of research and writing.

Margaret warmly thanks her husband, Jay; son, Sam; daughter-in-law, Marian; grandchildren, James and Nicholas; daughter, Martha; and son-in-law, Richard—a cheerful and encouraging group whom she loves dearly. Margaret also wants to acknowledge that her entire career was made exciting and wonderful by her teachers and colleagues, too many to name here but cherished by her. Working with Janja on this and an earlier book has been a great experience and is warmly appreciated.

Margaret extends her gratitude to the thousands of people she has met as a therapist, interviewer, and researcher during the fifty years she has been a psychologist. By sharing their lives in very special ways, those individuals allowed her to see how good therapy helps people and how some therapy can go awry. Learning about the experiences of so many was a great source of inspiration for this book.

Janja would like to acknowledge the following people for being there for her when life's little (and sometimes big) turmoils and traumas threatened to get in the way of working on this book: Darlene Frank, Pam Guthrie, Marny Hall, Felicia Phillips, Elizabeth Swenson, and Polly Thomas—thank you forever. Janja also thanks her two former therapists, Shelly Rosen and Betty Kalis, for being so down-to-earth and helpful in the past; and she extends a giant thank you to colleague, coauthor, and dear friend, Margaret, who so generously shares her knowledge and makes writing books together such a pleasure. Most especially, Janja thanks Kim for surviving with her through yet another book.

July 1996
Margaret Thaler Singer
Berkeley, California

Janja Lalich
Alameda, California

Introduction

This book was written to help consumers become aware of the vast array of psychotherapies being offered by a variety of practitioners in the mental health marketplace today. The therapies range from widely accepted, scientifically based treatments to traditional but less scientifically researched methods to those that typically are the creation of an individual and often have even less grounding in scientific validation and professional acceptance. Our aim is to explore primarily those that fall within the latter category.

The therapies described in this book have been and continue to be controversial; we are by no means the only ones who question and comment on these theories and techniques. We have selected the term *crazy* to describe some of these therapies, using the word as it is used in the vernacular, to refer to something as controversial, nonstandard, or "far out," and sometimes to depict fads or current enthusiasms. Some of these therapies will fade from the scene; others might be modified to meet the standards of the professional community; yet others might be driven out by consumer complaints and legal actions.

Our observations and investigations have led us to the conclusion that consumers need to become far more inquisitive and far more aware of their rights when selecting a form of psychotherapy or psychological treatment. You have the right to ask, Is this therapy accepted in the professional community? Is it based on science and on rational thinking, or on the conjecture and proclamations of the innovator? When dealing with innovative therapies, consumers should be informed by the practitioners that the procedure is still not accepted in the scientific community, or that it is surrounded by controversy, with proponents and critics clashing about the issues involved. In the final chapter of this book, we provide readers with guidelines and suggestions for evaluating a therapy or a therapist.

We have seen three types of results from these crazy therapies, which fall on a continuum of helpful to harmful, including sometimes a combination thereof. The first outcome is the placebo effect. Here, consumers think they're being helped. They might feel better even though there is no scientific reason or established clinical practice to support the apparent positive results. Consequently, individual clients may experience varied results from the same procedure, with some believing they've been greatly helped and others feeling no gain whatsoever.

The second outcome is loss. Consumers may end up wasting a lot of time and money pursuing dead ends and false leads. In some of these cases, clients may have fallen prey to unscrupulous, exploitative therapists; in others, they may simply have gone along with the enthusiasm of ill-trained, inexperienced, or faddish practitioners who themselves are caught up in believing in the curative abilities of a particular theory or treatment.

The third outcome is harm. Some consumers risk being harmed—psychologically or otherwise—by some of the therapies currently in vogue. Each year countless individuals throughout the land turn over their innermost thoughts and feelings to a trusted counselor, only to be exploited and abused by some of them. When we go to a mental health professional or someone claiming to have special knowledge, we don't suspect the worst; rather, we hope for the best. We go with open hearts and open minds. But here are some of the outcomes we've seen:

- "Joseph" went to a therapist for help with his anxiety
  and sleep problems. Dr. "P." led Joseph to believe that
  his problems were caused by his having been abducted
  by extraterrestrials. Joseph became convinced of this
  past occurrence and began to tell his "abduction" story
  to all who would listen, including the part about having skinny tubes inserted into his rectum while on the
  alien spaceship. Joseph's friends and coworkers tired of
  his endless tales, and Joseph eventually lost his job for
  inattention to his duties and lack of concentration.

- "Jennifer" was referred by her physician to Ms. "W.," a
  hypnotherapist, for treatment of stress-related
  headaches. Using extensive trance sessions, Ms. W. led
  Jennifer to believe that nearly four hundred human,
  animal, and other-world entities had invaded her body
  and were living and squabbling inside her. Prolonged
  treatment led to Jennifer's mental deterioration and
  multiple suicide attempts.

- "Jake" saw an ad for a therapist-led warrior weekend
  that boasted, "Find a new and healthy self. Never be
  fearful or physically anxious again." At the weekend,
  Jake learned that he would have to do combat with
  martial-arts black-belt experts. During the evening
  combat session, Jake was permanently injured; he is
  now facing emotional distress, prolonged physical therapy, and job loss.

- Mr. and Mrs. "Johnson" went to therapy for typical
  marital issues. Dr. "T." was a believer in aggressive
  methods of expressing feelings. Handing the couple
  some plastic bats, Dr. T. instructed them to fight it out
  as hard as they could. When the couple responded

rather limply, Dr. T. sat on the sidelines yelling at them, insulting them, and urging them to be more forceful. The couple ended up bashing not only each other but a great deal of furniture in Dr. T.'s office, as well as taking a few swings at him. Afterwards, Mr. and Mrs. Johnson felt silly and never went back, but the following week they received a bill for $5,000 in damages to Dr. T. and his office.

- "Carol," a young professional, was seduced by her licensed therapist, Dr. "K.," who violated professional ethical codes and state law. Even before the sexual liaison began, Dr. K. urged Carol to divorce her husband and wait for Dr. K. As a result of this affair, Carol lost custody of her children. Shortly thereafter, Dr. K. abandoned her. It was later learned that Dr. K. would frequently convince his female patients to enter into a relationship with him.

- "Shari" was told by a friend that the best thing that ever happened to her was the counseling she received at the "Rocky Mountain Road New Birth Center." Feeling troubled by her relationship with her teenage children, Shari called the center for an intake appointment. At the first session, Ms. "R." told Shari that her problems with her children would be solved by Shari reexperiencing her own birth trauma and then growing up again the right way (according to Ms. R.'s views). This would happen at a weekend session, Ms. R. informed Shari. In order to prepare, Shari was instructed to strip down to her underpants, sit on Ms. R.'s lap, and suckle her (rather suddenly exposed) breast.

Things happen in this world that are often too outrageous to think of as real. Sometimes they happen at the hand of a so-called healing professional. Through our work we have heard example upon example, like those just mentioned and worse, of maltreatment and exploitation by psychotherapists and counselors of all stripes. One of us, Margaret, has been a clinical psychologist for fifty years; the other, Janja, is an educator and consultant in the field of psychological influence and abuse. So you might conclude that we've encountered the bizarre and the arcane, the violent and the greedy, and we have. You might also think that we've probably gotten used to it, become hardened and cynical, but we never have. Instead, we hope to use what we've heard to educate psychotherapy consumers by exposing some of the misdeeds and illogical theories and alerting consumers to the controversial nature of certain therapies.

Abuse exists in many parts of our society, some of it perhaps much worse than what you will read about here. Yet we feel that these injustices, these instances of devastating emotional harm and financial loss, this psychological manipulation and in some cases physical and sexual abuse must no longer go unheeded. We seek to expose the questionable reasoning and behaviors that hide behind a mask of professionalism because we believe that, for the most part, the general public, the professional community, and the media are unaware of (and in some cases, we shudder to think, turning a blind eye to) the kinds of abuses that are rampant today in the fields of psychotherapy and personal transformation. We add "personal transformation" because over time we have seen that many so-called therapies actually have less and less to do with legitimate forms of psychotherapy as they have more and more in common with unscientific pop psychology theories and New Age techniques.

A key to understanding what goes wrong in these situations is to remember that the practice of psychotherapy has been around for hundreds if not thousands of years. There are known methods of treatment that work, that bring positive results. For example, it is generally accepted that cognitive therapy really works with depressed people, and that certain medications help those who suffer from anxiety attacks. Scientifically validated approaches to therapy are known and used on a regular basis.

Equally, rational and long-used counseling techniques may not all have been scientifically validated, but for decades they have met the requirements for the standard of practice in the general psychotherapy field. The broadly trained psychotherapist should have a sufficiently large armamentarium of techniques to use in helping clients without having to resort to idiosyncratic, untested, or unproven ideas that might prove harmful, diversionary, or useless.

There are many recent studies, most inspired by the advent of managed care, that have shown without a doubt that psychotherapy works—that is, that specific therapies work in specific situations. These conclusions have been drawn from studies based on scientific data and outcome measures. Over the years, reliable statistical techniques, objective diagnostic criteria, and structured, standardized interviews have been devised in order to allow us to research and evaluate the effectiveness of psychotherapy.

Yet, what we invariably see with some of the crazy therapies is a form of experimentation in the types of treatments prescribed and the techniques used. Certain practitioners are in effect toying with untested procedures. These therapists are not getting "informed consent" from their clients because they are not advising their clients that there are alternate approaches and methods of treatment, they are not advising their clients of the risks and side effects, and they are not informing their clients that they are being asked to participate in unproven experimental procedures. Aside from the unethical nature of such professional interactions, there is a degree of deception that is unacceptable. Some of it may be attributed to incompetence or lack of proper training. Some of it may be rooted in greed or ego gratification. And some of it may be based in evil intent. Whatever the source, there is no justification for the suffering and loss to the thousands who have been taken in by certain crazy therapies and their proponents.

We feel an urgent need to warn you, to warn everyone, about the possible risks lying behind that ad promising personal power or that business card handed to you at a social gathering, or the potential hazards of putting too much trust in a slick practitioner who lures you with a vision of the "ideal you."

Whether misguided or downright evil, some of the crazy therapies are difficult to discern if you don't have your antennae up. Keep in mind: just as there are no free lunches, there are no instant cures. And if something about your interaction with a therapist or counselor doesn't seem right, trust your gut instincts and go on out the door.

A Word About Terminology

In this book, the terms *patient* and *client* are used interchangeably to identify those seeking therapy, counseling, or some kind of advice or help. In general, "patient" is more commonly used when the person is seeing a professional with an M.D. or a Ph.D. degree, whereas "client" became more appropriate when people began seeing practitioners with master's degrees and briefer training.

For simplicity, the label *therapist* is used to identify those who are providing a service to someone seeking psychological treatment, although in many cases the practitioner may not be using that label or may not qualify for it. Nevertheless, for our purposes here, *therapist* is used in the broad sense of the definition—that is, a person providing or assisting in a cure or relief for something that ails a client. For variety, *counselor, healer, provider,* and *practitioner* are also used.

Names and details in all case examples have been altered to respect the privacy of the individuals involved. These cases have been drawn from coauthor Singer's fifty years of working as a clinical psychologist and of being someone to whom former clients of crazy therapies have come seeking clarity on that experience or requiring an expert witness for legal action they might be pursuing against their former therapist.

———————

Most therapists are admirable. These men and women are mature adults who have come to understand human complexity and human interactions, and they talk about them in ordinary terms. Research has shown that therapy can and does work, when based on sound methods and a trusting relationship between the therapist and client. Effective therapy that brings positive results generally does not require the application of some startling theory or technique.

Good therapists present a stable self and relate to clients professionally and maturely. They do not direct or order their clients and patients to obey. They help their clients to recognize and try out more useful, reasonable strategies for dealing with life. They have avoided joining in on trendy concepts and have remained solid, sensible humans while many around them have adopted some of the most bizarre schemes imaginable.

Many clients have been mistreated, harmed, disappointed, exploited, or worse by so-called therapists. Bad therapy has been carried out by credentialed persons as well as by quacks, charlatans, and self-appointed purveyors of various cures. Over the years, a number of therapeutic practices and training programs have evolved and in some cases disappeared. Fads, foibles, and odd therapies have come and gone. Yet today, more crazy therapies than ever are being added to the smorgasbord of self-improvement and self-help.

Because not all therapists receive thoroughgoing training and consistent supervision; because of a shortage of professional critiques and a disregard for criticism and standards of practice; and because of the growth of psychotherapy as a relatively unregulated industry, we find ourselves in a new era of therapeutic offerings. "Buyer, beware" has never been a more appropriate attitude for the person searching for a therapist or a method of relief.

By exploring in this book some of the explicit and implicit assumptions underlying a number of therapies, we hope to encourage a thoughtful reassessment of certain practices and trends. We hope to bring a touch of rationality to an area that has become polarized and impassioned.

We hope that reading this book will help the future client be a more informed consumer, one who is able to distinguish between the fanciful and the truly therapeutic.

STUDENT: What is science?

PROFESSOR: Looking for a black cat in a dark room.

STUDENT: What is philosophy?

PROFESSOR: Looking for a black cat in a dark room and there is no cat.

STUDENT: What is psychotherapy?

PROFESSOR: Looking for a black cat in a dark room where there is no cat and finding it.

"Crazy" Therapies

What's Wrong with This Picture?

"I was referred to a therapist by my regular doctor because I had some pains in my chest, neck, and head that he felt were related to stress," said "Glenda" quietly. "I was thirty-eight years old and had just moved to a new town, started a new job, and my kids were all crying because they missed their friends. My husband travels a lot on his job and he wasn't around to help the kids or me very much.

"The therapist, Dr. 'M.,' never asked me about my personal history or anything. She just said I needed hypnosis to uncover memories from my muscles of what had happened to me in the past. She said that memories are buried in our muscles as well as in our minds and that hypnosis would uncover those memories.

"Dr. M. hypnotized me the very first day. She had a lay-back chair that flattened out. She put a blanket over me and turned the lights down and told me how to relax, close my eyes, and give her what she called 'ideomotor signals' with my right index finger for yes and my left index finger for no. I must have been a good subject, for when I awoke at the end of the session, Dr. M. told me that she had discovered that I was a multiple personality and that I was suffering in my muscles and joints from the children within me fighting and trying to take over. Before long, the sessions sometimes lasted three or four hours and the bills ran up fast.

"The way she got me to meet more of these children within me, whom she called 'alters,' was by telling me I would go into trance and soon see a movie with me in it. Whoever was in the main role was me, and I was to pick a name for that alter. She fussed at me if I repeated a story or returned to an earlier story. Each session had to be the discovery of a new child within me, or some new episode in the life of one of the alters I'd already met. She gave me a book to read about body memories. She explained over and over that my pains were due to the inner children fighting and quarreling so much that I was stressed out. Eventually she and I found an older boy within me; we put him in charge of the younger children.

"My husband, children, and friends complained that I was 'losing it.' They tell me now, after I had to be hospitalized for a psychotic breakdown, that I would sit and talk like a little child and refuse to respond to them as myself. They said I sat and rocked back and forth, sobbing like a little kid.

"I remember coming home from the hypnotherapy sessions and telling crazy stories about things that never happened but had been in the 'movies' the therapist had me make up. After sessions, I came back and accused a number of relatives of wild, crazy things. Like I said my favorite old aunt was in a Satanic cult and cooked babies in a pot in the garage. I said that my mother beat me and locked me in the basement for days on end. I said that I opened the hall closet one day at my mother-in-law's house and found a woman's body standing upright and it fell out.

"I am in therapy now with a really sane therapist who is helping me learn what really happened and why I lost control. Much of what happened my husband and friends will have to tell you because I don't recall lots of time prior to going to the hospital. But getting rid of all the crazy memories that I made up or saw in the so-called movies during hypnosis still scares me. Sometimes I suddenly think how ever did I get to believing that stuff and I fear that I can't trust myself yet, even though I have been away from that hypnotherapist and her zany ideas for over a year now."

"Glenda," who thought she was going to a therapist to get some help with her everyday problems with stress, is no different from the thousands of people who turn to therapy each year. Society has in fact relied on some form of talk therapy for decades, if not centuries; it's a need that can be traced back to the oracle at Delphi. And it appears that this very human urge has only increased over time— at least in the United States.

Since World War II, therapy has been commonly accepted as a way to solve problems and change bad habits, causing our country to be sometimes labeled "the psychological society." For nowhere else in the world are psychology, self-improvement philosophies, and self-betterment programs so popular and widespread. No longer does a person need to have some pathology (the medical term for something abnormal going on) to seek psychological help or counseling. He merely has to enter treatment with one or another of the thousands of practitioners.

Millions of people need *good* therapy, and the majority of therapists are honest and conscientious. According to one researcher, "there are more than 250,000 accredited therapists in the United States and one in three Americans has visited one." Who knows how many there are who are not accredited or licensed, not to mention those who offer what might be called therapy of one sort or another but that in fact has little to do with what one normally thinks of as a "helping profession."

A book published in 1980 described more than 250 different kinds of therapies being practiced at that time. The number has possibly doubled since then. But adequate monitoring of the profession in general and healthy critical comment on particular practices have been lacking. Because of this, we've witnessed a proliferation of dubious theories and techniques, often reinforced by media exploitation of some of these "cures." Many new therapies are based on less-than-scientific research, sometimes after observation of the technique applied to only one or two patients.

Consequently, a number of credentialed therapists, paraprofessionals, and nonprofessionals alike have adopted some rather bizarre and silly notions. An abundance of exotic techniques are now widely used across the spectrum of so-called therapies. Yet many practitioners have no idea how much of their therapy—the theory and the techniques—is founded on myths or unproved notions.

The Scene Today

The general public today is confronted with a panorama of theories and practices said to address a variety of symptoms and disorders, ranging from the supposedly scientific to the ludicrous and unchallenged. An array of therapists, counselors, and healers promote the following techniques, among others:

Flower essence therapy

Chakra and aura readings

Sexual touching

Soul work

Humor therapy

Guided visualization

Karmic astrology

Alien-abduction therapy

White goddess healings

Crystal healings

Dreamwork

Mythmaking

Trance treks

Guided meditation

Tarot readings

Aromatherapy

Chemical inductions
(use of LSD, sodium amytal,
and other drugs)

Hypnotherapy

Angel therapy

Color therapy

Yoga

Past-life regression

Alchemical hypnotherapy

Channeling

Herbal brews

Drumming

Intuitive readings

Breathwork

Vibrational bodywork

Video work

Rapid eye technology

Overleaf charts

Ritual ceremonies

Shamanic counseling

Rebirthing	Facilitated communication
Intuition development	Hot tubbing
Fighting	Floating
Tours to sacred sites	Depossession

These techniques—for which a consumer can pay anywhere from less than one hundred to several thousand dollars—are purported to bring about results such as the following:

Inner-child healing	Spirit releasement
Clear frequencies	Disharmonious energies release
Revelatory past-life journeys	Inner-child bonding
Smooth life transitions	Spiritual healing
Parents' programming release	Inner purpose revealed
Alignment of fluid intelligence systems	Becoming a galactic human being
Reclaiming your missing self	Deep, transformative healing
The body's energies rebalanced	Sexual karma revealed
Insightful shamanic journeys	Lifelong happiness
Personal empowerment	Transforming dragons
Pain control	Soul retrieval
Planetary healing	Past-life integration
Soul integration	Knowing essence twins

These lists reveal the spectrum of offerings available today. How does a person evaluate whether something is legitimate or a waste of time, possibly beneficial or potentially harmful?

This book will survey some of the more popular and wild-eyed concepts and procedures that have taken hold in our society, and will examine and critique them as *healing* techniques. We intend to shed light on the potential dangers of some of these methods, including the increasing occurrence of iatrogenic damage, that is, damage to the client induced by the therapist.

We also hope to alert consumers to the peril of falling prey to those practitioners who push a technique that has little or no benefit to clients but keeps them coming back for more treatment.

Women in particular have been victimized by these therapies: rather than feeling empowered and more autonomous, some women have become dependent and needy, and some have been exploited and abused, psychologically and/or sexually, by self-serving therapists.

The treatment suggested for clients caught in a crazy therapy may include sitting in hot tubs with their therapist, moving in with the therapist's other clients, being hospitalized unnecessarily, or being subjected to prolonged trance-inducing techniques that interfere with their capacity to function.

Some of these crazy therapies are carried out in one-on-one meetings with a therapist, some take place in therapist-led group meetings with other patients who are supposedly suffering from the same problem, and some combine the two approaches. A mishmash of procedures and experiences are advertised by all levels of practitioners who imply or overtly state that they will provide mental, emotional, and social benefits equal to or better than traditional mental health approaches. Those who offer these therapeutic services range from well-trained, ethical persons with proper degrees and licenses to people with little or no formal training.

But watch out! The mere fact that some practitioners have degrees or a wall plastered with various fancy-looking credentials is no guarantee that their work will be ethical and competent. Therapists with degrees have been known to provide services that range from excellent to negligent to out-and-out quackery. The "flying circuses of psychotherapy" whirl into town, display their unproven techniques, and vanish, leaving behind certain insecure therapists who adopt every notion, from the quaint to the downright dangerous.

Who Are the Practitioners?

Because psychotherapy originally grew out of the reasoning and methods of medicine, clients generally expect a therapist to have been trained in one of the mental health disciplines. But the average consumer may be confused about the differences in training and educational background of psychiatrists, psychologists, social workers, and others who call themselves counselors, therapists, advisers, or healers. Here are some brief descriptions of the various types of providers.

Psychiatrists

Psychiatrists are medically trained. They have attained a degree in medicine (M.D.), usually after four years of medical school, generally followed by a year of internship (supervised medical experience) and a residency of five years or more (further supervised training in psychiatry). A medical license is required to practice psychiatry, but the title *psychiatrist* can be used by any medical doctor without approval from anyone. Some psychiatrists are certified by the American Board of Psychiatry and Neurology, meaning that after completing required residency training, the person passed certain oral and written examinations given nationally.

In addition to providing various forms of therapy (much like other mental health professionals), psychiatrists, because they are physicians, can prescribe medications. Other mental health practitioners must refer patients to physicians for medication. There are some current efforts to train certain psychologists to prescribe and treat patients with psychiatric medications. Time will tell how this proceeds.

Psychologists

Psychologists generally have a doctoral degree—a Ph.D., doctor of philosophy; an Ed.D., doctor of education; or a Psy.D., doctor of psychology—attained either at a university or professional school. (The freestanding professional schools, which have appeared in the United States in the past generation, are new training programs that vary in their accreditations and offerings.) Psychologists usually have a bachelor's degree plus four or more years of graduate training in clinical psychology, including supervised practical work in an agency or hospital, or under the supervision of experienced professionals. Master's-level psychologists are licensed in some states.

Social Workers

Social workers usually have two years of graduate school training beyond their bachelor's degree; a few have doctoral-level training (D.S.W.). The master's-level training includes field placement, which consists of supervised work experience. The credentials are M.S.W., master of social work; C.S.W., clinical social worker, and L.C.S.W., licensed clinical social worker.

A newer license is the M.F.C.C. (marriage, family, and child counselor), a California innovation, which is now available in more than thirty states. It usually consists of a two- to three-year program of coursework, along with three thousand hours of supervised field training. Once completed, the person must pass a written and oral examination. The M.F.C.C. has become quite popular of late as a master's-level certification to practice therapy.

We also see a whole host of other practitioners who offer psychological, emotional, spiritual, career, and financial consultation, advice, and therapy. Typically they don't have any of the background just outlined. This catch-all category would include some certified hypnotherapists; some personal-development trainers and seminar leaders; various types of personal "coaches"; spiritual advisers, clairvoyants, psychics, channelers, and those who commune with angels and spirits; shamanic counselors; some types of massage therapists, body workers, and breath workers; and various and sundry providers who primarily advertise their wares in New Age publications and operate by word of mouth. Many tend to use such tools as the *I Ching*, the enneagram, runes, astrology, hypnotic regression, out-of-body experiences, palmistry, and other devices to supplement their "therapy." They often attend and promote weekend workshops that advocate such techniques.

In going to a therapist, a person usually assumes that the therapist will diagnose, suggest a treatment plan, and outline the necessary program to help with the problem. Just as the mere presence of a degree does not guarantee that the therapist will be helpful or the best one for a particular person, neither is there any guarantee that a particular technique will work.

As with other human interactions, the relationship that emerges between therapist and client is more important than the degree, title, and other features of the therapist. Similarly, a particular theory or school of psychotherapy is outweighed by the satisfactory or unsatisfactory nature of the relationship between client and therapist. This fact remains extremely pertinent to much of the discussion in this book, as we will in many instances be taking a close look at the amount of influence a therapist can have over clients.

We also hope to make clear that in describing certain of these therapies we're not talking about merely one or two off-beat therapists or noncredentialed "healers" who are drawing their patients into ridiculous or far-flung procedures. The situation is more pressing than that. Although we're prevented from naming individuals or institutions, we have seen plenty of evidence that big names in the field—professors and trainers, as well as established and supposedly reputable teaching and training academies—are deeply involved in some of these crazy therapies, and are far from exempt from harming their clients.

And should you doubt the prevalence or popularity of what might seem at first glance to be farfetched techniques, just spend a little time lurking around the World Wide Web. Use the search engines and type in a key word, such as *rebirthing, alien abduction, past-life regression, channeling, facilitated communication,* or *shaman,* and see what comes up: hundreds and hundreds of entries, and new ones every day. If what people are posting, advertising, and talking about on the Internet is any indication of the heartbeat of the nation, then read this book carefully and use it as a resource to help you avoid being taken in by a psychological con artist.

Where Do They Go Wrong?

An inability on the part of the therapist to properly diagnose a client's problem or determine appropriate treatment is a recurring pitfall in some of the cases described in this book. This hazard is often rooted in the practitioner's "single cause–single cure" approach to therapy, which has led many a therapist down a dead-end trail and has created no end of problems for clients.

In life there can be many causes and contributing factors that bring on the various emotional disorders or discomforts that might lead a person to seek therapy. Each person's problems are unique. Therefore, a therapist should be thought of more as a custom tailor than as an off-the-rack salesperson. The custom tailor looks at and measures the client, discusses and plans with the client what the garment will look like, how long it will take, how many fittings are needed, and so on, so that the final product is made to fit the specific person.

The One-Way-Only School of Treatment

Some therapists, however, fall into a modus operandi in which they proceed as if there were only one cause and one cure for *all* mental troubles. They apply their one therapeutic approach to everyone who comes into their office. A Southern psychiatrist once remarked that, just as there are many cooks who think there is only one recipe for pecan pie (their own), many therapists think there is only one approach to helping with emotional and mental problems (their pet method).

A devotion to one-way-only notions of treatment often grows out of certain limitations in training programs, wherein many student therapists are exposed to only a very narrow range of treatment methods. The single-minded approach also seems to stem from the fact that during graduate school, residency programs, and anxiety-producing field placements, certain therapists-in-training solve their anxiety by simply following without question the dominant theory of their most powerful, best-loved, or most anxiety-provoking supervisor.

Increasingly, however, other sources of one-way-only approaches have been pop psychology books, weekend seminars, and "trainings" from self-proclaimed gurus. In these cases, the assumptions and beliefs are often deeply felt because they resonate within the therapist, who tends to identify with something in the "new" philosophy: being abused, abducted, repressed; feeling like less than a man or woman; having unhappy thoughts about his or her own childhood. Happy to find an instant cure, these therapists actually believe that these single cause–single cure ideas are true and effective.

Latching onto a pet theory of personality or human behavior does a great disservice to clients. Too often, clients are not told that there are many, many theories of psychology, behavior, and personality, each composed of numerous constructs and concepts. A theory, after all, is a mere formulation based on hypotheses; it is a creation, not a truth etched in stone.

Relying on Personal Beliefs and Assumptions

Beliefs and assumptions personally held by certain therapists are either inadvertently or intentionally imposed on the client, following in this vein of single cause–single cure. The therapists cling to their assumptions, using them as rationales for carrying out a personally motivated therapy. We do not propose to debate or challenge the existence of UFOs, reincarnation, spirit entities, and other notions involved in some of the therapies explored in this book. Our point is that some therapists themselves become fascinated with, invested in, and personally committed to belief systems that they then inflict on clients as if the assumptions associated with those beliefs were universally accepted and agreed-upon single pathways to cure. Some of the more common assumptions fall within the following several major themes:

1. Extraterrestrials exist and are abducting and experimenting on humans on a regular basis, and there is a government conspiracy to cover up this information.

2. All humans have lived one or more past lives, aspects of which interfere with our current life. A subtheme is that various "entities" (human and nonhuman)—spirit beings from "the other side"—reside within individuals and are the cause of difficulties in a person's life today.

3. Trauma and abuse experienced in early childhood is the root cause of all psychological and emotional problems. This includes having been subjected to incest and other forms of sexual abuse, having been raised by incompetent and "toxic" parents, and even having suffered through the trauma of the birth experience itself. A subtheme is that childhood sexual abuse, including participation in intergenerational Satanic ritual cults, is rampant.

4. It is possible to regress people to their birth moment, then "rebirth" them and bring them up correctly.

5. Emptying out the emotion attached to past and present experiences will cure people. The idea is that catharsis brings cure, and especially that screaming out in anger or pain brings a curative release, sort of like an ex-lax® for the mind.

6. Reliving traumatic experiences will cure people. The idea is to revivify and relive the remembrance, whether real or imagined.

7. It is acceptable for therapists and patients to have sexual relations, as it makes the patients feel better and is not harmful to them.

8. There is a human mental mechanism that prevents people who have suffered abuse and trauma from remembering this

aspect of their lives, and certain techniques can help people retrieve these blocked memories. As visions of specific events come forth in more and more detail, they become like a motion picture of the past abuse and are to be accepted as valid memories.

9. The world is full of certain magical powers. These powers can reside in spirit guides and angels, symbols and archetypes, inanimate objects such as crystals and wands, and potions and herbal treatments. Special, gifted individuals can also have magical powers.

Using Simplistic Techniques

Taking the dearly held assumption, some therapists will then concoct a treatment (or will have learned one at a workshop) based on their preferred belief system. Some of these treatments are terribly simplistic and may play out as follows:

Technique A

1. On the therapist's urging, acknowledge that your parents had a terrible influence on you and, just as the therapist says, your mother was especially cold and unloving.

2. Let the therapist hold you like a baby.

3. Put on a diaper and drink from a baby bottle, which you should carry with you at all times.

4. Now you are better, if not cured.

Technique B

1. Relax and let the therapist hypnotize you.

2. While in the trance state, go back to a past life (guided by the therapist) and describe who you are, where you are, and what is going on.

3. Look for and encounter the traumatic event that took place during this other lifetime.

4. Afterward, in discussion with the therapist, you will come to an "insight" about how your past-life experiences are interfering with present-day events and actions.

5. Now you are better, if not cured.

Technique C

1. Recall as much of the real-life incident that is troubling you as possible.

2. Imagine yourself back in the situation and feel the emotion you must have felt then.

3. "Let it all hang out" by expressing every primitive idea, emotion, and impulse that emerges, and this will make you spontaneous and free.

4. Now you are better, if not cured.

None of these techniques—neither A, B, or C, in and of itself—is a proven method of treatment. And you can take any of the assumptions listed in the preceding section and devise similar scenarios.

A common feature of new psychotherapies, as well as many of the older ones, is that one case—"the key case"—served as the starting point. It may be startling to learn that what is presented as tested scientific fact is instead a scheme built on one case. This single key case opened the door for the therapist to see the "one way" to deal with all psychopathology.

For example, the founding of Gestalt Therapy revolved around a sexually impotent young man who came to see Fritz Perls. When Perls learned that the otherwise healthy young man was in treatment with an ear, nose, and throat specialist, Perls supposedly suddenly recalled Freud and Wilhelm Fliess.

Fliess believed that there was a "nasal reflex neurosis" that involved the nose with a number of bodily symptoms in the cardiac, gastric, respiratory, reproductive, and other physical systems. Based on this notion, Fliess anesthetized areas inside the nose with cocaine and performed various surgical procedures on patients. Enamored of Fliess's ideas, Freud had his nose operated on by Fliess many times. He also referred patients to Fliess for nose surgery. One of those patients, Emma Eckstein, nearly died from botched nasal surgery; Fliess had left gauze in the surgical wound, which became infected. Author and critic Martin Gardner referred to this treatment as "Teutonic Crackpottery."

So, with Freud and Fliess in mind, Perls had the young man with impotence stop treatment with his physician for his nasal problems and alternate his concentration on his nasal sensations and his absent genital sensations. The nasal swelling decreased and penile tumescence increased. Perls claimed that this one case allowed him to see that he had to look at the "gestalt"—the total situation—and treat the patient in a context. Perls went on to advocate: "Don't think, feel" and "Lose your mind and come to your senses."

Psychotherapist Jacob Moreno noted how a woman who worked as an actress in his theater played a gentle, wistful, frail woman, whereas at home the woman was a volatile shrew who was irascible and hostile (according to her husband). After learning that, Moreno had the woman play disagreeable, violent characters. Her husband reported that their marriage improved as she became more reasonable, sweet-tempered, and relaxed at home. Moreno went on to use this one case to develop dramatic techniques and theatrical tricks, which he called Psychodrama.

Sandor Ferenczi came upon his idea of Privation Therapy when he discovered a woman patient masturbating on the couch by pressing her thighs together. He claimed that forbidding her to adopt this position on the couch led to significant progress, and he used it in general treatment. Freud read Ferenczi's paper and soon wrote his own, incorporating Ferenczi's ideas. Freud extended the theory to the point of saying that a client in therapy should be taken as far as possible under conditions of privation and in a state of abstinence. Other psychologists, such as Theodore Reik, adopted the notion, whereas Ferenczi eventually changed his mind and decided that love from the therapist—indulgence—is what's needed for growth.

F. William Gosciewski developed Photo Counseling after a difficult client brought snapshots to therapy. The client talked more freely about the photos than he'd ever talked about anything before, so Gosciewski extended this technique to others.

Philosophical Psychotherapy was based on work with two patients. The therapist, William Sahakian, instructed the patients to stop fighting their neuroses, to accept them and be philosophical about them. One of the patients declared himself cured. As a result, Sahakian led patients to change their philosophical outlook about their symptoms.

Unfortunately, when a one-size-fits-all therapist develops an overfocused, single-issue notion of the cause (or cure) of all, or almost all, mental problems, the risk to the patient is great. The patient's current life issues tend to be ignored. The patient's personal history gets revised and reinterpreted to fit the therapist's narrow notions. In effect, real therapy never begins because the therapist is too busy ignoring or reinterpreting what the patient wants and needs to deal with. Instead, the patient is led down a garden path by the therapist, and consequently the patient does not receive appropriate care, nor are the presenting problems dealt with. In a sense, these patients become pawns in a scenario that will ultimately be used to confirm the therapist's idealized theory, usually the latest fad therapy.

Using Faulty Checklists

Some therapists' opening maneuver is to get a brief history and then pull out one or another of the many checklists currently popular in the healing trades. Using the checklist, the therapist will indicate to the new patient that she meets many criteria of a person who has had certain specific past experiences and that therefore she suffers from x ailment, usually attributed to y past trauma. Two factors are questionable here:

1.   *Checklists are heavily loaded with universal items to which most people might assent.* On these checklists we see such phrases as "I dislike speaking before large audiences"; "I do not like going to the dentist"; "I frequently feel tired." Just about anybody could answer yes to many of these items, from which the therapist concludes patients are suffering from a particular disorder.

Such lists resemble cold readings done by magicians and mentalists. For years, stage performers have been known to perfect lists of universal statements to which people of a certain age, sex, educational, or ethnic group might respond as true about themselves. The tricksters also perfect their questioning and commentary skills to prevent the subject from becoming aware of what is happening. Today's practitioners of crazy therapies seem to have adopted similar skills in pulling the wool over their clients' eyes—and minds.

2.   *Reasoning backwards from checklist responses is not an acceptable, scientific way to evaluate behavior or diagnose disorders.* In essence, this approach leads to a "formula diagnosis," and once again fails to consider clients' individual differences. By making a snap diagnosis and asserting to the client, "You have features in common with persons who . . . ," certain therapists end up going off on ventures with their clients that tend to support the therapist's idiosyncratic beliefs by essentially training the patient to fit into preconceived patterns. The therapist leads the client into accepting the faulty diagnosis, which is cloaked in the therapist's authority.

In general, the many broad-based symptom checklists floating around the therapeutic community these days tend to do damage in their support of misdiagnoses rather than bring viable solutions to the clients on whom they are foisted.

By relying on personal assumptions and faulty checklists, more and more therapists fall into what might be thought of as "Procrustean bed" therapy. Procrustes, a character from Greek mythology, forced travelers to fit into his bed by either stretching their bodies or cutting off their legs. By making clients arbitrarily fit into one pet theory, these one-size-fits-all therapists are essentially showing a merciless disregard for individual differences.

Doing Harm

In some of the crazy therapies discussed in this book, we see a pattern of abuse and harmful effects on clients. These are described here in no particular order, as the consequences may vary for each situation, but as far as we're concerned, they're dire on all counts.

• *Most of these therapies are based on myth and fantasy,* not on scientific study showing solid evidence of beneficial effects for the client. Clients are taught to adopt a kind of magical thinking, which easily filters into all parts of their life and worldview.

As a result, clients may tend to look for instant cures for any life obstacle or situation, rather than relying on logic and sound reasoning. This can affect their daily life on the job, their relationships with their friends and family, and their studies, hobbies, and other interests.

For example, instead of hashing through problems with her teenage son who was entering the "teen rebellion" stage, one mother ingrained with this kind of thinking from her therapy sessions spent hours trying to "visualize" a happy household, unaware that her son was slowly sliding into a drug-filled lifestyle. Magical thinking can cause additional problems when clients find that they have lost touch with reality or are no longer able to function adequately in the real world.

• *There is rampant misuse and overuse of hypnosis and other trance-inducing techniques and exercises,* such as guided imagery, meditation, yoga, and relaxed breathing. Some of these methods may in fact be useful in the course of legitimate therapies, and may have a noticeable healing effect. But when misused and abused—as they so often are in odd, unfounded therapies adopted by poorly trained or single-minded practitioners—these procedures can in fact have a deleterious impact on clients. Practitioners of crazy therapies tend to rely on a lot of hypnosis, as it makes clients more suggestible and compliant.

- *Clients tend to waste time and money on these fad therapies.* Aside from what's already been spent, clients often need to start all over once they get away from the bogus care. Usually their original problems have not been taken care of, and often new problems develop because of the previous practices.

Sometimes the therapist abruptly ends the therapy when the client's insurance coverage runs out or the client can no longer afford the sessions. Ending a therapy precipitously, especially when instigated by the therapist, can often have detrimental effects on the client.

- *In some cases, clients are led to adopt religious or spiritual concepts* in which they previously had no interest and which may run counter to their personal belief system. Although the clients thought they were seeking psychotherapy, they were in effect put through a religious conversion.

For example, being convinced by a therapist that you have lived many past lives is essentially adopting the idea of reincarnation, a concept present in most forms of Hinduism but one that is not accepted in other religions. Unexpectedly taking on this belief during the course of therapy can cause certain clients to experience upsetting internal conflict, and they may not recognize the source of their difficulty.

- *Many crazy therapies rely on false notions of memory* and of the ability to retrieve memories. Therapists who didn't do their homework on memory and how it works tend to convey myths and misinformation to their clients, and in some cases set about tampering with clients' actual memories.

For example, some clients are led to believe that they were abducted by aliens, a "memory" they did not have until they went to the therapist and were subjected to many sessions of hypnosis. From this, they can spin off and come up with other "memories" and begin to have an entirely new view of their life or background, which often causes separation from family and friends, who may contradict these new discoveries.

• *Countless clients are harmed through sexual, physical, and emotional abuse.* Some of these we learn about when a client manages to escape the grip of her therapist and brings charges against the practitioner. But even then, most of these cases are settled out of court and never see the light of day, with the therapists rarely facing public censure, much less revocation of their professional license. At most, some might receive a professional slap on the wrist.

• *Numerous clients are not helped to become happier, better-functioning persons.* Instead, there are growing legions of conflicted, lonely individuals who find themselves bogged down in interminable therapy or who end therapy worse off than when they began. As mentioned earlier, they may have new problems engendered by the therapy, ranging from serious psychological difficulties to total estrangement from their families. They may even have adopted revised, fanciful, and often tragic personal histories; one female client, for example, came to believe that because she had been a prostitute in a past life, she now deserved to suffer from AIDS and die.

• *Many who've been exposed to a crazy therapy become disillusioned and distrustful of therapy or helping professionals.* After leaving the bad treatment, these people may fail to seek out help, which they might need. This can cause them continued distress in their lives, as they may never get a clear picture of what went wrong in the unhelpful therapy and may in some ways blame themselves.

To society's loss, there is an alarming laxity within the mental health professions when it comes to monitoring, commenting on, and educating the public about what is good therapy, what is negligent behavior by trained professionals, and what is or borders on quackery. Not enough attention is paid to the conduct (whether illegal, damaging, or just plain crazy) of the impaired therapist, the quirky therapist, the insufficiently trained therapist.

We open the daily paper and see advice about which movies are good, which books are helpful, which food products are healthful, but we find no objective guides for evaluating the efficacy of a particular treatment. One writer noted that "there is no equivalent of a Food and Drug Administration to monitor therapies' and therapists' effectiveness. There is no psychological FDA to root out unproved claims or dangerous practices. University selection procedures, professional societies, and state-licensing laws help, but they don't exert much control over the therapist's personality and technique. Until they do, let the buyer beware."

In the chapters that follow, we will highlight some of the controversial therapies that consumers are likely to run into. Some, like reparenting, have been around for decades; others have taken hold in recent years, and new ones are emerging every day. The number and types of crazy therapies certainly are not limited to those found in this book, but we hope that with these examples you will begin to recognize the characteristics of psychological zaniness and be armed to protect yourself from potentially harmful theories and techniques.

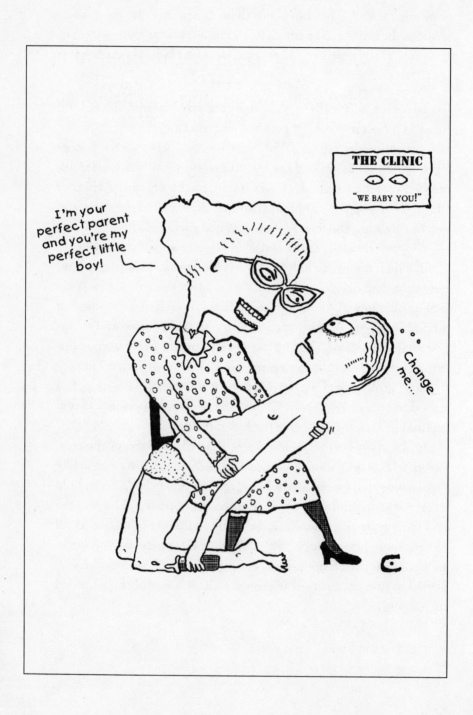

Back to the Beginning

Regression, Reparenting, and Rebirthing

"Rose," thirty-seven, married with two teenage daughters, saw a psychologist's poster advertising that patients would attain dramatic personal transformation, learn long-forgotten events, and achieve emotional intensity that would revitalize their lives. "Women—Prepare for the New Century Through Rebirthing and Reparenting," the poster proclaimed. Rose was intrigued and called for an appointment.

During the first session, the female psychologist asked Rose some about her personal and emotional history, but seemed to have little interest in what Rose was recounting. The therapist spent a great deal of the time explaining how her groups worked and the requirements. Rose was told that future sessions would be in the evening in a group setting. "Others of my children will be rebirthed that night," the therapist softly murmured. Rose was to wear old clothes and bring along a blanket, pillow, and baby bottle.

The group met in a large conference room without chairs or furniture of any kind. Large pillows, many blankets, and lightweight cotton rugs were stacked against the walls. Rose learned that she was one of four new "children" to be rebirthed that night. Four other advanced patients would assume the role of the "primary mother" of each of the new women.

The psychologist instructed each newcomer to lie on a spread-out cotton throw rug. Each primary mother showed her assigned newcomer how to get into the "birthing position": on her side, fetal position, chin tucked toward chest, arms against torso, legs drawn up. Each primary mother rolled her rebirthing candidate into the rug so that it formed a cocoon. Meanwhile the psychologist was telling them in the background that she would use guided imagery to regress them back to birth, and that they should visualize being in a dark, tight place that was squeezing in on them. They were to fight and wriggle their way out of the birth canal, just like at their first birth. She assured them that this time they would be birthed the right way, received with unconditional love. "I will receive you as my children," she intoned. "I will release you to your new primary mother who, one step at a time, will help you grow up right." Much squealing, wriggling, and crying out ensued as the primary mothers tugged at the wrapped women until each was "rebirthed." Eventually Rose was dragged over to a large pillow against the wall. Her primary mother lifted Rose's torso, and while cradling her fed her milk from the baby bottle.

The eight women met four times a week for a month. Rose's husband, "Fred," noticed that she was regressing rapidly in her daily behaviors. Soon she would not get up in the morning until he brought her milk in a cup and fed her. She lost the will to do the most simple self-care tasks, letting her hair become unwashed and unkempt, not showering, and rarely getting dressed. Fred and the daughters had no home life with Rose gone to the reparenting group four nights a week, where she wore diapers, crawled on her hands and knees, and babbled baby talk.

Finally, Fred called the psychologist, telling her that he felt that Rose had disintegrated into a regressed, depressed, enfeebled human who stayed in bed most of the day. The psychologist replied, "Everyone has to get worse before they get better." She suggested that Fred join one of her men's rebirthing groups so that he could understand and share with Rose. Before slamming down the phone, Fred yelled in anger, "But who is going to take care of all of us then if she and I both are lying in bed expecting to be fed!"

Over time, Fred began to fear that Rose had gone crazy. He convinced her to cancel further reparenting, and got her mother up from another part of the state to take care of Rose and the teenage daughters. After a few days, Rose, Fred, the mother, and the two girls met with a psychiatrist for an evaluation. A person meeting Rose for the first time who didn't know she had formerly been a sprightly, bright woman would have wondered if she were mentally retarded, severely depressed, or in some way demented. It took some months for Rose to recover, and she felt particularly bad when she saw the impact her regressed, stuporous behavior had had on her two teenage daughters, who like their father had been worried that their mother had "lost her mind."

Stories like these are plentiful, and practitioners of various forms of regression therapy combined with the use of mind-altering techniques are rampant in the United States and abroad. As of 1992, one "corrective parenting association" formed in the mid-1980s reportedly had 350 member therapists. This figure represents but a handful of the therapists and counselors who believe in these unfounded theories and use potentially harmful methods.

Leonard Orr, said by some to be the founder of rebirthing, claims to have talked to ten million "energy breathing students." Energy breathing is the goal of rebirthing, and Orr writes on his Internet home page, "People who have mastered their ability to breathe energy as well as air, report that they can breathe away physical and emotional pain, and long standing [sic] diseases." At his new location in Staunton, Virginia, Orr offers five-day Rebirther's Training sessions *every week of the year*. And who knows how many others get trained by these graduates?

Another well-known rebirther and early cohort of Orr is Sondra Ray. Information from her organization lists "qualified" rebirthers in New York, Georgia, Massachusetts, Connecticut (the location of Ray's center), Florida, Nevada, Michigan, New Jersey,

North Carolina, Nebraska, Missouri, Tennessee, Virginia, Puerto Rico, and Manitoba—so don't think that only people in "flaky" California get involved with these weird goings-on (Ray's list of rebirthers and their seminars includes only one contact in Los Angeles). As readers will soon discover, unscientific therapies are a national, and in some cases international, phenomenon.

In this chapter, we examine the use of regression as it relates specifically to rebirthing and reparenting, but the techniques have been adopted, adapted, and promoted in countless therapies by numerous practitioners, as will be evident in the chapters that follow. Proponents of regression therapies often refer to their work by a variety of names, sometimes making them hard to detect at first glance, especially for the uninformed potential client. In general, these therapists combine suggestion, guided imagery, and hypnosis to reinforce their encouragement of marked regression—a method that can be psychologically disastrous to many persons, as it was to Rose.

Because objective research on regression techniques is limited, the assumptions about regression remain merely myths based on anecdotal reports from enthusiastic proponents. In fact, Sondra Ray states several times in one of her books that there is no research and there are no accurate records or statistics; she even claims that this isn't her job: "Rebirthers consider themselves to be spiritual guides, not scientists." So much for reality checking or scientific verification.

Rather than helping clients to become stronger and more independent, most regression therapies, and in particular the rebirthing-reparenting sort, induce in the client an abdication of responsibility and a state of sickly dependence on the therapist. This is a blatant abuse and misuse of the power relationship inherent in the therapeutic process; it is in effect the exploitation of the client's emotional vulnerability. The "Mommy" or "Daddy" therapist who is supposed to parent the client correctly is in fact playing with fire, potentially entrapping and crippling their "children," and causing undue suffering and in some cases long-lasting damage.

Regression techniques continue to be used throughout the United States today—from San Diego to Seattle to Kansas City—as well as in Germany, India, England, Sweden, Canada, Belgium, and Holland, having been successfully spread via weekend seminars sold around the world by traveling trainers. On the whole, professional associations in the mental health field have ignored the practice, although there has been the occasional mild reprimand to practitioners of these therapies. Generally, it is only when enough damaged patients and their families have sought legal redress in the courts that the public has learned through the media about the egregious behavior and the sometimes disastrous consequences.

Where Do These Ideas Come From?

Most schools of psychotherapy believe that childhood and the early years of life have formative influences on the adult personality. But some therapies—regression, direct analysis, reparenting, corrective parenting, and rebirthing—are based on the untested assumption that a therapist can regress patients to infancy in order to reparent them, even rebirth them, and then bring them up correctly. Believers claim that these therapies are able to alter, repair, and even reverse the alleged negative impact of someone's early life experiences, simply by making babies out of clients and having them relive the experiences—only this time, supposedly, the therapist is going to carry out the parenting in the right way.

The underlying assumption is that an adult patient first needs to be regressed in order to act like and be treated as a small infant; then, through "corrective parenting" by the therapist, the patient will emerge as a more ideal person. As we have seen in the case of Rose and others, some therapists who engage in rebirthing and reparenting techniques feed adult patients from baby bottles; have patients suck on therapists' breasts, thumbs, and penises; instruct patients to wear diapers and to engage in such behaviors as being cuddled as an infant, being made to stand in the corner, and even being physically restrained and beaten, sometimes brutally, by the reparenting therapist. This type of therapy may go on for varying lengths of time. Some we've heard of lasted as long as seven to ten years.

This unfortunate and dangerous theory is grounded in a widespread tendency in our society toward "parent bashing," in which parents are blamed for not producing totally happy, satisfied, creative, wonderful offspring. For several decades, some professionals have ignored the fact that there are other significant influences on human personality—namely, genes, illnesses, physical conditions, and social and political conditions such as wars, poverty, crime, and natural disasters. Parents have been blamed for every misery their offspring have suffered: being fat, thin, sickly, depressed or schizophrenic, or just plain dissatisfied with their lot in life.

We can trace this tendency back to Freud, who readily blamed parents for his patients' supposed problems. The belief reached its zenith in the 1940s and 1950s within the ranks of traditional psychoanalysts. A primary wave of attack was on mothers. Some were labeled "schizophrenogenic" and accused of causing schizophrenia in their children, while other mothers were called "homosexual-inducing." By the late 1940s some therapists were proclaiming that their patients' parents were unloving, mean, intrusive, and controlling, and had in effect harmed, if not ruined, their offspring. From there, some therapists deduced the solution that the all-loving therapist would restore the patients by bringing them up properly.

Pioneers in Regression and Reparenting

Two therapists in particular, Marguerite Sechehaye and John Rosen, received considerable attention as forerunners in the use of regression and reparenting therapy in their work with schizophrenic patients. Colleagues in the field readily praised Sechehaye and Rosen for their innovative methods.

Sechehaye and Rosen began by claiming that their massive regression techniques, coupled with authoritarian control, would cure schizophrenia. Fortunately for them, the post–World War II period was an era when people were willing to justify extreme forms of therapy in an effort to "cure" schizophrenia. Because it was also a time when parents, especially mothers, were being vilified in the world of therapy, the severing of family ties and the regression techniques were tolerated, even lauded, by other therapists. They accepted the "logic" of thinking that perhaps rough treatment and separation from families would cure a major mental illness. But soon not only schizophrenics (who almost never have a constituency looking out for their welfare) were subjected to this treatment; almost anyone who went into certain therapists' offices was open game for being regressed and reparented to cure *any* ill.

Sechehaye was an academic psychologist and psychoanalyst in Geneva, Switzerland. She developed a method called "symbolic realization," with which she treated a twenty-one-year-old schizophrenic woman for more than ten years. Sechehaye had the woman live with her; she fed her and in general parented her in a warm way. For about seven of those years, the patient was acutely psychotic and cared for as a baby would be. Sechehaye had concluded that the woman's problems grew from a lack of maternal love.

Renee, the patient, referred to Sechehaye as "Mama." Holding an apple against her breast, Mama would then feed the girl by cutting a piece of the apple and having the girl lie against Mama's breast to eat. The raw apple was to be "breast milk" for Renee. Sechehaye's treatment was far more symbolic than the reparenting therapies developed by others, which became more and more overt, and sometimes even sinister, in their "mothering" practices.

John Rosen, a physician who had been analyzed but never trained as a psychoanalyst, originally professed in 1947 that his new method, which he called "direct analysis," led to schizophrenic patients "recovering" and having their "psychosis resolved." Claiming that his patients had not been loved during childhood, Rosen reported spending sometimes as much as ten hours a day with one patient. What was eventually revealed about what went on in those sessions is almost too horrific to imagine. Some of these techniques were tantamount to extreme violence and torture.

As a young psychologist in the late 1940s, I (coauthor Singer) had the opportunity to observe Rosen work with schizophrenic patients when he was a guest faculty member at the university medical school where I was working. I recall seeing Rosen do his direct analysis on some seriously ill patients. He yelled at them, threatened them, and verbally badgered and insulted them. This, as we all were later to learn, was only the half of it.

The selected patients were presented before hospital staff, medical students, and faculty. A nurse brought patients down from the wards, and one at a time Rosen began his direct analysis of their remarks. In front of such an awesome group of strangers, most patients looked frightened and puzzled, and became even more so as Rosen proceeded. Rosen's conduct was nothing like the expected demeanor of a physician speaking with patients, and he was far from polite. With little knowledge of the individual patient, Rosen began to ask questions. He responded to whatever the patient said with insult and bluster, including the use of profanities and scatological terms. The patients appeared stunned, but Rosen's manner conveyed that they must stay and take what he was dishing out.

I recall sitting in wonderment as I watched Rosen's onslaughts on patients during his demonstrations at the hospital. I kept asking myself, "What could be his rationale for what he's doing?" He claimed he was talking the language of the id, the language of the primary process, and that he was showing them he cared for them. But what logical connections were there between the diagnosis of schizophrenia, Rosen's conduct, and his assumptions that it cured patients? He wrote, "Sometimes, when I have the patient pinned to the floor, I say, 'I can castrate you. I can kill you, I can eat you. I can do whatever I want to you, but I am not going to do it.'" He went on: "The patient gets the feeling of having met a master who could do anything he wanted to him by virtue of his physical strength but will not do it because he loves him."

Later in the day I saw these same patients on the wards. Rosen's treatment had indeed produced regression. There they were, either sitting rocking in a mute, stunned manner with a staring gaze, or lying in various parts of the ward quietly sobbing. Prior to these sessions with Rosen, the patients had been up and about on the wards interacting with other patients and the staff.

The senior staff at the university medical school all seemed to endorse what Rosen was doing. Most of us underlings were appalled, and spoke to each other about how cruel and demeaning the "treatment" was, but we dared not speak out, I'm sorry to say. In fact, Rosen was extolled in the literature and at professional meetings where he demonstrated his approach as heroic and dedicated. In 1971 he even won the American Academy of Psychotherapy Man of the Year award.

An article by Rosen in a 1947 *Psychiatric Quarterly* reported on thirty-seven of his cases. Rosen claimed that all thirty-seven individuals recovered. Six years later in his book *Direct Analysis*, Rosen reported that thirty-one of the original sample were no longer psychotic and were doing well. Yet, in a follow-up study in 1958, nineteen of the former patients from Rosen's report were located by researchers at the New York Psychiatric Institute. They found that seven of the nineteen were not schizophrenic at that time, nor had they ever been; instead, six were evaluated as neurotic and one as manic-depressive. These independent researchers concluded that "the claim that direct analytic therapy results in a high degree of recovery remains unproven."

Finally, in March of 1983, thanks to the courage of a number of Rosen's former patients who came forward to speak out and expose the abuses they suffered, Rosen surrendered his medical license. He had been charged with "sixty-seven violations of the Pennsylvania Medical Practices Act and thirty-five violations of the rules and regulations of the Medical Board, [which included] the commission of acts involving moral turpitude, dishonesty, or corruption, as well as misconduct in the practice of medicine, practicing medicine fraudulently, beyond its authorized scope, with incompetence, or with negligence." In fact, unbeknownst to many, as far back as 1960 Rosen had lost a case in New York in which he had been accused of beating a female patient. From investigations, depositions, and testimonies given regarding the various charges against Rosen, information came forth about the kind of care patients were getting at Rosen's facilities. Striking, stripping, and beating patients was a regular occurrence. Patients were kept locked in security rooms without toilets, and at least two patients died. Both male and female patients were sexually abused by Rosen and forced to engage in the most atrocious acts with him and sometimes with other patients.

John Rosen had been highly regarded for years throughout the psychiatric community. To this day, some still uphold Rosen's work, when in fact Rosen and his direct analysis led to some serious abuses of patients and legal suits. Rosen may have lost his license, but the confrontational techniques that he professed live on, as we will see.

Baby Bottles, Berating, and Beatings

Many of Rosen's methods have filtered into the profession and are alive and well today in various therapies that regress and infantilize clients to the point of having them drink from baby bottles and be humiliated and punished in other ways. When asked by author and researcher Jeffrey Masson in an interview in 1986 if he still used the methods he learned from Rosen, a doctor replied that he used "physical methods that included shaking patients, sitting on them, and wrestling with them." Because there is more awareness and concern today about abuse and patients' rights, the doctor qualified his comments by saying that "he would use something like the cattle prod only experimentally."

Some regression therapists like to call what they do "little work." You know, making patients little again. Much of this "little work," as seen in Missouri, Minnesota, Washington, California, Colorado, Oklahoma, and elsewhere, can be linked to another controversial name in this field—Jacqui Schiff, once a social worker in Virginia.

Jacqui Schiff and Cathexis

In 1967 Jacqui Schiff turned her home into a care facility for severely disturbed young adults. A few years later she wrote a best-selling book—*All My Children*. In it, she chronicled how a young adult named Dennis became her adopted son, Aaron. Schiff had been seeing the young man in group and individual therapy for some time. One day he seemed very upset. Schiff's husband was present, and in the book Schiff describes what happened.

"Without another word, Dennis very quietly assumed a fetal position, cuddled into my lap, and attempted to nurse. We stared at him in astonishment. Both of us had been prepared for an outbreak of terrible anger. But Dennis's face was serene. Despite the beard, it was clearly the face of a baby of about nine months of age, a nursing infant." This event became a turning point for Schiff and her work.

Schiff's establishment grew as she took in more young adults to be reparented in this way, incorporating regression techniques into the setting. She referred to these young adults as "our babies." She wrote, "Now we put all our babies in diapers and feed them from bottles and let them sleep as much as they like."

Virginia authorities closed the place down in 1971 because the home was unlicensed and "endangered the health, safety, welfare, and lives of the patients." The Schiff facility moved to Alamo, California, where in 1972 an eighteen-year-old schizophrenic resident died after being placed in a bathtub of scalding water. He had been stripped naked, bound hand and foot, lowered into a very hot bath, and fatally burned.

Schiff's adopted son Aaron, who had become a therapist at the facility, pleaded guilty to a reduced charge of involuntary manslaughter, which was reduced even further to misdemeanor child abuse. One resident testified that she had been kept tied to a chair for six days and five nights. "They let me out twice to go to the bathroom," she said. She eventually managed to escape. When authorities refused to renew the license on the Alamo facility, Schiff moved to Oakland and set up the Cathexis Institute.

Jacqui Schiff was a member of the International Transactional Analysis Association (ITAA); to the dismay of some, within a few years her reparenting ideas had become accepted by the ITAA. In fact, in 1974, only two years after the scalding death just described, Jacqui and her son Aaron were given the Eric Berne Scientific Memorial Award. Before long, Schiff's reparenting theories became extremely popular among those who practice Transactional Analysis (TA), and study of the techniques was incorporated into TA training.

According to Alan Jacobs, a scholar and prominent ITAA member, "Schiff apparently believed that she had reached the point in her experience and knowledge about reparenting that her views and her judgment were unassailable." He quoted Schiff as having written, "My professional advisors offered no help; I was already beyond the range of their imagination."

However, all did not flow smoothly for Schiff, and eventually ITAA received an ethics complaint against her, after which she withdrew from the association. She went next to Bangalore, India, where she continued her reparenting practice, and later relocated in Great Britain. Through Cathexis-Europe, Schiff served as a consultant to reparenting programs in England, Germany, and the Netherlands.

Recently, the Schiffian method of reparenting gained notoriety in England. The local paper in Birmingham reported finding patients tied by lengths of rope to their therapists, crawling around on all fours making baby sounds; having to stand for hours, even overnight, in a corner; changing their names; and being denied telephone calls and mail. Patients were seen wearing disposable diapers, sucking their thumbs, and drinking from baby bottles, with some on a regime called "living room" in which the patient is kept in a room with another person until they have solved a "problem." In order to leave the room, a patient was required to be accompanied by another person no more than three feet away. Patients were encouraged to regard their therapists "as new and better parents, and to make open displays of physical affection towards them."

Reparenting techniques, despite this controversial history, are still widely used today. As recently as July 1995, Jacqui Schiff made an appearance at the ITAA conference in San Francisco, where she was given a warm reception and more than one hundred people waited in line to greet her and wish her well.

Not long ago, a California psychologist surveyed 267 reparenting therapists whose names were obtained from Cathexis Institute, New Directions in Education and Psychotherapy, and the ITAA newsletter. Eighty-six percent of the 267 reported using regressive work in their practices. Patients were being regressed to target ages of prenatal to thirteen years. The survey responses added up to some rather startling results, highlighted in Table 2.1.

Matrix in Missouri

Matrix (also known as the Mid-America Training and Reparenting Institute, Inc.), a Kansas City psychotherapy institute, took up the reparenting-regression techniques popularized by Schiff. During lawsuits against the clinic, it was revealed that the clinic had a supply closet with stacks of adult diapers, a kitchen with baskets of bottle nipples, and a pantry full of baby food and Zwieback toast. Wherever one turned there were bottle warmers, buckets of baby wipes, baby silverware, even a changing table! Handcuffs, ropes, and other physical restraints are also not uncommon sights in reparenting centers here and around the world.

Journalist Tom Jackman exposed Matrix in a series of articles in 1988. He described adult patients in the Kansas City facility sucking

Table 2.1.   Regression Therapy at Work.

98 percent held their regressed clients

98 percent played with their regressed clients

88 percent fed their "young child" client

22 percent spanked their regressed clients

82 percent punished clients by having them stand in a corner

46 percent bathed them

48 percent admitted to doing "toileting work" with them

 7 percent breast-fed clients

26 percent said sessions may be used inappropriately by the patient; in other words, some patients may become addicted to the process as an escape from adult problems, a place to hide rather than to grow

16 percent said patients' lowering their adult defenses and experiencing their younger child can lead to difficulty in their grown-up lives

15 percent reported patients developed unrealistic expectations about what their therapists can provide, including the illusion that the therapist will be the parent they never had, among other transference problems

34 percent were concerned about liability and the therapist's use of authority

16 percent were concerned about the use of physical restraint or confrontation

Few respondents mentioned the need for adequate training (a mere 3 percent), and only 1 percent mentioned the need for consultation or supervision.

on pacifiers, eating baby food, and drinking from baby bottles, with therapists coddling patients as if they were babies. Much of the therapy was done by unlicensed psychotherapists. Not only schizophrenic patients were treated there.

Between 1988 and 1994 at least four legal cases were settled by the organization—all in favor of the former patients who were mistreated and abused. The cases and the allegations against the Matrix therapists were as follows:

1.   *Charges: Negligence; breach of contract to provide competent professional services; intentional or reckless infliction of emotional distress. Settled out of court in 1994.* In this case, a woman in her freshman year of college away from home became depressed and had suicidal ideation. She sought therapy at Matrix. Allegedly the therapists had regressed and hypnotized the patient "to the mind of an infant, bottle-feeding, breast-feeding her and becoming her surrogate mother with the effect of replacing her biological mother." The patient said she was induced to suck on the therapist's nipple and on nursing bottles, to change her name, to address one therapist as "Mommy" and another as "Aunt Gail," and to buy a teddy bear that the therapist sprayed with her perfume as a reminder of her for the patient.

Among other charges were that the patient's "body was pinned to the floor and she was coerced to scream anger against her parents." On another occasion, the patient fractured her thumb when she was pushed to the floor by the therapist.

After several months of this regression therapy, the young woman was admitted to a hospital for being suicidal. She was returned to the therapy, and in about three months was rehospitalized for cutting herself on the arms, legs, and stomach with razors and scissors and beating herself with a belt. Further therapy ensued for a little under one year, at which point the therapists negligently terminated their relationship with the patient in violation of professional ethical principles, thereby allegedly triggering the patient's attempt to kill herself with a drug overdose.

2.   *Charges: Fraudulent misrepresentation; intentional infliction of emotional distress; negligence; malpractice; negligent hiring and supervision. Settled out of court in 1989.* A couple sought consultation at Matrix about their teenage daughter. It was later determined that she was an ordinary teenager, not in need of psychotherapy, but by that time all four family members (the parents and their two daughters) had been induced to engage in reparenting therapy based on

the diagnoses given them by an unlicensed therapist who repeatedly and falsely represented himself as licensed and as someone experienced in working with adolescents.

At one point the therapist falsely told the wife that her daughter's psychological problems were so serious that she may have to be "put into a group home." Later, the daughter was "wrongfully and with inadequate evaluation hospitalized for a so-called suicidal condition." The daughter was also encouraged and instructed by the therapists to move out of the family home.

The parents were wrongfully hypnotized on various occasions, were counseled to "distrust their own mental processes and to place their trust, belief, and reliance in direction and judgment of the defendants," and were subjected to "Game" therapy, "a form of physical, emotional and verbally abusive and demeaning interaction." The husband was told that he would suffer lifelong serious psychological problems unless he continued counseling with Matrix. Over time, the family had paid more than $12,000 to Matrix. (Matrix, by the way, was incorporated as a tax-exempt organization.)

3.   *Charges: Negligent acts, errors, or omissions in professional services provided to plaintiffs; intentional or reckless infliction of emotional distress; negligent infliction of mental distress. Settled out of court in 1989.* The lead therapist in this case was an unlicensed practitioner who had been denied licensure in three states and, in a prior legal case, had been banned from holding himself out as a psychologist. His degree was in education, not psychology. He is also one of the four persons charged in the case just described.

A couple married twenty-seven years entered family therapy with their two teenage children. During the course of four years in therapy at Matrix, the family members received 1,051 therapy treatments, for which they paid close to $55,000. Divided equally, that would mean each family member went for therapy 65 times each year, more than once a week.

Each was subjected to hypnosis, reparenting, and regression, including being made to swing a batlike instrument against cushions. There was also improper touching by the therapist. Shortly after the first year, the wife was hospitalized for "increasing depression, erratic behavior, and suicidal thinking." She was put on antidepressants for the first time in her life, and within days took an overdose of the pills because she felt betrayed by her therapist. During that year the wife lost twenty-eight pounds, her weight dropping to ninety-nine pounds. The therapist, who was counseling both husband and wife, directed the husband to file for divorce. As a result, the wife and two children lived in a motel. Meanwhile, the therapist instructed the wife to hospitalize the daughter for "not going to school and crying." During the course of therapy, the daughter, who'd originally been a B-average student, began doing less and less well, until she finally dropped out of high school.

Eventually, family members were alienated from one another, and the marriage and family broke up. Prior to going to Matrix, the family had not sought out therapy, nor had anyone experienced mental problems or emotional illness.

4.   *Charges: Negligent acts, errors, or omissions in professional services provided to plaintiff; intentional or reckless infliction of emotional distress; negligent infliction of mental distress. Settled out of court in 1988.* A woman received a flier announcing an art workshop. When she called to inquire, she learned that the workshop was taught at Matrix and cost fifteen hundred dollars. Enrolled as a student training to be an art therapist, she was told that seventy-five sessions of psychotherapy were required. For this, she personally was billed nine thousand dollars and was seen by nine different people, six of whom were unlicensed. Additional claims were sent by Matrix to her insurance company for collection.

The young woman was "hypnotized, mesmerized, and regressed to the mind of a baby"; she was told that she was a paranoid schizophrenic. The male therapist had her suckle his nipples and he had sexual contact with her, including fellatio, masturbation, and sexual intercourse.

_____

The lawyer handling some of the Kansas City cases wrote us the following: "My lawsuits have shown it takes about six reparenting sessions to begin to bring about profound and pervasive changes in self-image, affect, cognition and behavior." These changes have been shown to be for the worse.

The Case of Paul Lozano

Harvard medical student Paul Lozano committed suicide in April 1991 after being subjected to the regression-reparenting treatment of a Harvard psychiatrist, Dr. Margaret Bean-Bayog. At the end of his second year of medical school Lozano sought treatment for depression and was seen by Bean-Bayog almost daily for the next four years.

Bean-Bayog had never before used regression therapy with any patient, but she set about regressing Lozano to the age of three: "We invented a baby version of him." At Bean-Bayog's suggestion, she and Lozano role-played during his therapy sessions: she would be the mother, he the three-year-old baby. With no proof, but latching onto another popular trend, Bean-Bayog concluded that Lozano must have been sexually abused by his mother as a child.

According to the records, Lozano had no history of abuse or mental illness before he entered Harvard Medical School. He said at one point that his so-called memories were brought forth by him "as a means of retaining Dr. Bean-Bayog's interest and affection."

After his death, two books and numerous articles on the case appeared. The dead student's family sued the psychiatrist and accused her of seducing Paul and driving him to suicide. Documentation of what transpired in the therapy was never wanting, as Bean-Bayog kept copious notes, written right after each session with

Lozano. Lozano also spoke with other psychiatrists after the reparenting therapy, and volumes of testimony were accumulated during the preparation for the lawsuit and for the license revocation hearing (which was aborted when Bean-Bayog relinquished her medical license). Additionally, fifty-five pages "describing the most graphic sexual fantasies in Bean-Bayog's own handwriting were introduced as evidence."

There was some question about the kind and amount of sexual contact that had occurred between Bean-Bayog and Lozano. Dr. William Gault of the Newton-Wellesley Hospital, who was Paul Lozano's therapist subsequent to Paul's treatment with Bean-Bayog, was the first professional to be shown documentation of the reparenting therapy and the sexualized behavior that had occurred. Gault, referring to his talks with Paul, said: "Neither of us spelled out what we meant by sexual relations. . . . And if they did have sexual contact, I wouldn't think of that as having been one of the most harmful things that happened. . . . The harm was in the therapy itself."

Gault wrote to the Massachusetts Board of Registration in Medicine: "[Bean-Bayog] told him [Lozano] not to communicate with his family, and told and wrote him over and over that she was his mother, and that he was an infant. She sent him many children's book as gifts, as well as numerous cards and letters on which she said she was his 'mom' and he was her little boy. He says she openly masturbated during some of the therapy sessions. . . . His course of treatment was improper. During the past five years his life and professional education have been severely disrupted."

Not only Gault but other therapists who saw Lozano during his hospitalizations were unanimous in saying that medication and sensible, supportive therapy were indicated in light of the depressive states Lozano experienced when he first sought therapy. They believed that the kind of emotional, intense, and off-beat treatment he was given was not in his interest.

Born-Again Therapy

A variation—some might consider it an offshoot—of reparenting is the idea of rebirthing. These therapeutic schemes are organized around the birth process itself. Rebirthing therapists offer clients the idea that in ordinary human birth there is trauma, especially trauma around breathing. Some of these therapists have concocted rebirthing, which is a method of teaching patients to imagine going through the birth process in order to learn "proper breathing." Patients are told that the traumas of ordinary birth, suffered by us all, can be cured in this manner.

The Origins of Rebirthing

Leonard Orr, generally regarded as the founder of modern-day rebirthing, developed his theories by spending considerable time in a bathtub having "revelations." In 1974 he began to suspend friends in a redwood hot tub with snorkels and nose plugs. During these immersions, many of them began to get in touch with (as they said back then) certain of their own destructive behavioral patterns. A number of them said they experienced their own birth during the process. As Orr and his friends introduced it to others, rebirthing as a therapy began to spread.

After a time, Orr apparently came to realize that his very presence was an important part of the rebirthing event. He attributed this to the belief that he had released enough of his own birth trauma that other people felt safe to experience theirs with him in the hot tub. About a year later, Orr began working with the breathing pattern he felt happened at birth, but this time without using a hot tub. It then became apparent to him that it was the "rebirther" (that is, the person leading the session) and the method of breathing that were important, not so much the warm water.

Here's the theory in a nutshell: damage is done to the breathing mechanism at birth because the child is cut off from its supply of oxygen through the premature cutting of the umbilical cord. This initial panic ("breathe or die") remains in the person's subconscious as a nameless fear. The goal of the rebirthing process is to get the person to release this long-held tension and learn to take advantage of the fully functioning breathing mechanism. Once accomplished, the person can lead a full, happy, breathy life.

Rebirthing takes an average of three to ten two-hour sessions. Initially, rebirthees were promised both dramatic life changes and subtle feelings of contentment. Later, rebirthing was purported to bring on "permanent changes. . . . [It] releases deep body tension and thought patterns, . . . [causes] spontaneous remission of diseases, and just about every disease, from chronic lower back pain to cancer, has been released." Psychic abilities are supposed to increase and expand, not to mention that rebirthing wards off common colds and allergy attacks.

People have been rebirthed in ordinary home tubs in blue bubble-bath solutions, and in outdoor redwood hot tubs under starry skies. Others, like Rose at the beginning of this chapter, have succumbed to "dry rebirths," being rolled into a carpet on the floor and made to struggle to free themselves in order to "reexperience the birth process." Some have been wrapped in a series of blankets and rebirthed on an office couch.

One certified hypnotherapist who advertises on the Internet describes rebirthing as a form of hypnotherapy and as a "patterned breathing process which allows you to access and resolve blocks that are held in the body." Without qualifiers, she asserts that hypnotherapy is safe, and a trance state is a natural and familiar state, and that it can benefit you. She states that the technique of rebirthing combined with hypnotherapy will work for dealing with compulsive behavior, weight problems, anxiety, and phobias; that it will heal the child within related to abuse, abandonment, self-esteem, and improved relationships; that it will reduce stress and improve concentration; that it will improve health, pain, cancer, and chronic illnesses; that it will elevate performance in selling, communication skills, sports, dance, and art.

As far as we can tell, rebirthing is magic.

Major Leaders in Rebirthing

Sondra Ray and Bob Mandel are two big names in the rebirthing field. Their organization, previously called Loving Relationships Training, has recently taken on the new name Association of Rebirth Trainings International. Weekend sessions described as "educational and experiential" cost between $275 and $300. Participants are told that not only will they experience two rebirths during the weekend, but also "you will be helped to locate and release any negative decisions you may have made at your birth and which are still affecting your current life."

Sondra Ray, once a student of Leonard Orr, describes her own birth in this way: "When I was in the womb, I tried to communicate to my mother that I wanted to be born at home." She had also tried to communicate to her delivery team. Her mother heard her, she says, and she was born at home. The only problem was that Sondra was born on the kitchen table, to which she attributes her lifelong neurosis about food.

Bob Mandel, Ray's coauthor, describes his birth, too. His birth was "normal," he writes, but he mentions having been born in a Jewish hospital with Father Divine nurses assisting: "This might explain some of my religious confusion later in life, and my unending quest for my personal divinity."

In Ray and Mandel's book, a chapter is devoted to every imaginable type of birth: premature or late, unwanted, fast or held back, cesarean, wrong sex, induced, breech, forceps—you get the picture. The authors enumerate what they view as typical traits of those who were birthed in a particular way. For example, in the chapter on unwanted, unplanned, and illegitimate births, they suggest that if that's how you were born, then you may be addicted to rejection, or you may reject everyone who wants to be with you, or you may work to avoid being rejected by making yourself indispensable.

As discussed in Chapter One, stereotyping people and giving them all the same simple solutions seems to be a major characteristic of many of the odd therapies that have emerged over the years. Regression, reparenting, and rebirthing therapies fall on a narrow path. The innovators found themselves doing something: sitting in a hot tub, berating patients, or feeding them out of baby bottles. It felt good or worked for the therapists, so they made some assumptions in order to create an ideology that would support practicing the method on others. Without much thought, and little or no proof, the technique was expanded to become a "cure-all" for all people.

An additional factor that tends to make a risky situation worse is that some forms of therapy—which initially might gain support as "a breakthrough," "creative," or "innovative"—are not inspected critically by the professional community. Instead, these therapies are allowed to harm a number of patients until the courts are asked to evaluate the conduct of the therapists, the rationality of the therapy, and the extent of the damage done. Sometimes public inspection or legal redress never occurs, and the therapies continue to be promoted for decades, as we've seen here, with the on-going potential for outlandish or disastrous consequences.

Despite the widespread continuing use of regression techniques over the years, there are still only anecdotal tales to support any of the massive regressions described here (with the one exception of the outside study of the Rosen sample, which showed that the actual patient outcomes were contrary to what Rosen claimed).

Age regression, reparenting, and rebirthing are not proven helpful techniques. There is no scientifically established or objective clinical evidence showing them to be beneficial. So be careful! Think twice before going backwards.

to communicate with entities and disembodied spirit guides; learning about the "cosmic connections" between UFOs, extraterrestrials, and spiritual intelligence; and experiencing astral projection. Not only was there a five-hour television movie about the book, but MacLaine also took her show on the road, with a lecture tour and large group seminars. One financial writer for *Money* magazine estimated at the time that MacLaine would gross four million dollars for putting on seventeen weekend seminars.

There's no denying the influence that Hollywood box-office personalities have on the general public. If Shirley MacLaine is promoting New Age and occult philosophy, from belief in the power of crystals to channeling, astral projection, and spirit guides, it must be okay. Right?

Wrong.

Let's listen to one unhappy person. This gentleman called in to *Larry King Live* when MacLaine was a guest on the show to denounce the ideas being put out, saying that such ideas had completely "blown apart" his family.

> "My wife . . . in a time of depression went to a psychic healer and was told that in a past life I had murdered her and run off with her teen-aged daughter. I've not seen her in two years. I think she was looking for a crutch to avoid dealing with the realities of life—thinking things would be better the next time around. I think there's a certain group of people that can be damaged irreparably by this type of thought."

When asked to comment on this controversial therapy, Dr. Robert Phillips, deputy medical director of the American Psychiatric Association, said without hesitation, "This is, I think, charlatanism at its finest."

Our sentiments exactly. In numerous cases of which we're aware, clients have been harmed in a variety of ways. When the therapy ends, often because the client runs out of money or the client's insurance coverage runs out, the client is left stranded with a sense of victimization and unreality.

The past lives conjured up during therapy are rarely happy ones, and the fiddling with memory that goes on in these sessions tends to leave some clients confused and dysfunctional. Victims of this kind of therapy often have complaints such as, "Every day I have problems with almost everything I do because I keep wondering if something is real or not," or "I just can't get anything done anymore. I feel sort of paralyzed by the godawful scenes running through my head." Such negative aftereffects tend to occur because the type of vivid imagery invariably produced in hypnotic sessions of past-life recall are not easily forgotten: mass murder, rape, strangulation, burning at the stake, vicious physical assault. Scenes that would be X-rated in the movies become unforgettable repeat performances during so-called past-life work.

Linking such horrendous past events to something in the present prolongs and reinforces the detrimental effect. If even for a moment a person really believes, for example, that she was a prostitute in a past life, a victim of a gang rape by Viking warriors, or murdered by her current best friend, certainly the aftereffects of such thinking are not so readily erased.

We have never heard of a happy past-life account, the excuse being that clients are dealing with today's problems, so naturally they'd be rooted in past-life unpleasantness. Yet how "reliving" such nastiness can be touted as healthful, spiritual, and refreshing goes far beyond the scope of our imaginations.

The Concept of Reincarnation

Past-life therapy is based on the concept that we have lived many other lives before this one—essentially a belief in reincarnation. Past-life therapists tell us that identities and events experienced in our past lives are causing us hangups in this life and that we need to revisit our past lives and reexperience the trauma in order to get rid of the ghost, so to speak.

Although this therapy technique has become particularly trendy in recent years, few realize that first Colavida in Spain and then Albert de Rochas in Paris were using age regression during trance work as early as the late 1800s. De Rochas is said to have written the first book on the subject, published in 1911. Past-life work has always generated controversy and skepticism, and in 1921 one critic complained about de Rochas: "Subjects are so open to suggestion during trance that their ostensible memories of past lives would be merely responses to de Rochas' dominant and suggestive presence." Could this also be what's happening today?

Some of those who grant credibility to hypnotically induced past-life experiences often refer to the research of Dr. Ian Stevenson, a Canadian psychiatrist with an interest in the paranormal. Having traveled throughout the Far East, Stevenson based his findings on personal tales told to him (via a translator) of past-life visits to ancient lands and places. What's not often mentioned when citing Stevenson as a source of verification is that most of his tales came from the mouths of children.

Many defenders of past-life work also like to point to the famous case of Bridey Murphy as proof that a person can be hypnotized to remember past lives. In the 1950s, a soft-spoken housewife under hypnosis began telling tales of life in nineteenth-century Ireland, where she was a lass named Bridey Murphy. Her hypnotist wrote a best-selling book at the time, and for a while the Bridey Murphy fad swept the nation. Later it was discovered that she was in fact recounting stories told to her as a child by her Irish nanny. Despite the debunking of this "proof" of hypnotic past-life recall, countless people today are promoting past-life therapy as a cure-all.

We do not intend to challenge or offend the belief in reincarnation held by many as part of their belief system. We merely hope to call attention to those practitioners who are wont to use hypnosis and suggestion to induce a supposed past-life experience in their clients. We draw a distinction between religious or spiritual beliefs held by individuals and those therapy techniques that promote the acceptance of certain concepts because of the influence of a predisposed practitioner.

Past-life therapists seem to disregard or summarily dismiss the fact that the notion of reincarnation is a religious belief, not an accepted scientific tenet of psychology or psychiatry. Looked at in the cold light of day, past-life therapy is a form of spiritual or religious conversion intertwined with mental health counseling—although that's rarely how it's described by the practitioners. Rather, they would have you adopt an interpretation of reincarnation that tells you that we've all had past lives, that they affect our current lives, and that by remembering those awful things that supposedly happened to us centuries and eons ago, we're going to feel better today. It's a pseudopsychological approach to karma, a spiritual belief.

As with other odd therapies, past-life therapy involves leading a client to accept a belief system and the language that goes with the belief system. This practice shows no respect for either the scientific validation of mental health approaches or human individuality and freedom of choice.

It appears that past-life therapists are using their power position to indoctrinate. The patient comes in feeling bad, feeling needy and dependent, and wanting help. They may not know that this procedure isn't mainline, scientifically based, standard-of-practice therapy. As a result of going along with their therapist's recommendation, some patients end up adopting a new cosmology, including a new religious belief. What a hue and cry would be raised if a therapist told his or her patient that unless the patient accepted a certain political party's ideology, or joined the therapist's church, the patient could not receive therapy from that practitioner.

On this topic, John Kihlstrom, a professor in the Department of Psychology at Yale University, wrote: "In the final analysis, people who do religious healing should do religious healing, and not call it psychotherapy. After all, genuine faith healers don't call what they do medicine." He goes on to say that past-life therapy essentially "brings the occult into what is supposed to be a scientifically based therapeutic method."

Shaping Responses Through Hypnosis

One of the problems with past-life, future-life, and some of the other therapies described in this book is the misuse of and overreliance on hypnosis as a therapeutic tool. Hypnosis, when used responsibly, can indeed be beneficial. However, as with any procedure, in the wrong hands it can be misrepresented at best and harmful at worst. It is not magic, nor does it bring about instant recovery from troubling symptoms. Unfortunately, at present, the practice of hypnotherapy is not monitored sufficiently.

In the United States today there are anywhere from ten to fifteen thousand lay hypnotherapists, many of whom became certified by taking perhaps a weekend seminar or a brief series of courses. There are no licensing requirements, no prerequisites for training, and no professional organization to which those who hypnotize others are accountable. You can be a real estate agent, a graphic artist, an English teacher, or a hairdresser and also call yourself a hypnotherapist by hanging a certificate on your wall that states you took as few as eighteen hours of courses in hypnosis.

This lack of oversight leads to all sorts of abuses and malpractice. Inadequately trained people using hypnosis may find themselves practicing psychotherapy without a license. They are unable to diagnose serious psychological difficulties their clients might have; should they sense that they are in over their heads, many tend not to refer clients to more qualified professionals; and many are generally not aware of the common pitfalls of using hypnosis. They are also often the same people who tend to latch onto whatever "personal development" trend may be in the wind.

As with the use of hypnosis in general, a recent investigative report into past-life therapy substantiated the fact that almost anyone can call himself a past-life therapist after only a few hours of learning some basic techniques. In response to this, Dr. Dorothy

Kantor, president-elect of the American Psychological Association, said, "You wouldn't go to a doctor for a physical ailment who you thought had five sessions of training. . . . It makes such light of human emotion."

Hypnotic Imaginings = Reality

One argument used by promulgators of past-life therapy is that while in trance subjects describe places or situations they have never been in, studied, or talked about; how else could they so accurately describe these past eras or cultures unless they had been there? Here are some startling examples:

> DR. G.: Can you tell me where you find yourself?
> MIKE: A farm.
> DR. G.: Can you perceive what you are wearing?
> MIKE: Farmer's clothes.

Dr. G.'s verification: Mike is a skeptical reporter, a big-city guy who'd never even been to a farm. Here's another example.

> DR. G.: Where are you?
> CAROL: It's the South.
> DR. G.: What is happening now?
> CAROL: The Civil War.
> DR. G.: What is your name?
> CAROL: Sarah.

Dr. G.'s verification: Carol later learned from her 105-year-old grandmother that Carol's great-great-grandmother was named Sarah, and no one in the family had ever known about her before.

Aw, c'mon.

Bruce Goldberg (Dr. G.), the dentist turned past-life therapist, claims that the field of past-life regression/progression hypnotherapy is "the only one accepted by the APA that is based on a hard science." When we telephoned the American Psychological Association to verify this, reading directly from Goldberg's book, the APA spokesperson soundly denied Goldberg's claim. The APA doesn't take a position of accepting or not accepting, she told us. She said that it was inaccurate of Goldberg to say that, and that the statement in his book was misleading the public.

Goldberg's 1994 book was the basis for a made-for-TV movie, *Search for Grace*. It features Goldberg's client Ivy, who discovered forty-six past lives during forty-five hypnotic regressions. Some of Ivy's past lives were as a craftsman in ancient Rome, a fourteenth-century shepherd, a Polish pianist, a prostitute during the French Revolution, a tormented housewife in the mid-1800s, and a Roaring Twenties party girl. But that's not the half of it. In therapy, Ivy also discovered that her present lover had killed her more than twenty times in her previous lifetimes.

While most hypnotically induced imagery is vivid and convincing (as Ivy's past-life recall surely was to her), there is also the fact that most of us in modern society have been exposed to videos, movies, novels, photographs, and textbooks of various eras and historical characters that would provide us with material that would influence any hypnotic recall—just as this material influences our dreams. As much as some might like to think that all past-life scenarios are pure memories, it's hard to ignore the impact of all the stimulation around us—best-selling books, talk shows, TV movies, the news, glossy magazine articles, and plain old word-of-mouth tale-telling that filters in over the years. All of this has some effect on all of us in some way, and one effect is that it can fuel our imaginations. Equally influential in our lives are our relationships with peers and authority figures—one authority figure being our therapist.

Therapists—lay or professional—who rely so heavily on hypnotic and other trance-inducing techniques fail to consider the *demand characteristics* of the situation. That is, in their eagerness to have their brand of therapy work, some practitioners don't consider three very important factors:

1. The patient's knowledge of or supposition about what the therapist hopes to hear

2. The active, leading questioning done by the therapist

3. The therapist's shaping of the responses given during the patient's trance state, and the shaping of the interpretations afterwards

Therapists who expect a certain result can inadvertently or directly shape responses in numerous ways: through voice tone, through when and what they respond to, through how they word their questions, and so on. This shaping behavior will no doubt affect what is touted among certain hypnotherapists as the spontaneous emergence of uniform or grossly similar responses from clients. If all your clients are suddenly talking about space aliens or past lives, then it must be real, right?

Is This How Memory Works?

Therapists who believe, and convey to their clients, that everything that comes up during a hypnotic trance is spontaneous and comes from within the person are misleading clients. In reality, these therapists are influencing what happens during trance—a widely recognized and not uncommon phenomenon in the use of hypnosis in general. Many of these therapists appear to ignore the entire literature on influence that has become available over the years; for them, all the scientific work done on memory, hypnosis, and interpersonal influence falls between the floorboards like dust.

To add to the confusion and, in some cases, the intentional misrepresentation, many of these same therapists have an unswerving belief that human memory is like a video recording of everything that ever happened to a person. This stance runs contrary to decades of scientific research demonstrating that memory is reconstructive and *not* akin to a videotape; that not everything is recorded, much less retained or accompanied by the exact emotions experienced at the time of the event.

Past-life therapy trainer Hans TenDam writes: "The way to recall past lives is the same as to recall lost memories of this life. This way is called age regression. Full regression, originally a hypnotic state, brings back memories, but more intense, more like reliving than remembering. . . . We experience the situation just as it happened at the time." TenDam also emphatically states: "We all have a complete and uninterrupted memory of everything we have consciously and unconsciously experienced."

In most past-life therapy, hypnosis is used to lead clients into reverie and trance states during which the therapist asks a series of suggestive and leading questions that allegedly promote regression into past lives, where the patient will discover and relive traumas. The fact that these "rediscovered" stories may not be true or even historically accurate does not bother most practitioners of this type of therapy. Listen to what some of them have to say:

- "Even without conclusive proof, the benefits for personal empowerment, healing and enlightenment are tremendous."

- "Actually, whether the former lifetimes that are 'relived' are fantasies or actual experiences lived in a bygone era does not matter to me as a therapist—getting results is important."

- "Disproving hypotheses like imagination, pseudo-memory, and deceit is neither useful nor interesting."

Eighty people paid two hundred dollars each for a day of training in past-life regression at a recent workshop led by Brian Weiss. He taught the attendees some meditation and self-hypnosis techniques and told the group in a gentle tone that they could remember "everything," that people using past-life therapy get better.

Weiss handles the question of whether patients' material is actually recollection from past lives or simply subconscious imagining by saying: "You can't go into the laboratory [for proof]. . . . In therapeutic terms, it doesn't matter [where the images come from]. As a therapist, what it is becomes secondary."

Weiss claims that past-life therapy works and that's all that matters. Yet, on a scientific level it has been argued by other professionals such as Yale professor John Kihlstrom that "there is absolutely no acceptable evidence . . . not even a single clinical study with anything like an acceptable design, showing that past-life regression has positive therapeutic effects. . . . Scientifically oriented psychotherapists have an affirmative professional obligation to employ only techniques that are known to be safe and efficacious."

Therapist As Agent of Influence

In one of his books, Weiss includes instructions on how to "guide your subconscious mind to uncover the most pertinent childhood, past life, or perhaps in-between-life memory for you to experience." The notion of in-between-life as described by Weiss is akin to the idea of entities lost in space, floating in limbo, never having made it to "the other side," which we explore in the next chapter on entities therapy.

Weiss offers a script to read onto an audiotape, and a list of words to use for free associating. The words are, on the whole, ones likely to call forth the type of tales Weiss reports that his clients spontaneously produce in trance—for example: war, peace, desert, soldiers marching, church, spear, mob, hanging, execution, slave, king, knives, cave, body, funeral, pain, birth, and so forth.

As to whether or not the therapist influences the patient, past-life therapist Edith Fiore boldly states: "Sometimes it takes a bit of prodding on my part for the images to emerge and for you to find yourself 'there.'" And Bruce Goldberg explains that he gives patients a "conditioning" tape to listen to at home so their memories will become more accessible.

The theories of past-life recall didn't stand up to the test of four scientific studies carried out by Canadian psychologist Nicholas Spanos and colleagues. The conclusion was that "past-life identities are interpersonal products whose characteristics are geared to the expectations of significant others. One particularly important source of such expectations is the hypnotist." Despite what past-life regression proponents and well-wishers might say to defend the practice of this questionable technique, there is no scientific evidence to support the myth that the recall of past lives is possible through hypnotic induction or related techniques.

Meanwhile, on various Internet newsgroups, practitioners of all stripes are offering words of advice and encouragement regarding the use of past-life hypnotic regressions. Some advise the use of assistants or questioners, and others don't—although almost all indicate the importance of going into some form of altered state in order to access past-life material.

A Cure for Everything and Everyone

Some practitioners caution that "past-life therapy is not for the weak-minded or frail-hearted." But many therapists using this method are prone to try it on every customer. "In my experience several thousand clients have relived one or more past lives," said clinical psychologist Glenn Williston, one of the more prominent practitioners in this field. Another leader, Helen Wambach, reported that by 1978 she had done hypnotic past-life regression with one thousand persons. Clinical psychologist Fiore boasts: "I have performed between twenty and thirty thousand individual past-life regressions."

Because most past-life therapists assume that current life problems are related to events that took place in past lives, they contend that the client must confront certain past-life scenes and discharge all the emotions attached to the scenes in order to release themselves from their present-day troubles. An example might be a client who learns that being fearful and cautious is a remnant from a past life in which she had been stoned to death as an adulteress or witch.

Most past-life therapists argue that even though the trauma itself is important, what's more important is the continuing residual emotional reaction to the experience that comes down through time to bother the person today. These therapists appear to believe some version of Williston's theory that "programmed reactions . . . become fixed in the subconscious and passed on through Soul memory."

Some patients come to therapy ready for such work because the therapist has a reputation for doing past-life work. These patients expect hypnosis or some form of trance technique to be used, and look forward to exploring lives lived long ago. On almost any night on the Internet, you can find individuals asking into the yonder for recommendations from others for therapists who "do past-lives work."

Clients who didn't start out with past-life treatment in mind may find after a session or two that their therapist will suggest that past-life regression through hypnosis is the way to understand the unconscious and the origins of their symptoms and moods. By reliving the past-life traumas, clients are told, they should be able to comprehend and thus free themselves from puzzling fears and symptoms.

Some therapists—such as Fiore, Williston, and Weiss—make available model transcripts of themselves directing a person through a past-life trance regression. Others—like psychic researcher Brad Steiger, mystic Frances Steiger, and metaphysical teacher Ted Andrews—present do-it-yourself books with instructions on how to tape-record your own voice reading the various hypnotic inductions to play back later. But Morris Netherton, considered a pioneer in the field, insists "this is not a do-it-yourself-process." Netherton believes the presence of a therapist is crucial: clients are dealing with "memories of death" and can end up in some pretty scary places.

Most past-life therapists, however, maintain that past-life regression is easy if the subject is open-minded and willing, and has rapport with the therapist. One person who claims to have done past-life work for twenty-two years wrote on the Internet talk.religion.newage newsgroup that "for most people remembering past lives is as easy as remembering what they had for lunch yesterday."

Past-life therapy has been recommended by its practitioners for a panoply of symptoms: phobias, allergies and asthma, anorexia

and bulimia, atypical forms of psychosomatic disturbances, alco-
holism and drug abuse, homosexuality, epilepsy, cancer, sadism,
and masochism, although Netherton cautions that "it cannot
repair tissue damage."

Fiore mentions curing, or at least discovering the causes of,
patients' sexual and marital problems; fears of jumping overboard,
of getting lost at sea; snake phobia; fear of the dark, of fire, of train
travel; sleep disorders; smoking; eating disorders and compulsions;
and so on. She found "chronic headaches, including migraines, to
be the result of the patient's having been guillotined, clubbed,
stoned, shot, hanged, scalped or, in one way or the other, severely
injured on the head or neck. . . . [and those] with chronic, intract-
able abdominal pains relived having their bellies run through with
swords, bayonets or knives. Even the origin of menstrual problems
has been traced to trauma, usually sexual, in a previous life." Fiore
proclaims: "There is not one aspect of character or human behavior that cannot be better understood through an examination of
past-life events."

This approach to therapy presumes that almost all emotional and
behavioral problems stem from a single type of trauma. Such reasoning falsely assumes that everyone is the same and that there is only
one cause and one cure for all psychological ills. Here the cause is
past-life trauma, and the cure is past-life regression therapy. Everyone
has been stamped out like a cookie, and with another cookie cutter
people can be reshaped. Therapists who use this single cause–single
cure approach have lost respect for human individuality.

As for the opinion of one professional organization, Dr. Mel Sab-
shin, medical director of the American Psychiatric Association,
offered this statement: "The American Psychiatric Association
believes that past-life regression therapy is pure quackery. As in
other areas of medicine, psychiatric diagnosis and treatment today
is based on objective scientific evidence. There is no accepted scientific evidence to support the existence of past lives, let alone the
validity of past-life regression therapy."

Is the Trauma in the Past Life or in the Therapy?

Some personal stories of past-life therapy can illustrate the potential for loss of time and money, as well as for psychological harm.

Getting Scalped

"Paul" was referred by his internist to a psychologist for tension, worry, and recurrent headaches. In the first session, the psychologist said that he practiced past-life therapy to eliminate specific symptoms one at a time. He told Paul to lie back in a reclining chair, close his eyes, and give his personal history.

The therapist asked Paul to pick which symptom he wanted to work on first. Paul chose his headaches, because they kept him from enjoying life. The therapist asked him to think of a scene just before his birth. Paul told the therapist that his forehead felt hot, that he felt as though he were pushing against something with his head. The therapist told Paul that he was back in the birth canal, trying to be born. Paul felt woozier and woozier as he listened to the therapist tell him he would soon feel the forceps that were used to deliver him. Paul felt intense pain around his head, sunk deeper into a "passing out" feeling, and soon realized he was back to room-level awareness. The therapist congratulated him on being a good subject.

"We know now that part of your headaches are connected to when you were born in this lifetime," said the therapist excitedly. "But let's go back more and see what happened to you in past lives."

Paul closed his eyes as the therapist spoke of "going back, back, to when your head began to hurt really badly." Paul saw himself running, trying to escape from an Indian who hit him over the head with a tomahawk. Next he was in a place resembling Hawaii. Enemies were chasing him toward the edge of a cliff high above the ocean. He dove off the cliff. He landed on his head on rocks and died. Paul then saw himself riding on a horse in military uniform and striking his head against a tree branch and falling off his horse into white light.

At two sessions a week at $150 per session for a year, Paul spent more than $15,000 on this treatment—all of his savings. His symptoms didn't go away; in fact, they got worse. He became spacey at work and eventually lost his job, at which time the therapist stopped seeing Paul because he could no longer pay.

Being Buried Alive

"Ruby" was referred to therapy by her internist, who told her he hoped that talk therapy would prevent the need for antidepressant medication, which he was planning to prescribe for her if talk therapy didn't alleviate her symptoms. He sent her to a psychologist who had recently moved into the same medical building.

Ruby entered treatment expecting to talk about her current life problems, which were great: her husband had developed crippling arthritis and was having to change his work from being an electrician to being a salesman in a hardware store. Ruby was caring for her aged mother and two small children, while attempting to enter court reporting school. Ruby, who came from a family with a number of relatives on medication for depression, was worn out and demoralized.

The therapist turned out to be a past-life therapist. She told Ruby they would do trance work and learn the source of her depression; they set up a series of appointments. In trance, Ruby saw herself as a man in ragged clothes helping build a pyramid in ancient Egypt. She was so tired from laboring up an incline with a large stone slab in her arms that she fell into an open chamber. As she was lying there dying, she heard the slave master tell the other workers to simply seal the chamber and leave her there.

The experience was so terrifying that she canceled the other appointments by phone the next day, telling the psychologist she was cured. Ruby went back to her internist, who apologized for the odd treatment, put her on medication, and referred her to another psychologist better known to him.

You Have Been Here Before Already Tomorrow

Meanwhile, some therapists are supporting the idea of future-life progressions. Glenn Williston states that "our future selves affect us as much *now* as our past selves. . . . You can influence your past and future personality aspects by knowing the truth *now*, and all are affected *now*."

Bruce Goldberg, the dentist from Baltimore, claimed in 1982 that he knew of "no other therapist in the country who does progressions"—that is, who takes clients forward in time. Progressions require more conditioning, Goldberg unabashedly tells us, because humans are programmed to think of the future as mysterious and inaccessible. "Yet," he writes, "if we weren't supposed to know the future, progression simply wouldn't work." And it has worked big time for him: he claims to have done thousands of progressions as well as regressions with his clients.

Having heard so many of his clients talk about the future, Goldberg makes sweeping but rather benign predictions for the future, which include the following:

- Twenty-first century: Earth will undergo major geographical changes; scientific progress will be most evident.

- Twenty-second century: much advancement in medical science will be evident.

- Twenty-third century: sophisticated computers and video equipment are household appliances.

- Twenty-fourth century: a small-scale nuclear war results in a reduction of the world's population.

- Twenty-fifth century: androids perform all menial tasks.

He describes the twenty-sixth century as what could be regarded as absolute bliss.

Goldberg assures clients that they never have to worry about getting stuck in the future. As with regressions, he says no one has ever been harmed. As a safeguard, though, Goldberg uses a special protective shield. He has the client "imagine a pure white light entering the top of the head and filling the entire body. . . . That is all there is to it," writes Goldberg, who states that this white light wards off any harm or negativity.

———————

Although perhaps a lucrative practice for the practitioner, past-life therapy appears to offer the client a multitude of contradictions, problems, and potential risks. Essentially, past-life and future-life therapies encourage patients to adopt a kind of magical thinking that teaches them to evade rather than cope with reality—which is what therapy is supposed to be about. Even though there may appear to be some short-term benefits in the relief gained from the cathartic release of screaming, shrieking, and crying during the "re-experiencing" of hideous past-life traumas, there are also risks.

Oftentimes patients tend to become dependent on the therapist for more and more regressions. In some cases, patients who are extremely suggestible (that is, dissociative-prone persons) may not find their way back so easily from the deep hypnotic trance episodes. They may get lost in a kind of irreality and find that they are less functional than they were before seeking therapy.

Even those who experience some short-term relief may in time find their original symptoms resurfacing; they realize that they hadn't really gotten to the root of the phobia, aversion, or whatever the regression was supposed to have cured. So, a disheartening feeling of not really getting anywhere is added to the loss of time and money spent on the past-life therapy.

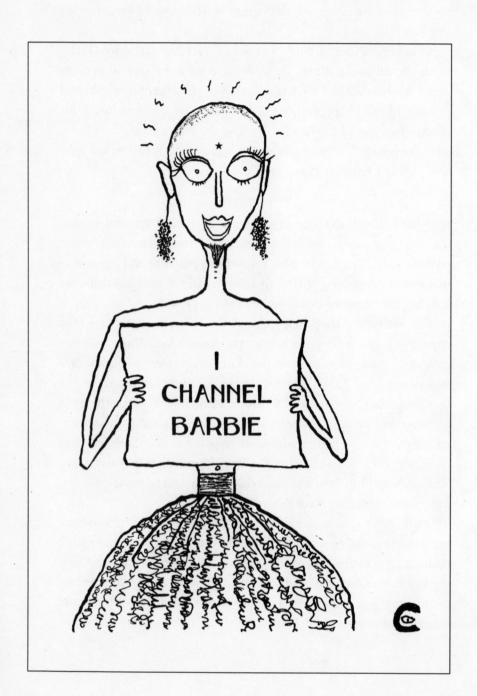

4

They've Got You Coming and Going

Entities Therapists and
the Channeling Connection

Entities therapists teach their clients that certain beings did not at the point of death "pass over" or fully transition from life on earth to another plane or afterlife. Instead, they took up residence as spirits, or entities, living in the clients' bodies. Depending on the situation, these therapists may wait a few sessions before introducing this idea and claiming that they will help rid the client of the spirits and the trouble they are causing.

The terms *entities, spirits, discarnates, earthbounds, walk-ins,* and *possessors* are used interchangeably by the practitioners of this trade. A few therapists advertise that they also deal with ghosts—spirits outside the client—as well as with those inside a person.

These therapists assert that cure rests on the use of hypnosis and regression therapy to recall the spirits that have invaded the person, and that the spirits are the origin of the client's conflict, pain, or other symptoms. Some entities therapists also tell clients that the clients' descriptions of their parents indicate that they too may have been invaded by entities. At some later point, the therapist and client begin the exorcism ritual, by which the entities are dispatched, freed, and sent out of limbo into eternity. In most cases these exorcisms are emotional and quite violent proceedings. Here's a typical example of what can happen in this kind of therapy:

Visualizing Fiery Deaths

"Jason," a twenty-nine-year-old accountant, went to therapy because he felt lonely and his job was very stressful. He saw an ad in a local paper offering a combination of treatment and training in hypnosis. Jason thought such a program offered a twofold hope: he'd overcome his loneliness and learn another career.

Dr. "R.," a licensed psychologist and director of the institute, said the institute's work was based on theories that mental energy gets knotted up inside a person. Through hypnosis a person can learn to relax, untie the knots of stress, and gently free oneself from the effects of "incompletions." The object was to release spirit entities, those human, animal, and mystical creatures that invade us and take control of our lives.

Although skeptical about entities and such, Jason said, "I knew the man had a Ph.D., and he was very positive and made lots of reference to scientists. He assured me that this was the therapy of the twenty-first century, that only recently had science discovered the effects of entities on the human psyche. He said I so impressed him he would be my personal therapist."

Dr. R. would say at the beginning of each trance session, "You will only remember what you need to." Toward the end of the session, Dr. R. would "awaken" Jason and tell him which entities had been found. Some were little children who were terrified of other entities, which sounded like those creatures in the bar scene in the movie *Star Wars:* erect walking creatures with fur, fangs, and claws, making odd guttural menacing growls.

After a few months, Jason's coworkers noticed his seeming preoccupation and absentmindedness and asked whether there was anything they could help with. Jason seemed worried, blue, and slowed down. Then one day his boss confronted him with evidence of Jason's gross errors and slow output. The boss told Jason that he didn't want to fire him and suggested he see a doctor.

Jason started to reflect on what was going on with him. He realized that he couldn't keep track of his thoughts and was often getting lost going home on the freeway. He was unable to keep the entities out of his daily waking mind. Most nights he would just sit and go into trance, working over the scenes in his mind. Jason told Dr. R. what the boss had said and also expressed his own concerns. Promising to "release" the entities and get Jason feeling better, Dr. R. suggested an all-day Saturday appointment.

On that day, while hypnotized, Jason visualized a gathering of entities in a large barn. A bolt of lightning struck, setting the building on fire. The entities were burned in vivid, terrifying ways. Jason watched as horribly scarred and blistered creatures emerged, chanting "Jason, Jason."

The session left Jason confused and spacey. Nothing around him seemed quite real. He felt estranged from his surroundings, and even felt that his own hands and legs weren't part of him but were some new foreign things. He called a psychiatric clinic and asked for emergency help.

Some entities therapists work alone, incorporating the entities idea into their therapy techniques after having attended one or more weekend seminars on channeling. Therapy may entail months of getting clients to locate, name, "experience," and release (or get rid of) what sometimes turns out to be a multitude of inner entities.

Other therapists work collaboratively with a "channeler," a special person who claims to have the ability to communicate with and speak for entities and long-gone beings. The entities supposedly exist on a reachable plane, from which they can be contacted by a tranced-out channeler. In such cases, the therapist, client, and channeler meet together. While the client is in a hypnotic trance, the therapist is told by the channeler, who also goes into a trance state, which entities are present within the client. Later this information is conveyed to the client. Occasionally clients are told that helpful entities reside within the channeler or that the channeler can be useful in convincing some of the client's entities to assist in the process of getting rid of the other bad or troublesome entities.

Sometimes a therapist will refer clients to a particular channeler for private sessions without the therapist included. Information and insights from the channeling sessions are then followed up on in therapy, as in the following example.

Spirit Advises Wife to Flee

"Kathy" was married and had two children. She had been seeing a therapist because she felt some dissatisfaction at being home with two young children and anger at her husband, who worked long hours and, in Kathy's opinion, left her alone too much. Her licensed, credentialed therapist recommended that she see a channeler for a few sessions to contact a spirit entity so that Kathy could learn more about what the future had in store for her.

After a few sessions, the spirit (via the channeler) told Kathy to leave her husband and hide herself and the children from him. This loss, intoned the spirit, would lead to Kathy's husband's demise from a fast-spreading disease he would contract. The spirit advised that the inheritance from the death would enable Kathy to lead a free life, with enough money for herself and her children. On learning this, Kathy's therapist did nothing to counteract the channeled spirit's wild advice, and Kathy left town surreptitiously, as instructed. Her husband finally located her and the children and learned this tale from her. The family remains in disarray, with Kathy continuing to see the therapist and the channeler, and the husband seeking legal and psychological help for himself.

The fees for this combination of channeling consultation and therapy are, of course, double: a payment for the therapist and one for the channeler.

Simply put, entities therapists combine ages-old trance mediumship with a form of modern-day exorcism. They seem to have little trouble finding a vulnerable population on which to foist their theories, for surveys show that 23 percent of Americans believe in reincarnation, 14 percent believe in mediums, and 42 percent believe they have been in contact with someone who died. That's anywhere from 3.5 million to 10.5 million people who might make the leap to accept communication with the dead as a therapeutic practice, not to mention those like Jason, who don't start out with this propensity but are convinced by their therapists of the existence of other-world entities and of the usefulness of these entities as a means to cure whatever ails the client.

This book is not the place to debate the validity of the trance channeling phenomenon. Rather, we will focus on the impact of this technique and related theories.

Speaking with the Dead and Long Gone

Since antiquity, people have claimed to communicate with or produce remarks from the dead. Traditionally, these clever people have been called mediums.

Two famous mediums popular in the United States and Europe were the Fox sisters, who in 1848 claimed they were communicating with a Mr. Splitfoot, the spirit of a man murdered in their house some years earlier. Margaret Fox, age fifteen, and Kate, twelve, worked out a tapping code for disseminating wisdom and answering questions (one tap for no, three for yes). Forty years later, in 1888, Margaret confessed that she and her sister, with the assistance of a servant girl hiding in the basement, had produced the rappings with their toes.

A wave of mediums appeared in the 1870s. These mediums introduced into their seances automatic painting, automatic writing, rapping in the room, the levitation of small tables, mysterious touches on the hand or cheek, billowing curtains, luminous forms floating in the room, and chairs or other objects moving about—all of this supposedly emanating from spirits acting through the medium. Some mediums alleged that the smoky or foglike luminous effects in the dimly lit room were the "materializations of ecto-plasm," a material "proof" of the spirit's existence.

From 1885 to 1915, Eusapia Palladino, the best-known medium of the day, gave hundreds of seances and was caught in blatant fraud a number of times. Nevertheless, certain doctors and academics kept on believing that she cheated only part of the time.

The most widely known American medium is Edgar Cayce, who died in 1945 but whose books are still available. Cayce was suppos-edly communicating with the minds of both living and dead peo-ple but his voice always remained his own. In that sense, he was somewhat different from other mediums, and for some believers he was considered far superior in that speaking in his own voice was supposed to mean he was completely in tune with the entities.

More recently, *channeler* rather than *medium* became the popular term to use in relation to this fad, no doubt stemming from mod-ern-day familiarity with the television term for the electrical fre-quency on which a certain station appears. Also, being a channel through which disembodied spirits can communicate tends not to convey the sad aura of a dead person speaking, as is the case with mediums. Use of the word *channeling* was a definite improvement for the more positive-minded attitude of the Age of Aquarius.

The Channeling Connection

Trance channeling in general has become so popular that one observer wryly described the present-day scene as the "rush hour of the entities." The mainstream media, tabloid papers, and alternative and New Age publications carry stories about and advertisements for channelers galore. Who, for example, hasn't enjoyed Hunk-Ra, the entity made famous in the "Doonesbury" cartoon strip?

Not a weekend goes by without an opportunity to attend a seminar with a channeler. These seminars are especially geared toward professionals, possibly because they can afford it; they also pay to come back for more, bringing along their friends and colleagues. Because a significant number of mental health professionals attend these seminars and engage in private sessions with channelers, some odd combinations of therapy have emerged. Some channelers themselves claim a professional background, listing master's, doctoral, nursing, counseling, or divinity degrees. Thus, they themselves become the psychotherapist, providing counseling services to their clients.

Channelers abound in many areas, with individuals from Hawaii to Scotland advertising the entity or entities they channel. Some researchers say that there are tens of thousands of channelers worldwide, with approximately one thousand in southern California alone. Books about channeling can be found in most bookstores, alongside books that were purportedly channeled to the author. A recent estimate puts the number of published "channeled" books at more than one hundred thousand.

How Does It Work—Or Does It?

Researchers of channeling are found in the fields of parapsychology, ESP, psychic phenomena, and psychology. One advocate, Arthur Hastings, former president of the California Institute of Transpersonal Psychology in Menlo Park (a community adjacent to Stanford University), defines channeling as "the process in which a person transmits messages from a presumed discarnate source external to his or her consciousness."

Former Rutgers University professor Jon Klimo is often regarded as the foremost researcher on channeling. Taking a somewhat favorable stance, Klimo uses this definition for channeling: "a phenomenon in which otherwise ordinary people seem to let themselves be taken over by, or in others ways receive messages from, another personality who uses them as a conduit, medium, or channel for the communication. . . . Such personalities usually purport to be from some other dimension or level of reality, often claiming to be more highly evolved than we on earth are. Much of their information seems intended to hasten personal and planetary growth."

Most channelers lay claim to a single entity who speaks only through that channeler. However, one entity—Michael—is unique in that he (it?) is described as a "'recombined entity,' made up of more than a thousand 'old soul' fragments." In the San Francisco area alone, at least six individuals claim to channel Michael. One person advertises Michael as a "light-hearted . . . nonphysical group of teachers, whose goal is Unconditional Love . . . often with humor."

A wave of channeled publications followed the appearance in 1970 of *Seth Speaks*, a book supposedly channeled through writer and poet Jane Roberts. Seth described himself as "an energy personality essence no longer focused in physical reality." That same year, Richard Bach wrote the best-seller *Jonathan Livingston Seagull*, a book said to have been dictated by a spirit entity that appeared to Bach in the form of a bird.

Another remarkable publication, *A Course in Miracles*, first came forth in 1975. Helen Schucman, a psychologist at Columbia University, claimed that for seven years, starting in 1965, she had been the channel for the voice of none other than Jesus. According to Schucman, "the Voice" began by saying, "This is a course in miracles . . ." with such force that Schucman felt compelled to take notes. The Voice's dictations resulted in a twelve-hundred-page work, including a teacher's manual, which was published in three volumes by several of Schucman's colleagues. Initially, hundreds of thousands of sets were sold by word of mouth. To date, the current publisher claims that more than a million copies of the three-volume set have been sold.

The *Course*, or ACIM (as it is sometimes referred to by its advocates), has been wildly popular and regarded as helpful by many since the 1980s. Yet in discussions or reviews it is rarely mentioned that Schucman was raised in a metaphysical environment, that she professed to receive signs from God as early as age four, and that the *Course* was little different from much of her own previous writings that weren't "channeled."

By the nineties, channeled entities seemed to be a dime a dozen, each trying to have its own peculiar twist. Some disclaim individuality, such as Jach Pursel's "Lazaris," for example. Lazaris says he is "not now and never has been physical or human. Nor is he a person as we would define it, but rather a group being living in another dimension from ours where time and space as we know it do not exist." Lazaris has been channeled by Pursel since 1974, usually speaking at weekend seminars that now cost at least three hundred dollars and in expensive private sessions organized by Concept: Synergy, a company run by Pursel, his ex-wife Peny, her new husband, and a staff of devoted assistants.

One particularly well known channeler claims to speak for an entity named Ramtha, a warrior who lived 35,000 years ago who introduces himself as "The Enlightened One." Ramtha came to prominence when actress Shirley MacLaine consulted him through his channeler, J. Z. Knight, a Washington State former cable TV executive and breeder of Arabian horses. Once again, MacLaine, through her prominence as a celebrity, lent an aura of credibility and respectability to a controversial phenomenon. By praising her contact with Ramtha and writing about it in her best-selling *Dancing in the Light,* MacLaine contributed greatly to Knight's vast popularity.

Other entertainment personalities claim to contact spirit guides such as Mafu, a "highly evolved being from the seventh dimension, last seen on Earth when he incarnated as a leper in first century Pompeii." Mafu is channeled by California homemaker Penny Rubin.

Today, the Internet serves as another outlet for channelers and their entities. Not only are channeled documents posted on various newsgroups, but one can also find frequent messages such as this one on the sci.psychology newsgroup:

We are starting a discussion group in the L.A. area, to be hosted by a teaching entity speaking through a full trance channel. The focus of the group will be Spiritual Self Exploration and Relationships. . . . Energy dynamics, dreams, past lives and other subjects are all likely to come up. . . . We have been trance channeling since 1989. The entity who will host this group has completed all of her physical incarnations except for one. . . . The entity is able to help people identify core issues in their lives, and typically gets right to the point, without judgment, if you are up for that. . . . Whether you are interested in psychology (including if you are a professional) or channeling, or psychic/spiritual realities, or if you simply want to explore something new, you may find this discussion group to be an opportunity worth pursuing.

Speaking of channeled sources, Harvard theology professor Harvey Cox said, "They are so cuddly and friendly. They seem to be yuppified versions of the demons and spirits of another time." Not all so cuddly and friendly, though, as those persons who have experienced them in a crazy therapy can attest.

How Do They Sound?

Several years ago a colleague in another part of the country, Carl Raschke, and coauthor Singer had independently watched or listened to videotapes or audiotapes of more than one hundred channelers. This was when channeling was first getting widespread media attention. Raschke and Singer learned of their mutual work only when they both appeared on a national television program.

From their studies, they each noted that most channelers spoke in pseudo-British accents, even when claiming to have lived thousands of years ago in Atlantis, Egypt, or North America. What seemed odd was that these "ancient" types were speaking a form of modern English with an American pattern to it. Some channelers speak like actor Yul Brunner in *The King and I*. Others appear merely to omit words, sounding a bit like actors doing a poor imitation of a foreign speaker; and still others speak in hushed, breathy sentences, much like a tired older man, and also leave out words, creating the impression that English is not their native tongue. In studying tapes of certain channelers going on for more than an hour at a time, an attentive listener can hear that the entity's accent diminishes and sounds more ordinary and American as the human channeler wears down a bit.

You, the reader, might be tempted to ask if the entities being channeled are real. Researcher Brooks Alexander asked that question and concluded: "There seem to be four basic options: (1) the entities are real and are telling us the truth about themselves; (2) the entities are real and are lying to us; (3) the entities are a 'dissociative reaction,' a mental dysfunction unrecognized as such; (4) the entities are a conscious fraud for the purpose of gain."

Swiss psychiatrist Carl Gustav Jung commented that "the communications of 'spirits' are statements about the unconscious psyche, provided they are really spontaneous and are not cooked up by the conscious mind." As for Carl Raschke, a professor at the University of Denver, his conclusion about trance channeling was a bit more pointed: "It's a form of mass psychosis that is leading to mass acceptance of the irrational."

With a sigh of relief we came across a posting on the Internet that spoke very much to this point. It was written by someone who was hoping to raise some pertinent issues relating to what he called "various newage [sic] philosophies." The author outlined some questionable patterns that he found lurking behind some of this thinking couched in terms of planetary cleansings, highly evolved beings, and galactic order. He ended with this apt summation:

> And how come the sources that many newagers channel
> are all saying different things? Can't they get it together
> up there on the higher levels? I have listened to a few

different tapes from "higher levels" and "ETs" and much of the information is contradictory. Why do newagers seem to assume that "higher dimensions" are better? If the information being channeled is contradictory, isn't it possible that the higher levels are filled with practical jokers and clowns just like this level is?

Maybe someone can tell me what all this is about. I kind of like this level and I agree with Thoreau . . . "One world at a time."

Are You Possessed?

Clinical psychologist Edith Fiore, introduced in Chapter Three, has compiled a list of the ten most common signs of possession. As with other such symptom checklists, this one is sprinkled with near-universal human problems. Fiore's ten signs are "low energy level, character shifts or mood swings, inner voice(s) speaking to you, abuse of drugs (including alcohol), impulsive behavior, memory problems, poor concentration, sudden onset of anxiety or depression, sudden onset of physical problems with no obvious cause, emotional and/or physical reaction to reading *The Unquiet Dead* [Fiore's book on possession therapy]."

At one point Fiore commented that "at least seventy percent of my patients were possessed and it was this condition that caused their dis-ease. Most of these people were relieved—through depossession techniques—of more than one entity." Some, she says, had been taken over by more than fifty entities.

Fiore claims to have treated more than five hundred possessed patients during the seven years prior to the 1987 publication of her book. She writes of having performed "twenty thousand hypnotic regressions with over one thousand patients." Using hypnosis and regression techniques, Fiore boasts of instantaneous cures of her patients:

- As for one patient, "Following the regression, her life-long depression lifted completely."

- Another suffering from sexual problems was regressed and at the next session reported "a complete cure!"

- Yet another "stated that she was totally free of her symptoms."

- And still another came back after her first hypnotic regression "free from all the fears she had had."

At first Fiore treated her patients with past-life therapy, but then she decided that her patients were "unwilling mediums" actually possessed by spirits or entities. She came to this realization when her patients said things to her like, "My husband says I'm two completely different people, especially before my period." So much for PMS-related mood changes. A statement as innocent as "That's just not me!" was proof to Fiore that she had before her a possessed patient—a subject to be hypnotized, in which to find spirits residing, on which to perform her exorcism ritual, which she calls depossession.

Unlike some of the other entities therapists, Fiore is very sympathetic to the lost souls. "My therapeutic goal," she explains, "is to help the possessing spirits, since they are in the greatest pain, even if it means that my patients must be burdened a little longer while we work on the willingness of the possessors to leave." This of course prolongs the therapy, and the question remains: Who's paying for this? The half-dead spirits or the living client?

The Impact on the Client

Although variations exist among entities therapists, one of the more common features is that these therapists appear to have developed a twist on the currently faddish diagnosis of multiple personality disorder. Instead of diagnosing a patient as a single person fractured by trauma into multiple selves, with the goal being to eventually integrate all the "alter" personalities into one, here a patient is told that she is one person but has been invaded by entities or walk-ins, or possessed by spirits or discarnate beings—whatever label the particular therapist chooses for the supposed invaders. The process of therapy then evolves into a sort of exorcism, a rite in which demons and devils are allegedly banished from the host.

With the help of some more personal stories, the reader can see why entities therapies should be of concern.

Turned into a Killer

"Cindy" entered therapy for mild depression and tiredness. At the time she was working two jobs and taking care of her home and family. In an early session, Cindy's therapist hypnotized her in order to discover the so-called entities that he believed had invaded her mind and body.

He told her that there were a number of therapists treating people for multiple personality disorder (MPD) but that he and his colleague were in the avant-garde of the therapy movement because they had made a great discovery. Regular MPD therapists, he explained, were telling clients that their one personality had fragmented and that they were to stay in lengthy therapy to work at integrating the various sub-personalities into one unified self. In contrast, he had discovered that MPD was really caused by spirit-world beings invading a person, and the therapist's role is to uncover the roster of entities in the patient and help get rid of them.

Cindy had to be hospitalized after one prolonged hypnotic session, as she was in a highly disturbed psychotic frenzy. In her mind, with the aid of the therapist's word pictures, Cindy killed off hundreds of entities within her through drowning, gaps in the earth swallowing people, explosions, and other violent acts. Afterward, she was left with feelings of terror and remorse. Cindy is now in therapy with a stable, realistic therapist who is helping her understand the trauma done to her by the fantastic therapy of her first therapist.

Thrown over the Cliff

"Beth," age twenty-eight, was married and the mother of three small children. Her husband's job necessitated a move from the Midwest, where they left behind Beth's large, warm family and all her friends. She'd never been away from them before. The move left her lonely, tired, and depressed. Wanting to adjust to the move, Beth sought therapy.

The symptoms and history she presented to the therapist would have been diagnosed by an ordinary therapist as an adjustment disorder with depressive features; in all likelihood Beth might have been referred for psychiatric evaluation to see if medication would help relieve her depression. The therapist might have provided supportive and rehabilitative therapy during a fairly brief period of time. Instead, something else transpired, for the therapist Beth ended up seeing had become enamored of channeling and entities therapy after attending a series of weekend seminars.

Sessions began with the therapist teaching Beth to relax while listening with closed eyes to several guided-imagery stories. He would say, "Listen to my words and imagine yourself in the scenes my words create." He then described panoramas of animals, children, adults, and mythical creatures, with vivid portrayals of detailed costumes from various historical times. The therapist would urge Beth to "get acquainted" with the people and creatures in the scenes.

Beth said it was like being in a movie watching herself interact with these people and creatures. After the imagery portion, the therapist quizzed Beth about her experiences with the stories. During the third or fourth session, he said, "Your symptoms and response patterns match those of other patients I've treated who had been invaded by entities." He led her to accept his interpretation that what she was seeing in the imagined scenes was the source of her depression. He'd make statements like, "Recently, psychotherapists and channelers have discovered that there are millions of entities that have been caught in another 'plane.' They exist as spirits that invade humans on a regular basis, causing tension and distress."

Beth's continuing therapy involved identifying the entities and discovering what in their lives they had not "completed." "Soon we'll begin to free the entities from being caught in their in-between existence," the therapist assured Beth. "This will allow them to move on to a peaceful eternity and a peaceful life for you." Beth's job, he told her, was to get the people and creatures to "complete" whatever was keeping them from going on to a full crossing over.

They proceeded to "discover" and discuss more than one hundred entities supposedly dwelling in Beth's mind. At the point of death—usually in the most desperate of circumstances, such as soldiers dying on medieval battlefields, people being swept away by floodwater, mothers drowning while attempting to rescue their children, and animals caught in caves from which they could not escape—all had become doomed to travel in this dimension between life and death.

Beth was directed while in trance to lead her entities to the edge of a high mountain cliff, where a terrific windstorm blew them over. Beth described hearing the screams of people she witnessed falling to their end in the ravine below the cliff. She came out of the trance state terrified by its seeming reality, and feeling that she had literally murdered the mass of poor creatures. Instead of feeling cured, to the contrary she felt she had killed them; that she, in fact, had not released them to a pleasant afterlife where they would not invade anyone else again, as the therapist had promised. She felt more anxious and tense than ever before in her life. Listening to the therapist effusively congratulate her on the many "completions," she could not bring herself to tell him how desperate she felt.

She barely slept the next three nights. Finally, in a state of near panic, she called a psychiatrist, who prescribed brief medication.

Beth remained in therapy with the psychiatrist for some months, going over the trauma and anger she felt toward the entities therapist and his theory. She was especially upset by the fact that she went into therapy to deal with her sadness at moving and had been subjected to the wrong kind of treatment. In addition to the cost of all this, she lost months of her life absorbed in the entities work and its consequences, which were increased anxiety, confusion, anger, and bewilderment at how she had gone along with what in retrospect she sees as a bizarre therapy.

Sucked into the Sea

At age fifteen, "William" had been in a tragic holiday boating accident on a lake, in which several men lost their lives. He had come to terms with that event as well as his subsequent fear of boats, water, and drowning. He later served at sea in the navy. Returning to civilian life, he married, and at a later time sought therapy after the death of his mother, who had been a lifelong asthmatic. He was depressed and wanted to talk about his grief, his job, and some everyday stresses of life. His therapist turned out to be an entities therapist who began using hypnosis to help with William's depression.

Before long, William was told by the therapist that from his own channeling work he could tell that William needed to meet and deal with his entities, which had appeared during "deep hypnosis." William liked the therapist, and because he had never been in therapy before, he went along with trying to visualize the alleged entities.

After about four months of twice-weekly sessions, William and the therapist had "discovered" several hundred men, women, children, animals, and science fiction–type creatures. There were so many beings that only a few were named. The therapist decided that they should narrow down the number of entities in order to help William move faster toward recovery. "Releasing the entities will release your symptoms," the therapist told William. He was instructed to visualize a scene in which about one hundred of the entities would be released.

The scene, visualized from the therapist's words, was near a beach. Somehow William and the entities were in a dreamlike swirl of water. He saw something like the funnel of a tornado dive into the water, as the entities were pulled down by a sucking force. Among them he saw the faces of his friends killed in the boating accident and of his mother—all being captured and pulled down by the swirling waters. William came out of the hypnosis in a terror, feeling for the first time that he had been the cause of the deaths of his friends in the long-ago boating accident, as well as responsible for sending his mother to this other-world place where she'd been destroyed.

William felt tormented, and he sought help after telling his wife what had happened. His wife was enraged that William couldn't even think of his beloved mother anymore because of all the turmoil and anguish produced by the therapist-directed visualizations and the process of "releasing" the entities.

Misuse of Hypnosis, and Other Ethical Issues

What seems astonishing is that some past-life and entities thera-pists, as well as others who use hypnotic regression techniques, have no grasp of the fact that through trance visualizations they are caus-ing their patients to feel as though they had killed or destroyed liv-ing beings during the so-called releasing process. Much of this stems from the misuse of hypnosis. If therapists using trance induction fail to recognize how the patient is responding or being affected, it is likely that things will go awry.

For some reason, entities therapy almost always tends to include violence and harsh imagery. The images visualized during trance can be so scary and vivid that often the hypnotherapist's later explanations to bring the client back to reality simply don't penetrate the client's mind. The client tends to remain stuck in the very concrete and vivid early portion of the session and therefore continues to be troubled by the destructive images.

One major flaw here might be that some of these therapists use the finger-signal technique as their way of maintaining high control of the situation. In such cases, the patient is instructed only to raise one finger or another, rather than speak, to indicate an affirmative or negative response to the therapist's questions. In that way the patient is kept silent, rotely responsive, and under the therapist's influence. But this type of interaction can have an additional detrimental effect in that the therapist doesn't really know what's going on with the client, and the client can get lost in an isolated state.

Besides this misuse of hypnosis, the behavior of certain therapists raises other ethical issues. For one, they are offering a quasi-religious/spiritual schema under the guise of scientific psychology. They are in fact teaching their own brand of a life-after-death philosophy. By introducing this belief system as a necessary part of therapy, entities therapists, like past-life therapists, may be encroaching on the religious beliefs and rights of their clients.

Second, there is no scientific basis on which they can rest their therapy scheme, and they generally fail to warn clients that it's an untested therapy.

Third, they rarely alert the client to the likelihood that the process of dispersing the entities will be extremely emotional.

Fourth, these therapists bypass working on getting to the root of the actual symptoms that brought the client to therapy in the first place.

Most entities therapists appear to have little or no concern for these ethical issues or for patient rights. All told, entities therapy seems to be yet another potentially hazardous route for the consumer.

5

You Were Abducted by ETs—
That's What the Matter Is

Certain therapists have become entranced with the idea that UFOs and alien life exist. In so doing, their interests appear to have overridden their role as unbiased and objective therapists and have turned them into hunters for "experiencers," or those individuals who are not only believed to have been abducted by extraterrestrials but also to have been experimented on like lab animals. Believing as they do in this phenomenon, these alien-abduction buffs, like other Johnny-one-note therapists, tend to project their beliefs onto their clients, conveying to clients that their personality problems are due to the trauma of having met up with alien creatures, or extraterrestrials (ETs).

As with other fad therapies, more and more practitioners—both lay and professional—have jumped on the bandwagon, or spaceship, as the case may be. Most recently, Harvard psychiatrist John Mack's book *Abduction: Human Encounters with Aliens* hit the bestseller list. In 1992, a conference held at the prestigious Massachusetts Institute of Technology (M.I.T.) brought together several hundred mental health professionals, scientists, and experiencers. This meeting garnered even greater publicity for the subject of alien encounters and resulted in a 683-page publication of the conference proceedings and a 478-page book by C.D.B. Bryan, a respected journalist.

The conference was cochaired by John Mack and M.I.T. physicist Dave Pritchard. According to Bryan, Pritchard told him: "It's not that M.I.T. endorses the conference. It's that they endorse the principle that the faculty should be given enough rope to make fools of themselves." Although many other professionals might be looking on with a great deal of skepticism, books by professionals with respectable credentials nevertheless lend a certain credibility to this phenomenon.

Edith Fiore's 1989 book on her experiences as an alien-abduction therapist includes a list of twenty-six hypnotherapists working with abductees. In his 1994 book, Richard Boylan, a prominent name in this field, listed forty knowledgeable counselors who work with experiencers of close ET encounters. Boylan, whose name appears first, will have to remove himself from the list, however, because in August 1995 his California psychologist license was revoked on seven counts of gross negligence with three patients. " 'Space alien' shrink loses his license," announced the news headline. According to the State Board of Psychology, quoted in the article, Boylan "abused his role as a therapist when he imposed his personal views on the existence of extraterrestrials into the dreams and memories of two patients."

Still, the number of people doing alien-abduction therapy is growing by leaps and bounds, as is obvious with even a cursory review of ads in New Age and alternative newspapers, magazines, and circulars, or Internet postings such as the following: "I have my MA in Transpersonal Psychology and I specialize in working with clients who have had UFO abductions and/or UFO experiences. My practice is limited to the Boulder/Denver area, but I am willing to consider doing some therapy over the phone with clients in other states. I am also in the process of starting a local support group. . . . Serious Inquiries Only Please."

Here is another: "Abduction Experience? Explore safely with regressive hypnosis by professional hypnotist David Bolton, using techniques developed by Dr. David Jacobs. This offer is only available in the United Kingdom and a small fee of £20 will be charged. If you are interested, email . . . for further details."

Most ET therapists tend to believe that alien abductions of humans are a widespread occurrence. "We can estimate that an average of more than 3,000 close encounters (CE-IVs) occur in the United States every 24 hours," writes Boylan, explaining that this is a very conservative estimate. At that rate, Boylan and others in his camp are suggesting that more than one million U.S. inhabitants are being contacted by ETs each year. Possibly the gentleman featured in the following headline from the *Arizona Republic* was one of them: "Confessed killer says UFOs made him do it, will defend self at trial."

ETs Are the Cause of Your Trauma

A therapist who has an overriding special interest in a single source for personal distress can soon, if not immediately, jump off the path of paying attention to the patient's presenting problems and instead focus on those special interests. As a result of such single-mindedness, the diagnosis tends to be shaped by the therapist's favored theory of causality—in this case, trauma based on a supposed encounter with a UFO or an ET.

Similarly, the patient's own recounting of his or her past history is molded and reinterpreted by the UFO-fascinated therapist as one indication after another that ETs were involved in long-forgotten episodes in the patient's life. The patient's personal history and family experiences are reframed to fit the therapist's notion that alien creatures are the source of the patient's current symptoms or personal discomfort.

Let's look at some examples of people who went into therapy with alien-abduction therapists.

Dreaming Up ETs

"Ellen," in her forties, with a good marriage and three children, went to a psychologist because of crying spells. When she began therapy, a number of factors were predominant in her life: (1) she was depressed over recent surgery that changed her lifestyle, (2) her father had recently died, and (3) she was worried about how the future would be with her children grown and gone.

The therapist failed to refer her for evaluation for possible antidepressant medication, and at no time during therapy dealt with Ellen's depression. Instead, he told Ellen that she was "jumpy and nervous, a posttraumatic stress disorder case." The therapist was especially interested in any repetitive dreams Ellen had. She told him of one dream in which she saw herself running from some unseen thing or person; she remembered first having this dream at about age ten. (Note: This type of anxiety dream is frequently reported by children and adults alike.)

The therapist hypnotized Ellen. After the first trance induction, he told her that hypnotically retrieved material revealed that her recurring dream was not a dream at all—she had actually been chased by extraterrestrials and had "repressed" the rest of the scene until just now. According to the therapist, the "hypnotic retrieval" indicated that what Ellen had described was really her first meeting with space aliens. The therapist then invited Ellen to join his therapy group as well as to continue individual therapy with him.

Oddly enough, this therapist "found" that most of his patients had had such encounters; therefore he had them meet each other in groups. Eventually, the group became cultlike in that the therapist, his family, and the patients who could afford it took trips together to attend UFO meetings, visit locations connected with UFO sightings, attend lectures on UFOs in various cities, and vacation at spots associated with UFO events.

Meanwhile, Ellen was never treated for her original problems, and ended up wanting to seek further therapy with someone else in order to recover from what she eventually decided were nonsensical ideas about ETs thrust upon her by the first therapist. Unfortunately, Ellen had used up all her insurance on the alien-abduction therapist and had to wait until the following year before she could get into a healthy therapy with a reasonable practitioner.

Incest Cover-Up by ETs

"Marian," age thirty-one, had been molested as a teenager by a young male neighbor. She had always remembered it and wished that it had not happened, even though she said it was "no big deal." She sought therapy because she was experiencing panic attacks, which developed after being in a severe auto accident. Marian was troubled by episodes of uncontrollable fear, rapid heartbeat, and excessive anxiety over leaving the house lest she experience a panic attack and find herself unable to get back home.

The psychologist she went to appeared uninterested in her panic attacks and her terror at being in motor vehicles; he never referred her to a physician for possible antianxiety medication. He showed great interest, however, in the sexual episode with the young neighbor. The therapist explained that he researched UFOs, ETs, and their experimentation on humans. He informed Marian that her childhood dreams were not normal but reflected contact with ETs as well as incest. He supported his theory by saying that he sensed her "loss of boundaries," which he found to be similar to that of other patients who had been molested by parents and ETs.

The therapist recommended that he hypnotize Marian to recover her repressed memories of the ET experience and the incest. Initially Marian protested that the ET idea seemed farfetched, and she insisted that there had been no incest, only the one molestation by the young neighbor, which she said she had not "repressed."

The therapist chided her, "If you really want to heal, you'll do this work. When you're ready to work on your issues, you'll start taking some risks and extending yourself beyond your comfort zone."

There followed nearly two years of hypnosis in which the therapist told Marian of "recoveries," which she described as a series of
"phantasmagoric dreamlike images" that she vaguely recalled after
each hypnotic session. The therapist interpreted these as evidence
that Marian was an "experiencer" of ETs. He also told her that her
parents had been programmed by ETs and that her father had raped
her, and then the ETs with their advanced technologies had wiped
out her memories of the rape.

Marian participated in group sessions with the therapist's other
patients, whom he said were all incest and ET experiencers. The therapist told them that his contact with other UFO researchers indicated
that the patients all needed to be very watchful because secret government agencies were trying to find out "how much is known about
ETs." He also had all his patients confront and accuse their parents
and stop having any contact with them.

Marian finally went to another therapist for help with her panic
and agoraphobia which, having been ignored by the ET therapist,
had increased to the point that Marian could not work. She also
became terrified that secret government agents were spying on her,
a consequence of the ET therapist repeatedly telling her they were all
being watched.

Marian retracted the incest and ET stories and reconnected with
her family after getting away from what she called "the constant bom-
bardment of tales of ETs from the therapist and the group." She said
some of the group patients had been with the therapist for much
longer than the two years she was with him, and they were all working on writing their life stories of the ET contacts.

Spawning Alien Life

"Harold," age twenty-six, sought therapy for long-standing depression,
loneliness, and dissatisfaction with his job. He hoped his therapist would
focus on helping him change jobs. The therapist informed Harold that
therapy with each patient began with a two-hour hypnosis session so

that the therapist could learn all about the person's past experiences and locate the source of problems in this "most direct way."

In the second session, the therapist told Harold, who recalled almost nothing of the hypnotic session, that as a young man Harold had been abducted by an ET and taken on board a UFO, where his sperm was taken for experimentation. The therapist indicated that Harold's loneliness and depression were related to his wondering if he had an offspring somewhere in space whom he had never met. The therapist held out great hope to Harold that if he were contacted again by the ETs, he could arrange to meet the child if indeed the crossbreeding of alien and human had resulted in a viable life.

Harold continued in therapy, was asked to join the therapist's group sessions, and soon found himself being indoctrinated into thinking along with the therapist and the rest of the group that there was a government conspiracy to hide what was known about ETs. Harold said the therapist and the group spent most of the time talking about their contacts with ETs, and used military jargon such as "debriefing," "rendezvousing," and "psy warfare."

At one point Harold was asked to go on a group trek to drive around some military installations where the therapist claimed alien ships were secreted and where bodies of space aliens who had died in crashes were kept in a preserved form, hidden from the world at large. The group was hoping to be able to sneak in and view the museum of alien life.

Harold's depression worsened, and eventually his general practitioner put him on antidepressant medication, suggesting that Harold see a vocational counselor. He eventually sought out a self-help group for people who have been abused by therapy and began to understand the negative impact of his sessions with the alien-abduction therapist.

Alien Probes and Therapist Prods

In alien-abduction therapy, as in other enhanced-memory therapies, the therapist sets the context for the patient by indicating that she regards ETs and the so-called close encounters as central to the patient's problems. The therapy generally involves repeated use of hypnotic techniques, putting the patient into a trance state. Sometimes patients are primed by being given UFO literature to read prior to the hypnotic sessions. Could anyone doubt that this would have an influence on the "memories" later "retrieved" during hypnosis?

In her book on alien-abduction case studies, psychologist Fiore indicates that her initial training in hypnosis was most brief: "I stumbled onto hypnosis accidentally in 1973 . . . at a weekend seminar at Esalen Institute at Big Sur, California. We took a self-hypnosis workshop, and I experienced going into a hypnotic trance for the first time. The following Monday, in my office, I tried it out with a courageous patient and have been using hypnosis ever since."

After having used hypnosis for fourteen years with her patients to elicit their UFO experiences, Fiore tells us in her book that while speaking at a conference on psychical research, she met a professor who also used hypnosis to work with alien abductees. Later, Fiore had him hypnotize her to explore the one UFO dream she had experienced, because she wanted to determine if the dream was perhaps a reflection of a personal UFO encounter—which, she explains, is often the case with her clients' dreams. (In other words, during therapy with Fiore, some clients may discover that what they always thought of as dreams are in reality close encounters.) Sure enough, these two decided that Fiore had been contacted.

Yet, in the same paragraph, she backpedals and says, "To this day, I am not convinced that I 'remembered' an actual happening. I had read a great deal on the subject and had done so many regressions with my patients that I could not separate fact from fiction." How then, one might ask, does she help her clients to make that separation?

Elsewhere in the same book, Fiore tells a patient that she has never seen a UFO, although she tries very hard. She says, "I travel long distances a lot, on planes, and I usually take the red-eye. I'm always looking out the window, but I've never seen one either."

Fiore's book ends with a contribution that may set a new standard for odd self-help suggestions. The author writes: "You can discover your own close encounters. By now you realize that your subconscious mind has a perfect memory. *Everything* you have ever experienced is recorded in your subconscious memory banks exactly as you perceived it. . . . You can retrieve memories. Therefore you can discover your own close encounters of the fourth kind [with] a simple, time-honored method for exploring forgotten memories."

The reader is instructed to take a small weight, hang it on a string, and learn to "will" the pendulum to swing back and forth for "yes," sideways for "no." Fiore declares that once you've mastered this, you'll have "a wonderful tool for exploring your own subconscious mind!" There follow fifty questions about UFO/ET experiences so that readers can decide if they've had an encounter. Fiore warns, "If you become upset while working on your list of questions, stop for a while. . . . If you are entirely too upset to continue, you have already answered a major question by your reactions. You probably have had one or more encounters and should seek help."

Context as Influence

In alien-abduction therapy, the client is usually told that hypnosis will be used in the attempt to uncover forgotten ET experiences. And as we have seen, clients often are given literature on ETs and UFOs to read before the next session. In the field of psychotherapy, such preconditioning and expectation are called the "demand characteristics" of the situation.

Demand characteristics are those features of the therapy that will be experienced by the patient as cues or subtle incentives to act or respond in certain ways. As discussed in Chapter Three, certain therapists remain blissfully unaware of, fail to consider, or deny the impact of the following:

1. The powerful influence of the setting

2. The therapist's power position

3. The nature of hypnotic imagery

4. The patient's fantasies about each of the above

When we go to a dentist, podiatrist, or accountant, we expect the professional to be interested in teeth, feet, or finances, respectively. How can ET specialists not be aware that their reputations and interests precede them?

Social psychologists and hypnosis researchers have for some time studied the demand characteristics of professional interactions. Psychiatrist Martin Orne writes, "The cues as to what is expected may be unwittingly communicated before or during the hypnotic procedure, either by the hypnotist or by someone else, for example, a previous subject, a story, a movie, a stage show, etc. Further, the nature of these cues may be quite obscure, to the hypnotist, to the subject, and even to the trained observer."

As Orne noted, the patient responds to cues of all kinds. These actual and imagined properties determine and color both what is revealed and the participants' demeanor in the situation. The personal stories earlier in the chapter showed us what happens to those clients who are not consciously choosing an alien-abduction therapist. And these therapists tend to gloss over why other clients seek them out or are referred to them.

When a person goes to a therapist known and spoken of in the community as an expert on ET abductions, the client is already influenced, or primed, by such ideas. She may feel, for example, that the therapist will only like her or work with her if she reports ET abductions, and that her pain and distress no matter what their origin will be treated only if she presents ideas the therapist is interested in, and she knows he is interested in ETs. Similarly, a lonely patient who feels insecure and unworthy may be fantasizing that she will become part of a new, emerging "special group"—that is, those allegedly abducted and experimented on by space aliens. Being a "contactee" will allow her to be a "special person."

Practitioners of this type of therapy, as well as those evaluating what is transpiring in the field, must acknowledge the very real possibility of this priming and influencing of patients through the therapist's reputation. (See, for example, Chapter Three on past-life therapist Brian Weiss's purported thousand-person waiting list. Surely those people have an expectation of what might occur when they finally see Dr. Weiss.) And aside from the influence of ads, articles, and direct contact with others, we must not forget that this is the electronic age.

Television talk shows, twenty-four-hour radio call-in programs, and Internet newsgroups continuously update and comment on what is new and trendy. Abductees report on their experiences with ETs in all those venues. Therapists appear on talk shows supporting the "experiences." Viewers learn which therapists provide such therapy, and pick up on the general scripts.

Many of these therapists disregard how clients who present themselves as having had such experiences could have gotten their material from all the myriad sources operating in our society. Some therapists, however, don't seem to bother at all with reality. Fiore said, "I have no desire to prove that the experiences really happened, any more than I do with my patients who 'discover' they've been sexually abused."

How Did UFOs Get Mixed Up with Therapy?

Throughout history people have claimed to have had contact with otherworldly creatures: spirits and ghosts; beings from the sea, the sky, and the lower world; gods, witches, werewolves, and dwarves; flying machines, monsters, and devils; angels, fairies, demons, and leprechauns. Occasionally, people have claimed that beings of one kind or another transported them to other spheres, or that they observed or were the subjects of strange and improbable acts done by these beings.

The historical background that contributes to the current combining of UFOs, ETs, and psychotherapy began after World War II. The first publication reporting a person being taken by a UFO was published in 1957; it described an alleged abduction in Brazil. In 1966, John Fuller reported on an American case, which is considered to be the real introduction of this phenomenon to the American public: on September 19, 1961, Barney and Betty Hill, a couple returning from Montreal to their home in New Hampshire, reported that their car was "flagged down by small gray humanoid beings with unusual eyes" who were in a strange craft. The Hills felt they could not account for two hours during this journey.

For two years afterward, Barney had trouble sleeping and Betty had frequent nightmares. They reported after considerable hypnosis that they had been taken from their car onto a craft where sexual examinations were performed on them. They declared that the beings communicated telepathically in English and instructed the Hills to forget what happened.

Because of Fuller's book and a made-for-TV movie about the Hills' experience, the alleged encounter was big news, in spite of the conclusion by the psychiatrist who saw the Hills: that Betty and Barney Hill had experienced a shared dream or fantasy, or folie à deux. There was a growing interest in "experiencers" and close encounters, or CE-IVs, as they came to be called in the world of people fascinated with UFOs. A close encounter of the fourth kind is supposed to be "a physical visit to the immediate location of a human being by one or more extraterrestrial, three-dimensional, intelligent beings (ETs), usually for purposes of communication, education or removal to a UFO craft for special procedures."

Claims of abductions multiplied during the 1970s and 1980s. UFOlogist Budd Hopkins (also a painter and sculptor) and historian David Jacobs are said to have interviewed "nearly five hundred people reporting such encounters" during a seventeen-year period (from 1975 to 1992). Jacobs, a professor of history, performed more than 325 hypnotic sessions with abductees.

One of the climactic moments at the 1992 M.I.T. conference was the presentation of the results of a 1991 Roper national survey, used by many abduction proponents as the source of their figures to show the supposed prevalence of alien activity, contact, and abductions. Richard Boylan, for example, who is quoted near the beginning of the chapter as saying that there are three thousand ET contacts every day in the United States, based his estimates on the poll, during which the Roper organization carried out a wide-ranging survey of 5,937 adult Americans. Seeded within the survey were eleven questions on UFO-related and other "unusual" experiences. Hopkins and Jacobs made calculations of the number of yes responses to the seeded questions and presented their conclusions at the M.I.T. conference: that at least 2 percent of adults (one out of every fifty) in the United States may have had UFO abduction experiences.

Arriving at their own base estimate of 185 million people after certain demographic exclusions, Hopkins and Jacobs announced in effect that nearly four million Americans have had ET encounters! The idea for the poll and the publication of the results in a sixty-four-page booklet was backed by Las Vegas entrepreneur Robert Bigelow.

When abduction proponents present these figures today, rarely do they mention the reception of the data at their very own conference. Journalist Bryan, who was there, described the audience reaction: "Following Hopkins's Roper Poll presentation, the M.I.T. lecture hall is in an uproar. Scientists in all corners of the large room protest that the survey is 'full of holes!'" Criticism centered on the faulty assumptions, lack of scientific basis, and lack of systematic pretests. One psychology professor asked why anyone "should pay attention to unvalidated poll data." Indeed.

Unfortunately, many in the counseling field are being influenced by the alien-abduction fad, which is reinforced by media publicity;

without thinking twice, many practitioners are foisting it onto their clients. The practice of alien-abduction therapy is supported and encouraged by the likes of John Mack, whose professional reputation certainly holds sway with others, particularly those with less training.

Mack wrote an introduction to the pamphlet analyzing the Roper survey results. In it he urged mental health professionals to "learn to recognize the most common symptoms and indications in the patient or client's history . . . fears of the dark and of nightfall; nightmares . . . ; a history of small beings or a presence around the patient's bed as a child, adolescent, or adult; small cuts, scars or odd red spots" of unknown origin. Again we see lists of broad-based symptoms that could as easily be attributed to other causes.

At the conference, and later in a letter to the American Psychiatric Association, Richard Boylan sought to have the aftereffects of alien abduction officially named as a syndrome by the committee revising the *Diagnostic and Statistical Manual of Mental Disorders* (*DSM-IV*), the diagnostic manual used by mental health professionals. Boylan described this so-called epidemic condition as "the psychological and emotional sequelae of the experience of being contacted by (and temporarily taken away by) extraterrestrials." He devised a checklist of twenty items, stating that a person having any four or more would meet the criteria for the disorder. Naming the condition Close Extraterrestrial Encounter Syndrome (CEES), he asked that the alleged syndrome be included in the forthcoming *DSM-IV* as an Adjustment Disorder, Not Otherwise Specified, 309.90. Boylan's syndrome was not accepted by the committee.

Fact, Fiction, or Urban Legend?

Therapists who support the idea that ETs abduct and experiment on humans on a regular basis and that the "remembering" of these incidents by clients will cure a variety of ills display some gross errors in reasoning. Let's look at John Mack's writings and statements about the subject. Remember, Mack is a medical doctor, a tenured professor of psychiatry at Harvard Medical School, supposedly trained in scientific reasoning. He not only disregards the contextual settings in which he meets these patients, but he also posits logically indefensible explanations for why he accepts their tales without question.

Mack's explanation for his acceptance of what he heard from alleged abductees can be summarized as follows: (1) the stories, told by individuals who had not communicated with each other, were consistent; (2) they had come forth reluctantly, fearing that their stories would be discredited or that they would be ridiculed; and (3) they did not seem psychiatrically disturbed. "There was nothing to suggest that their stories were delusional, a misinterpretation of dreams, or the product of fantasy," he wrote. Mack relies on these features to justify his acceptance of abductees' reports. At the same time, he also carefully states: "I am not presuming the physical reality of the person's experience."

Like other alien-abduction therapists, Mack gives us a variety of catch-all symptoms and indicators. These include, among others:

- The memory of a "presence" or "little men" in the bedroom

- Vivid dreams of being taken into a strange room where intrusive procedures were done

- Awakening paralyzed with a sense of dread

- Intergenerational abduction experiences

- Fear of night, hospitals, flying, elevators, animals, insects, sexual contact, of being alone, of the dark, of exposed windows at night

- Odd rashes, nosebleeds, cuts, lesions, rectal bleeding, sinus pain

- Difficult pregnancy, gynecological complaints, gastrointestinal complaints

Is everyone covered? Do we all know somebody, including ourselves, who can now explain away something, if not everything, by having been abducted by ETs?

Mack says that in order for him to take an abductee seriously, the person has to show sufficient sincerity and appropriate emotion in telling the abduction story. Of those included in Mack's sample for his book, two are two-year-olds! What exactly is appropriate emotion for a two-year-old recounting his or her abduction by ETs?

Various researchers have cited numerous refutations and alternate explanations for the kind of thinking Mack now represents. For example, because many experiencers report that their encounters with UFOs or ETs were sleep related, it's likely that these so-called experiences are simply night dreams and hypnagogic imagery. Those who describe frightening experiences accompanied by full-body paralysis possibly went through the rather common experience known as sleep paralysis, which occurs in 15 to 25 percent of the population. Sleep paralysis is typically accompanied by feelings of suffocation, the sense of a presence, and hallucinations.

As for alleged encounters that are not sleep related, the person's suggestibility and interests must be considered. In one study of people who claimed to have seen UFOs and of other people who claimed actual encounters it was learned that "subjects in both groups believed more strongly in the reality of UFOs than did comparison subjects." Those who described more elaborate experiences also held other esoteric beliefs.

Another important factor is that there are no corroborating witnesses to abductees' tales, except for experiencers who are married or closely related and vouch for one another.

The total lack of any physical evidence also bears some weight in any kind of objective evaluation. One detractor wrote: "Before you become too alarmed, however, it is important to realize that in spite of the millions of words that have been published—hundreds of books, thousands more articles about UFOs . . . there is not now, nor has there ever been, any physical, i.e., solid material evidence of any shape, form, or fashion to prove that such extraterrestrial vehicles have ever existed or currently exist. Perhaps the most damning evidence of all is the fact that if such extraterrestrial vehicles perform in the manner described, they violate all the laws of physics as we know them." Even Mack says that "the experiential data, *which, in the absence of more robust physical evidence,* is the most important information that we have" (emphasis ours).

In trying to make some sense out of this phenomenon—that is, what some might consider a rather widespread belief among primarily U.S. and British citizens that they've been abducted—there are several factors to consider. If so many people in the United States claim to have had a UFO abduction experience or an encounter with an extraterrestrial being, what's going on? There are plenty of theories, aside from those put out by people who simply believe it's all true.

Some say that those who put forth such stories are akin to people who engage in sadomasochist activities: that they are looking to experience a loss of self, a loss of control, including pain and humiliation. What could be more humiliating than a bug-eyed creature sticking a pipe up your behind?

Some say that those who believe they've been abducted were actually sexually or physically abused. Rather than face the real perpetrator, they blame poor old ET. Still others say that those who believe they were abducted by aliens have also fabricated that they were sexually or physically abused by a human. Lots of vivid imaginations out there.

Our assessment of the widespread nature of this belief in alien visits and abductions is a little more down-to-earth. As we've presented here and elsewhere in this book, we believe that much of it comes from therapist prompting, only this time the Procrustean bed is a spaceship.

Some of it also comes from the fact that information and ideas travel so rapidly today, thanks to television and computers. In the San Francisco Bay Area, for example, there are eleven hours of talk shows every day on regular TV (not including cable stations). People are very much influenced by what they see and hear on those shows, which love to cover such juicy topics as ordinary citizens having been whisked off in souped-up space vehicles and felt up by an alien or two. Later, people tend to forget where they heard about the incident; this is called "source amnesia" and is a very common occurrence.

Still others take up the belief because of its popularity. The idea of UFOs and "things" from outer space has been with us for centuries. In the past few decades, the belief has become something of an urban legend—that is, it's become part of our cultural makeup. Certainly the monumental success of Steven Spielberg's films on the subject—*Close Encounters of the Third Kind* and *E.T.*—has added to the acceptance of the idea by many millions.

Doing Harm

Whichever side of the fence one wishes to be on in this discussion, one nevertheless must not ignore the potential for damage and the real damage being done to clients who end up in this kind of therapy.

Alien-abduction therapists are spreading fears, encouraging magical thinking, and instilling paranoia in their patients. Some of these therapists adopt sinister theories such as those Hopkins puts forth: that aliens are among us in order to carry out genetic study, and we humans are merely part of a massive breeding experiment. They get clients to believe they've been experimented on or impregnated, or that they have given birth to starchildren. Clients are led to believe that they've had probes shoved up their noses, rectums, and penises, or that implants were put inside their heads and various internal organs and under their skin.

Others, like Boylan, profess that the U.S. government is engaged in psychological warfare against its own citizens. Part of these "PSY-WAR operations," as he calls them, are to dress short humans in alien costumes and have these "aliens" abduct people in order to confuse them and make them think they were abducted by real ETs. Clients are frightened into believing that they have been or might be subjected to electroshock, torture, drug injections, and cultic ritual sexual abuse.

Alien-abduction therapists are misdiagnosing and in many cases ignoring serious psychological problems that should be attended to. In some cases, they are actually causing psychological difficulties in their previously normal and stable clients. All in all, this is not a therapy we would recommend. If you're interested in outer space, rent *Star Trek* or go to the local planetarium. And if your therapist makes alien-sounding suggestions, tell him to go fly a kite.

6

Cry, Laugh, Attack, Scream—
Cathart Your Brains Out

"In the first session, we gave our histories and told the therapist about the escalating fights we were having. I had tried to choke my wife one day while she was in the shower. And right before we went to Dr. 'C.,' my wife was so mad she came at me with a pointed candelabra. We were hitting each other and screaming all the time. The kids were getting quiet and terrified, and the oldest one, who was ten then, wanted to leave home because she thought we were going to kill each other in front of her and her brother.

"Our family doctor had referred us to Dr. C. We saw him only two times. He told us in our first session that we needed to 'ventilate' in his presence and that he would provide interpretations of how our angers and behavior grew out of us not having 'worked through our childhood traumas.' He assured us that we would come to have insight about what motivated us, and that would reduce our conflicts and angry fights when we were alone.

"Dr. C. asked us lots about our childhoods. In the last part of the first session, he had us stand up and argue and shove each other. After he observed us, he said we weren't really getting down into our deep emotions, which he said had to be achieved before we'd get better.

"We were already sore with each other about something when we got there for the second session. Dr. C. said, 'Good. Now I want you both to really let all your anger out.' My wife had already ticked me off calling me a redneck on the way over. She always belittles my background, even though I'm a highly educated, highly paid professional now, as is she. Still, she always sees her family as more classy and more everything, and puts me and my family down every time we get into an argument.

"Well, there we were in the office, and the doctor said, 'Go ahead, let all your anger out,' and again my wife called me a stupid redneck, saying it was embarrassing for her to have to see a psychiatrist. No one in her family was crazy and I was a great embarrassment to her and them. I just lost it and hit her. She grabbed a lamp and came after me, and I defended myself by grabbing an umbrella to fend off the lamp blows. We really broke up a lot of stuff in the doctor's office—a table, some pictures, a window. Dr. C. became alarmed and threatened to call the police. He said he was referring us to someone more experienced in dealing with violent families. Things look pretty grim at the moment. And on top of everything else, we just got a bill from Dr. C. for $3,000 for the so-called therapy and the damages."

Some therapists promote the idea that airing your feelings will correct many problems, both intrapsychic and interpersonal. Emotional ventilation is supposed to relieve inner miseries. These therapists seem to assume that negative or bothersome emotions are like moths in old clothes: shaking the old clothes out and hanging them on the line to air them will make the moths go away. But is the same true for feelings?

Of course it can be helpful to talk about how we feel or to tell a therapist about our deepest or most troubling thoughts. Indeed, under certain circumstances with certain persons, beneficial results may ensue. But first, remember that talking and acting out are two different things. And second, this rather widely held notion that expressing feelings willy-nilly is just great is simply not backed up by research. Yet, a host of therapy procedures are derived from assuming that this ventilation brings genuine, positive healing.

The venting notion did not originate with therapists; it has roots in the Greek concept that watching a stage play and emoting along with the story serves a cathartic purpose. Aristotle felt that viewing a tragic drama would allow catharsis to occur for the audience, draining off especially pity and fear.

Psychotherapists use two terms—*catharsis* and *abreaction*. Catharsis is a purifying or figurative cleansing of the emotions. Abreaction is the release or expression of supposedly repressed ideas or emotions that are believed to be causing conflict in a person. Letting out thoughts and feelings in words, behavior, or the imagination is the desired aim.

Variations on Letting It Out

Letting it out, or venting, may take many forms, and as with other crazy therapies, most practitioners who hold that catharsis is curative tend to add a personal twist. Although most people probably associate painful feelings with some kind of cathartic experience, one innovation, the Mystic Rose, incorporates laughing and silent meditation into the process. Based on the teachings of the late guru Bhagwan Shree Rajneesh, the assumption behind Mystic Rose is that extended fits of laughter and crying jags are doorways to personal transformation. Rajneesh had a large following and a lively commune in central Oregon in the 1980s. One historian noted that many Rajneeshees came from the "caring professions," were social workers and psychotherapists.

A current version of Mystic Rose in Marin County, California, offers a three-day short course for $250. Each day is made up of three hours of laughing, followed by three hours of crying, followed by three hours of meditation. Enthusiasts can also take a three-week course of the same daily regimen. The Marin therapist who is leading these sessions said in a local news report that "there's no analyzing, no therapy. It just allows [feelings] to heal. It's very simple."

Another local psychotherapist quoted in the same story offered some words of caution. Dr. Gerald Amada said, "It sometimes poses a risk for people to express intense feelings if they don't have a context for those feelings, if they don't get a sense of perspective about them so they're not just feelings. Catharsis is not in and of itself curative. It's naive to think that it is."

As we have seen, over the years all kinds of notions have been put forth. Letting it all out in one way or another became a goal in and of itself. And if clients were resistant, their therapist or their fellow group members would prod them on, sometimes not so nicely. Most recently, with the advent of inner child therapy, generally attributed to John Bradshaw and his admirers, props of all sorts have been adopted to encourage the patient to play the role even more fully. Therapists themselves have engaged in this behavior, often serving as role models for their clients.

At a recent meeting attended by coauthor Singer and several thousand mental health professionals, a number of women and two men were wearing baby carriers with teddy bears or dolls in them. When asked about the carriers, each person claimed that she or he was nurturing the "child within." Some elaborated, saying they carried the doll or the bear to remind themselves to cater to their own inner child and not be caught up in just doing what they were supposed to do, but "to do something special for myself all day long." Others said they were giving the doll all the care, warmth, and closeness they never got from their families. Another said, "I have to constantly remind myself to be good to myself."

One woman stood out with the most unusual doll. She had a huge stuffed monster doll hanging over her arm. The creature was made up of a mixture of clothing and fur and had a completely distorted monster face with protruding eyeballs and scary teeth. The woman's nonverbal behavior was also eye-catching. She strode in long, strident steps, much as musical comedy singers would stride onto the stage announcing some feat. Bouncing on the woman's arm as she angrily strode along, the large doll was very ugly but obviously expensively made.

When asked about the doll, the woman replied: "It's my monster mother. I carry this day and night so I won't forget what a monster my mother was to me. My therapist has me do this because I

keep thinking good things about my mother and forgetting how she was. But I say now: 'This is my monster mother. I won't forget what a monster my mother was to me!'" She was engrossed in the role and delighted to vent venom on her monster mother. She strode off, the doll dangling and banging against her thigh.

This kind of venting—whether of hatred, anger, frustration, sadness, or even joy—if taken too far can result in extreme behavioral problems, exacerbated personal difficulties, and emotional instabilities. Often the client gets a lot worse before getting better, and he or she usually gets better only when the venting behaviors are stopped.

Merge, Purge, Cathart

The cathartic method as a mental practice within the field of medicine was introduced in 1877 by Josef Breuer, perhaps best known for his theory of hysteria and his use of hypnosis. Later, these ideas were taken up by Freud. These two men felt that hypnosis allowed the airing or expression of emotions that were attached to ideas and early-life memories not easily available to the patient. (Freud eventually rejected the use of hypnosis in favor of his technique of free association.)

Much of the background and beliefs about psychotherapy as it is practiced today by many therapists grew out of theories of personality developed in the late nineteenth century. Those outmoded models of how the mind, emotions, and body work were based on the hydraulic models of that time. When Freud, Jung, Adler, and others were theorizing, feelings and the mind were conceptualized as akin to fluid in a bottle that would leak over the top if the bottle got too full.

Twentieth-century science brought us other models—such as cybernetic and systems models—that more nearly represent how the complexities of the human mind and body are organized. The simple water-pressure, hydraulic model is an inadequate, inaccurate model for human functioning. Yet the impact of the period in which those early pioneers in psychotherapy wrote continues to color and actually to distort some of the constructs used today to explain behavior. One misconception is that letting it all out will make everything better.

The cathartic idea was reinforced both by the age-old folk belief that seeing a tragic drama would assist people in releasing pent-up emotions and by the perpetuation of the unfounded theory that such emotional purging was a universally useful and efficient technique. The last quarter century has seen the emergence of all sorts of "let it all out" therapies, ranging from therapists teaching people to scream and beat pillows to therapists encouraging clients to confront each other in groups and in other ways "abreact" and "cathart." The idea of expression through vividly emoting is central to these ventilation therapies. The faulty assumption is that it is beneficial for a person to air anger and hostility.

Attack Therapy

Attack therapy is an outgrowth of ventilation theory. Here the patient becomes the subject of verbal abuse, denunciation, and humiliation. This assault may come either from the therapist in individual sessions or from peers in a group context. Sometimes both methods are used. This negative and destructive development in therapy was encouraged by two major influences. First came the growth of unmonitored group therapies, which took hold in the late 1950s and continue to this day. Second was the widespread popularity of some form of therapeutic *encounter*. The actual therapeutic value of much of this type of work with clients is highly questionable.

In the 1960s and 1970s the world witnessed a kind of free-for-all approach to psychotherapy. As life became faster paced, so did the quest for a quick and radical cure for all problems, including psychological and emotional ones. Groups, which until that time were quite sedate and conventional, suddenly turned into "marathon" encounter sessions that went on for hours, days, or entire weekends. Therapy—whether one-on-one or in a group setting—took on a confrontational and piercing quality. In many cases there was no history taking at all, simply an almost coercive thrust to deal in the "here and now," often with a stress on nonverbal techniques. As one critic put it, "Tact is 'out' and brutal frankness is 'in.' Any phony, defensive or evasive behavior . . . is fair game for . . . critique and verbal attack."

It seems that with the acceptance of this pressing immediacy, all sense of propriety and ethics was thrown out the window. There were no rules, no standards, no guidelines in this milieu where the overarching goal was to express and experience feelings. It's not surprising then that more violent and active psychotherapy techniques would arise in this out-of-control climate, and that the abreactionist school of thought would be adopted by so many—mental health practitioners and purveyors of self-improvement programs alike.

Theories on screaming, pounding, fighting, sitting on the hot seat, and group confrontation were put into place in a number of therapy centers. The popular therapies emerged out of Esalen and other "human potential" centers, growing out of groups like the Living Theater and the Theater of All Possibilities and evolving into myriad innovations like Bio-Energetics, Gestalt Therapy, and Psychosynthesis. Model confrontational programs, such as Synanon and its clones, were being praised left and right.

Another variant of the confrontation therapies appeared in the commercially sold large group awareness training programs such as Mind Dynamics, Direct Centering (aka Bayard Hora Associates, aka The Course, aka Naexus), Arica Institute, Insight Seminars, and Lifespring. These programs were sold to hundreds of thousands of customers over two decades, and some still exist in old, revised, and new forms. Marketed to individuals, organizations, and business and industry as experiential education, they typically use powerful psychological and social influence techniques, not always bringing about the advertised claims of success and profit to the buyer, and sometimes bringing psychological distress to the clients.

Varieties of these confrontation therapies and self-awareness programs are still with us two and three decades later; in fact they're going strong, as shown by the following case histories. These examples also illuminate the mixtures of regression, attack, and let-it-all-out styles that can be found in the therapeutic marketplace today. Sometimes one can't help but wonder who's acting out here: the client or the therapist.

Pump Away the Pain

"Bob" had been in a cult for a number of years. After exiting, he suffered from periods of dissociation in which he lost his ability to concentrate and felt spaced out and distracted. He went to a psychologist, who said that in addition to talk therapy she did bodywork and that eventually he would be given instructions in the latter. She had him read a book by Alexander Lowen, the father of Bioenergetics. She explained to Bob that Lowen believed that emotional disturbances are rooted in muscular tension and that problems are dealt with by getting rid of the tension.

After a few sessions of history taking and general discussion, the therapist said they should start meeting at her house, where she had a special room for the bodywork. These sessions, she said, would have to be in the evening. "Have you read the books, Bob?" she asked. "I am ready to teach you how to release your aggressive anger, and you'll understand if you've done your homework that *any* form of release is acceptable."

When Bob arrived at the therapist's house, she showed him to a room with no furniture except exercise horses and pillows scattered about the floor. She instructed Bob to strip to his undershorts, then told him to lean back over the padded platform and make pelvic thrusts resembling sexual movements. "What are you angry about, Bob?" she'd ask quietly, then louder and louder. She would look on and analyze his movements, recording notes. Bob felt there was something very bizarre about the woman's demeanor, and something didn't seem quite right to him. For example, at the second session, the therapist sat cross-legged on the floor in front of Bob with her skirt pulled up to her thighs.

After about three sessions Bob stopped going, feeling that not only were the therapist's actions too peculiar but also that she had no rationale for what she was having him do. It seemed to Bob that the atmosphere was becoming very sexualized in a hard-to-explain way, which was making him more anxious than when he started therapy.

Healing Through Humiliation

"Kevin" was new in town; he had a master's degree in business and a good job that kept him extremely busy. He was lonely, and he wondered if the move had been sensible. He had had a good rapport with a college counselor so he thought some therapy might help, as a chance to thrash around these ideas. Someone at his job referred him to a psychologist whom we'll call Dr. Dominate.

Kevin soon found himself seeing Dr. Dominate twice a week for individual therapy and twice a week for group. Dr. Dominate put all his patients into his groups, and always had several going at any one time. Kevin's therapy bills and the time involved precluded his making other outside contacts. Dr. Dominate also directed his clients not to change anything about their lifestyle without discussing it with him and getting his approval. Even when a woman Kevin admired joined the group, the good Dr. Dominate forbade Kevin to date her. Dr. D. taught the patients in individual therapy that each of them had had a weak father and a domineering mother. Then, in the group, he said that he would be the strong father and they would all learn better roles than they had with their "wimp-dads" and "bitch-mothers."

Individual sessions with Dr. D. were set up to induce Kevin to like the doctor and want to get his approval. After a month of one-on-one sessions, Dr. D. started Kevin in the group and had him sit in the "hot seat" numerous times. The other group members were encouraged to shout out everything they saw, felt, or sensed about Kevin that was a reflection of what he had learned from his wimp-dad. Dr. D. would rage at the group for being easy on Kevin, who was called all sorts of obscenities and derided for everything from how he looked to his work, his car, and his voice. Kevin said the yelling, the rage, the vitri-olic nature of the attacks were "out of this world. It was hard to believe that ordinary persons could be stirred up by Dr. Dominate to be so frighteningly angry in their attacks on me and on others when they were in the hot seat."

Kevin felt decimated after the first group session, and he wanted to talk about it in his next individual session. Dr. D. was kind, saying, "We are all here to help you, and the others are just being honest. I'm being honest. We're all trying to help you grow." Kevin became depressed, demoralized, and discouraged, but stayed in therapy because Dr. D. would be the all-loving father in individual sessions.

Kevin was not the only target. Dr. D. broke confidentiality repeat-edly, revealing in group sessions things conveyed to him in private, using these revelations to goad the group to attack whoever was in the hot seat. Dr. D. revealed that one group member's penis had a defect and looked odd to his woman friend. Dr. D. took delight in humiliating both men and women in the group. A woman in the group who was always well groomed and attractive was attacked for being a carbon copy of her "artificial mother" who had trained her to please her "wimp father." Dr. D. would also pass unpaid bills around to humiliate anyone behind in their payments to him. He said that men who wore mustaches and beards, as several did when they first began therapy, were basically gay men hiding that their mouth was their vagina. Kevin said that he felt shocked and sorry for the several men who then shaved off their beards to escape Dr. D.'s attacks.

Kevin left the therapy and the group after three years; several years later he still suffers from the effects of the traumatic ways he was attacked and the deceptiveness of Dr. Dominate. At this time

Kevin is still too distrusting of therapists to seek any further counseling. He felt he could trust his general practitioner and was on medication for depression for a long while.

Training Attack Therapists

Violations of ethical practices and attacks on the individual sometimes occur when therapists themselves are in training. Some centers and institutes that offer training programs and licensing
supervision have been known to be the hotbeds for not only certain
crazy theories but also the perpetuation of abuses by those in power
over the trainees.

When the young man in the following example went to his sister who was studying to be a therapist, he got more than he bar-
gained for.

"Joel," an eighteen-year-old college freshman, became depressed
and called his sister, a graduate student in psychology. She urged
him to get their parents to send him to therapy with her supervisor.
Not long after, Joel's sister and twenty other therapist-trainees
dropped out of their graduate schools and went to live on a farm with
the psychologist and her husband. Joel was instructed to come
along in order to get the therapy he needed. There, the students
worked as house and yard help, at the same time getting their parents to pay for the "therapy." Most of the students had been invited
to participate in this live-in program by the female director of this
group, who was a licensed therapist and part-time instructor at a
nearby graduate school.

The trainees began the day with a confessional attack group in
which each person confessed any negative thoughts or feelings they
had about the therapist from the prior day. Then they were attacked
verbally by the group for their "negativity"—clearly a damned if you
do, damned if you don't situation. Joel, who was there solely as a
patient, later described the environment as totally controlled, day and

night, with endless confession-confrontation groups. Scorn was heaped on him when after a month he asked when he was going to see his therapist. He was told that this was the best therapy in the world; that the director was the world's leading authority on psychology; that she was being paid to cure him and others of their negativity, their egoism, and their inability to be selfless and open. Joel ran away and phoned his parents, telling them about what was going on at the therapy farm.

Discussing it later, Joel said he was depressed when he arrived there and had expected counseling or therapy to "help build me up." What he found didn't resemble anything he'd ever experienced before. But he said, "I went along with the program because it was run by a credentialed person who had all these graduate students around her. I thought it was just because of my resistance that I didn't feel about her as everyone else did. Every minute of every day was organized around her plans; there was no time to rest, think, talk freely with others. After weeks of these attack sessions, I felt totally confused and without emotions because nothing I said or did seemed to be acceptable to the therapist or the group. I did my best to emulate others to avoid being put in the hot seat, but my turn always came—it seemed my role was to serve as a practice dart board for the trainees. The director would get them all revved up against me."

When not in the confrontational sessions, the trainees listened to endless lectures by the head therapist and sometimes her husband. She claimed her theory was the path to "complete emotional expression and sane living," not just for her protégés but for the world. She harangued the trainees that as soon as they were able to "replicate her" and go out and teach the world how to live by her "treatment methods," the change would go beyond anything yet contributed by therapy or education. She referred to her theories as "the work." She explained to them that they wouldn't be perfect therapists or be able to share her work with the world until they replicated her ways, her language, and the exact emotions she showed. They would spend hours in exercises led by her that were an amalgam of primal scream and confrontational attack therapy.

What About Scream Therapies?

One variant of let-it-all-out therapy became all the rage in the 1970s. It was known as scream therapy, and many professionals and celebrities were taken with it—probably the most well known was singer and songwriter John Lennon. The popularity of scream therapies, at least to some degree, might be attributed to the times.

The 1960s and 1970s were times of demonstrations, protests, barricades, and cries of "revolution." Primal Therapy was a method that would let the customer feel, experience, and let out all those feelings of rage. Arthur Janov, the originator of Primal Therapy, even titled one of his books *The Primal Revolution*.

A number of scream therapies have gained considerable attention and followings. First were Janov's Primal Therapy and Daniel Casriel's New Identity Process. Nolan Saltzman then developed Bio Scream Psychotherapy out of Casriel's work. There are yet other variations and formulations that have developed over the years. Each of these therapies is touted by the originator as opening the road to happiness and mental health.

Primaling with Arthur Janov

Arthur Janov, a psychologist and psychiatric social worker, claims to have "discovered" primal therapy. It is another one of those therapies based on therapist observations of the conduct of one patient. At least Janov reports confirming the idea on a second patient. He then taught, and continues to teach, the method to countless others, professing that this is the best and only useful therapy to cure mental illness.

Janov said that he came to regard the primal scream "as the product of central and universal pains which reside in all neurotics. . . . Primal Therapy is aimed at eradicating these pains. It is revolutionary because it involves overthrowing the neurotic system by a forceful upheaval. Nothing short of that will eliminate neurosis, in my opinion."

Janov's original cases were two young men named "Danny" and "Gary." Danny was a twenty-two-year-old college student, whom Janov described as a "poor student, withdrawn, sensitive, and quiet." During therapy Janov instructed Danny to call out "Mommy! Daddy!" Danny refused at first, but Janov writes: "I persisted, and finally he gave in . . . he became noticeably upset. Suddenly he was writhing on the floor in agony. His breathing was rapid, spasmodic; 'Mommy! Daddy!' came out of his mouth almost involuntarily in loud screeches. He appeared to be in a coma or hypnotic state. The writhing gave way to small convulsions, and finally, he released a piercing, deathlike scream that rattled the walls of my office."

Soon Janov tried the technique again on another patient. Gary called for his mommy and daddy until "he was breathing faster and deeper. His calling turned into an involuntary act that led to writhing, near-convulsions, and finally to a scream," wrote Janov in his best-selling book *The Primal Scream*.

From these experiences, Janov concluded that all neurotics have "Primal Pain." Janov liked to capitalize certain words (as one critic remarked, "to underscore the monumentality of his concepts"): Primal Pain, Primal Therapy, Primal Theory, Symbolic Primal, Primal Scream, and so on. Unlike the rebirthing proponents we met in Chapter Two, Janov believed that "not all birth is traumatic; it is traumatic birth which is traumatic. The trauma is laid down in the nervous system, producing enormous lifelong tension."

Two years after writing his first book, Janov's certitude about having found the one cure-all was established—at least in his mind. In the first lines of his second book, Janov wrote: "Primal Therapy purports to *cure* mental illness (psychophysical illness, to be exact). Moreover, it claims to be the *only* cure. By implication, this renders all other psychologic theories obsolete and invalid. It means that

there can be only one valid approach to treating neuroses and psy-
choses." A few pages later he writes: "Primal Therapy methods are
replicable in the hands of any competent Primal Therapist who can
produce Primals and cures consistently." Yet Janov's World Wide
Web home page warns, "It must be emphasized that this therapy is
dangerous in untrained hands."

A colleague of Janov's claims that Primal Therapy is neurosis in
reverse, that children experience hurt and pain early in life and
respond only partially to that hurt. He described a "Primal" as a
two-phase response pattern: first, a person screams and cries in
agony to a peak followed by a tapering recovery phase. Then he
reexperiences an early-life painful event in the form of a vividly
recalled memory. At the end of a completed Primal, the patient is
described as "slightly euphoric, very lucid, and profoundly calm."

New Identity Process

Daniel Casriel calls his work New Identity Process (NIP), a
"totally new psychiatric delivery system necessitated by the clinical observations uncovered while using the technique of scream
therapy." Casriel claims that suppression, repression, or the under-
utilization of feelings results from cultural and parental injunc-
tions that can block happiness throughout one's life. He teaches
patients that there are five basic human feelings: pain, anger, fear,
pleasure, and the need for love. Patients learn to use three basic
attitudes: "I exist," "I need," and "I am entitled to my feelings/to
fulfill my needs."

According to this theory, smothered feelings prevent the experience of emotional well-being. So patients are brought together in
group therapy, and by screaming they learn to feel and express feelings and to demonstrate the basic attitudes just noted. As with
many therapy inventors, Casriel feels that his plan is universally
useful for all except the brain damaged, explicitly noting that it
is for "normals," delinquents, alcoholics, addicts, and character-
disordered and "functional" schizophrenic persons.

Bio Scream Psychotherapy

Nolan Saltzman began Bio Scream Psychotherapy as a more supportive, warm use of screaming than he felt was produced by Janov's or Casriel's versions. Saltzman thought that Casriel's method was highly confrontational and too hostile and humiliating for many patients. Saltzman calls his process "Scream/Love" or "S/L." He wanted screaming to lead patients to abandon defenses and to feel supported in a warm, empathic group.

Saltzman's scream therapy can be done in one-on-one sessions with the therapist or in a group setting, with the good feelings and support coming from the therapist or the group to the screamer. Saltzman promoted three venues for screaming.

In one method, patients are taught modal phrases, such as "I'm scared," "I hurt," "I'm angry," and "I feel good." One phrase is selected and repeated louder and more rapidly until the therapist leads the person to a complete release.

In a second method, the patients are directed to figure out what they want to say to a significant other (such as mother or spouse) imagined to be sitting before them in a chair. The therapist helps patients identify their emotions related to what's being said. Then patients are to repeat that over and over until the scream evolves.

A third method involves having patients lie on a mat on the floor. The therapist may hold a patient's hand while evoking the scream.

Saltzman is more modest in his claims for who can profit from his Bio Scream method, saying that it is not for psychotics and that it is not a miracle cure.

The Center for Feeling Therapy

Several therapists who had been with Janov broke away and started their own practice, called the Center for Feeling Therapy, in Los Angeles in 1971. One of the founders, Joseph Hart, is quoted as saying, "When we left Janov, forty percent of the patients came with us. After working with them, we found that most had been *faking* their Primals. They were simulating regression, just as some of Charcot's patients had done in France in Freud's time. It's hard to say if they were consciously faking, but they had learned to do what their therapist wanted."

Even with this apparent understanding, Hart and his colleagues proceeded to develop their ideas of "feeling therapy." Hart and cofounder Richard Corrierre referred to themselves as the Butch Cassidy and Sundance Kid of psychology. They and other center leaders claimed that patients could reach the next stage of human evolution only by following the therapists' dictates.

The Center for Feeling Therapy followed Janov's method of having the new client stay in a secluded motel room alone for three weeks of intensive daily sessions. A new client of the center met with a therapist in marathon three- to seven-hour individual sessions in which the person was attacked, criticized, and belabored. Deprivation was enforced during this period and afterward. Alone, when not in therapy sessions, the client was not to smoke; drink alcohol, coffee, or tea; watch TV or listen to the radio; or talk on the phone. These techniques made the therapy seem mysterious and frightening, and caused the client to enter into an anxious state.

Over the next ten years the center grew quite successfully. There were 350 patients living near one another and sharing homes, hundreds more were nonresident outpatients, and still others communicated with center therapists by written correspondence. The central theme foisted on clients was: if you do not live from your feelings, you are insane.

The leaders wrote books and lectured, and their power over the patients grew until at its demise the group was described as a cult and charged with scads of alleged mental, physical, and sexual abuses (some of which will be discussed in the next chapter). All twelve therapists associated with the center lost or surrendered their licenses.

Catharsis Therapies Today

Today there are several high-priced institutes where a person can both engage in and study variations of scream therapy, and a number of therapists still bill themselves as doing primal or scream therapy in individual or group sessions or sometimes a combination of the two.

Promotional flyers promise the following: "The emotional atmosphere of the group elicits deep feelings, and thereby accentuates the gains of individual therapy." But here are some examples of what can happen when all that emotion gets going.

"Matt" Learns Anger

"A couple of years ago, my wife, 'Betsy,' was in a women's support group which was into exploring feelings and expressing everything. It was a continuation of an important interest Betsy had developed in college. She complained that I was too taciturn and needed to get into primal or some other really expressive therapy where I could learn to feel and to show my feelings.

"So I began therapy with a female therapist recommended by Betsy's women's group leader. Neither the philosophy of the therapy nor the techniques seemed to grab me. The therapist assured me that I would become a new person when I finally achieved a 'primal.' I would never be moody again, she said. The therapist also advised me that I didn't have to see my parents ever again since they had so failed me. I tried to tell her about my happy childhood but she'd rasp at me, 'Matt, you are in denial!' I really had had a good childhood. I loved my father and mother and two older brothers, and in the therapy sessions I simply couldn't locate deep pains or feel the required deep rage against them the therapist said was buried in me.

"I went through the motions for about eight sessions, both seeing her in individual sessions and dutifully attending what I call 'group laydowns.' Pandemonium reigned at these weekly gatherings, with unleashed screams and moans, including mine. My voice got scratchy from my efforts at screaming out, trying to get a primal.

"The therapist urged me over and over to feel my anger. She then left the area for a better job and I was spared further treatment. My wife, oddly enough, thought I had made great progress and let up on trying to get me to see anyone else. All I can say is that I felt like a phony trying to please the therapist, trying to scream like she wanted, trying to feel deep pain and deep anger. All I could tell was that it got to the point that when my wife began to badger me about something, I began to express almost instant anger toward her and really told her off fast.

"Betsy was caught in a bind. She had wanted me to be more expressive, so I told her how the therapist was priming me to show anger and deep pain and not to fear showing anger. When I began to have a sharp tongue and lash out at her when she provoked me, she painfully asked, 'Did Ms. Therapist show you how to be kinder to your wife?' 'Of course not,' I'd reply, 'she just taught anger and pain as the emotions she wanted me to show.' My wife never pushed me to go to more therapy; in fact, she dropped out of her groups and became a much happier person. You know, that therapy could have broken up a marriage and turned me against my family. I guess I was just lucky that it didn't really take."

"Carl" Loses His Wife

" 'Rita' had been depressed when she was in junior high school, again in high school, and two times during college. Two of her sisters and her mother were on medication for depression and doing fine. We married when we were both twenty-four. I had known Rita since grade school. My folks knew her parents. They were from the South, bright and talented, but they had, as they put it, 'the family condition,' meaning some of them were prone to periods of black, hopeless depression. It was mainly Rita's mother's family, but actually both sides had some depressed people. These depressions seemed to snap on like a light, and turn off just as abruptly. All in all, the relatives were okay folks; none was what you'd call 'neurotic'—by that I mean complaining, sour, lazy, things like that.

"Rita and I had a good marriage, until I got transferred to the West Coast. Rita went into a moderate depression. She didn't want to go on medication like so many in her family. She saw an ad in a local giveaway paper for a clinic offering a whole roster of therapies. She went, and the woman who was her therapist told her that scream therapy would be the best for the type of depression Rita had, that she would not need medication ever if she completed the program, and that this treatment emptied out all the pain and sadness.

"Rita came home from her first meeting feeling encouraged. But soon her therapist wanted her to stop talking with any relatives on the phone. The therapist even started bad-mouthing me, saying I lacked 'complete feelings' and needed therapy also and that Rita might have to separate from me to get well. This was unbelievable. The therapist had never even met me! Rita felt her therapist knew something about me that she, Rita, didn't know; maybe the therapist treated someone from where I worked or something, Rita said, because the therapist would be so forceful about how bad I really was.

"Things got worse and worse. I would leave Rita breakfast on a tray and a sandwich for lunch before I went to work each day. She only got out of bed to go to therapy. I tried to talk with her therapist and let her know how sick Rita was, but the woman wouldn't speak with me. I even left a message saying I was afraid Rita would kill herself, she was so down. I spoke with a psychologist who shared an office with Rita's psychologist and asked him to tell the woman I was worried and felt Rita needed to go into a hospital. I told him Rita was not allowed to talk to any of her family, so none of them could help me persuade Rita to see another doctor. He gave me a song and dance about how Rita's therapist couldn't talk with me, it would break confidentiality. He said I shouldn't expect to ever speak with her.

"After each session Rita seemed worse. She said she was trying to get back every memory of every sad time she could recall throughout her life and reach a 'primal,' whatever that was supposed to be. One afternoon after her therapy Rita called me at work and asked me to come home, saying 'I want to take you with me.' I thought she meant back to her therapist or somewhere she needed to go. When I got home I called out to her and she softly replied 'I'm up here. I want you to go with me.' As I started up the stairs I looked up and she had a gun in her hand. She shot at me and I fell back with a shot in the leg. I heard another shot and a thud. I crawled to the phone and got 911, and the police came. Rita had put the gun in her mouth and blew her head off. I can't forgive myself for not making her go to a real doctor and get the medications she had had before, like had helped her and her family."

Counter Theories to Letting It All Out

Catharsis theory in all its forms has been challenged repeatedly over the years. Evidence that expressing angry, violent behavior does not drain it away but increases the chances of its recurrence has been presented in the scientific psychology literature for years.

Leonard Berkowitz of the University of Wisconsin points out that acting out hostile feelings in the ways advocated by such therapists actually increases hostility: "The therapist or group members usually approve the patient's display of aggression. As a number of researchers have shown, these rewards heighten the likelihood of subsequent violence."

Such research is apparently not read or accepted by the many therapists who continue to ply their ventilation trade.

In 1956 Seymour Feshbach demonstrated that the Freudian ventilation notion was incorrect. Feshbach gathered a group of little boys who were not aggressive or destructive. He gave them violent toys, had them kick the furniture and "otherwise run amok during a series of free-play hours. This freedom did not 'drain' any of the boys' 'instinctive aggression' or 'pent-up' anger; what it did was lower their restraint against aggression. On later occasions, the boys behaved in much more hostile and destructive ways than they had previously."

Ventilation by yelling and other acts of aggression does not help either children or adults to become less angry or aggressive. Couples urged to yell at one another feel *more* angry after practice, not less. Researchers in family violence and violence in general have been reporting for years that all the urging to vent pent-up anger only teaches people, both children and adults, to act out irrationally, to simply rehearse and demonstrate angry, aggressive acts.

The human organism learns as it acts; the more a certain behavior is practiced, the more it becomes a part of the person's automatic acts. Practicing being angry, then, is more like practicing swimming or riding a bicycle. One gets more proficient at it. Riding a bike does not rid one of the riding urge, rather it trains an expressive skill— and so does venting anger over and over. Demonstrating anger or any other feeling does not erase the event or the interaction that elicited the anger or other emotion in the first place.

The best remedies for "handling" anger generated by frustration or irritation with another person appear to be those that help people of any age better understand why another person acted as he or she did. Encouraging mild, placid, and rational people to "let go" and ventilate their rage only makes them feel worse if they do.

When therapists urge patients to express and release their anger—"Let it all out. Just ventilate and you will get it all out"— they are relying on that outmoded hydraulic model. They are viewing clients as though they were bottles nearly full of vinegar, which if emptied would magically refill with champagne. Those old-fashioned ideas that draining off the pressure will eradicate the anger, clear the mind, and allow the person to move on as a "new" being never were scientifically sound, nor are they today.

We are not saying that bottling up all of one's anger, resentment, or frustration is the way to deal with such feelings. Rather, we believe that rational therapies assist clients to find ways to talk with others, to change situations, and to identify socially useful and mature means to reduce anger-producing interactions and situations.

From a social influence vantage point, the let-it-all-out and attack therapies can have a major impact. Usually clients will have paid a fair amount of money for a therapy that might sound odd or bizarre to their realistic friends. Therefore, clients will feel a need to defend their actions and commitments, having made an open affiliation with the therapeutic practice and the therapist. During the course of the therapy, clients regress, become dependent, have their self-esteem and sense of self attacked and diminished, and to some degree lose touch with their previous everyday reality orientation. Nothing is the way it used to be.

Social psychology is filled with data showing that once a person makes a commitment in front of others about a position or belief, it is more likely that the person will cling to that position. Imagine the degree of commitment made by the people you met in this chapter: at their therapist's command, they rolled and moaned, beat cushions and each other, screamed, yelled, laughed, cried, insulted others, and were themselves humiliated and insulted.

It is definitely harder to recognize problems with a particular decision when a person has spent money, told family and friends about it, and invested the extraordinary amount of energy called for by these therapies. Participants may be less prone to admit to the therapist, to others, or to themselves that they still have problems or have not become totally fixed as promised by the therapist who is saying, "See, something dramatic is happening."

In effect, clients are simply practicing expressing rage, anger, and pain in a dramatic scene that the therapist directs by reframing the clients' activities to reflect what the therapist would have clients think is occurring. Because clients are persuaded by the status, power role, and credentials of the therapist, they tend to accept the therapist's verbal explanations and assurances. Caught in the web of their own commitment to the therapy and the influential urgings of the therapist, once they begin to participate, people find it difficult to get away from these crazy confrontation therapies. Only later do some clients realize that they've been had and, in certain cases, badly abused.

In general, if your therapist is telling you that you have to get worse before you get better, is tearing you apart rather than building you up, is letting group members insult and ridicule you, is insisting that you must go deeper and deeper and deeper to feel the feeling, or is doing anything that smacks of old-fashioned ventilation theories, get out as fast as you can and look for a supportive therapist who will listen and respond with human decency.

7

Therapeutic Seductions— or Sexual Hanky-Panky

At twenty-eight, "Jasmine" was abandoned by her husband after the birth of their second child. "You're no longer sexy," he said; he'd found someone else and was moving on. Jasmine couldn't help but feel depressed, and she decided to see a therapist. The therapist took only the briefest history, never learning of the many abandonments Jasmine had suffered in her early life, or how her husband's recent abandonment had exacerbated her fears, feelings of inadequacy, and distrust of men.

By the fourth session the therapist began telling Jasmine jokes. He seemed less interested in talking about Jasmine than talking about his marriage and other clients. This type of talk went on for many sessions. Afterwards, Jasmine said that because she'd never seen a therapist before, she didn't know how to judge what was going on. She assumed he was telling her about other clients and his home life to make her "feel special, or as a compliment."

In one session the therapist said to Jasmine, "I know a lot of men who'd be really happy to have a woman like you." He began telling her more intimate and especially sexual secrets of other clients. Soon he began phoning Jasmine between sessions, then bringing her gifts of flowers, candy, and jewelry. Because Jasmine had very little social life due to the demands of her job and single parenthood, she began thinking about the therapist all the time. One day she realized that her depression wasn't any better, her self-esteem was as low as ever, and nothing professional seemed to be happening in the therapy sessions. She called the therapist to tell him that she was ending therapy.

To her surprise, the therapist showed up at her house that weekend. He took her by the hand and led her into the bedroom, where they had sex.

After that incident, the therapist would call Jasmine at work, begging her to come over, saying he needed her. They would engage in sexual acts in his office. Eventually he would call her to pick up food or his dry cleaning, or to purchase items for him and deliver them to his office. A woman colleague at work who'd been covering for Jasmine when she'd leave early learned what was going on and helped Jasmine to see how she was being used and abused. Not too long after that, Jasmine took legal action against the therapist because the problems she went to therapy for had never been addressed and she was even less able to function because of new problems brought about by the therapist's behavior.

The Hippocratic Oath (circa 460 B.C.) makes explicit the moral and legal responsibilities of physicians to refrain from instigating or involving themselves in sexual activities with clients.

> I swear by Apollo the physician and by Aesculapius to keep the following oath: I will prescribe for the good of my patients and never do harm to anyone. In every house where I come I will enter only for the good of my patients, keeping myself far from all intentional ill-doing and all seductions, and especially from the pleasures of love with women or men, be they free or slaves.

The ethical codes of mental health professionals grow out of that early tradition, also prohibiting sexual behavior between therapist and client. This is true for the American Psychiatric Association, the American Psychological Association, and various mental health providers, and is even stated in many state laws.

Yet, in the past twenty-five years sexual activity between therapists and clients has become a major issue. Before then, few books or articles were written about therapist-client sex. Training programs rarely touched the subject, apparently assuming that future professionals would never engage in such behavior.

But a nearly nine-hundred-page annotated bibliography called *Sexual Intimacies Between Psychotherapists and Patients* appeared in 1990, which showed that there is certainly a problem. In that same year, another huge book of 837 pages appeared, titled *Psychotherapist Sexual Involvement with Clients: Intervention and Prevention*. Included in this volume are the results of nineteen of the largest studies of sexual contact between more than eight thousand psychologists and psychiatrists and their patients. Sexual contact includes erotic kissing, erotic hugging, erotic touching, and sexual intercourse. Roughly 10 percent of each discipline self-admitted sexual contact with patients.

In another study on the subject, Dr. Peter Rutter lumped together physicians, psychotherapists, lawyers, clergymen, and teachers. Using data from the 1986 report of the Bureau of Labor Statistics indicating that approximately four million men are in those professions, Rutter wrote: "If we use the minimum figure of 10 percent of these men who exploit the women under their care, and if we assume that these men each had sexual relations with only one protegee, we arrive at a total number of 400,000 victims. But because the studies show that most men who exploit are repeaters who exploit many women, we can multiply this figure (again conservatively) by three to arrive at the not unreasonable figure of over one million women in this country who have been sexually victimized in relationships of trust."

Of all the complaints filed with the California psychology licensing board in each year from 1990 through 1995, more decisions were made regarding cases in the category of "sexual misconduct" than any other violation. And a recent study of trends in health care listed sexual abuse as one of the top four causes for personal injury claims made against insurance companies for psychiatric malpractice. Awards to plaintiffs ranged from $35,000 to more than $8 million, and the average award was $502,800.

These sexual encounters are not merely some sort of illicit affair. They are sexual liaisons instigated by those who have more power in the situation. Rather than establishing safe and healthy boundaries, these abusing therapists throw professional ethics out the window. Clients are induced to submit to the therapist as the authority figure and are expected to rely solely on the therapist's perspective. The therapist's worldview and personal needs and desires are forced onto the client through the therapist's encouragement of a dependent relationship, sometimes reinforced by the peer pressure of a group setting.

The worldview in this case, either explicit or implicit, is that it's okay to have sex with your therapist. If the patient resists, or complains about the stress and conflict the sexual activities may be causing her, most times the blame is thrown back on her by the therapist. Often these therapists lash out with a personal attack couched in psychological jargon.

Ellen Plasil, a woman in therapy for five years, wrote of her experiences. She gives a vivid picture of her utter dependence on her therapist and his response to her complaints about having had sex with him.

> "You're scum," he muttered slowly with quiet venom. . . .
> "I'm thinking about throwing you out."
>
> I knelt on the floor . . . "Please don't throw me out,"
> I whispered in desperation. . . . "I'm sorry. Really sorry.
> I'll do anything to make it up to you, but *please, please*
> don't throw me out."
>
> "You're not even half the woman I thought you
> were—and I didn't think you were much to start
> with. . . . You violated my first rule. You didn't tell me
> everything that was going on inside your head. You

didn't tell me about the guilt, the doubts, or this turmoil you say you were experiencing. And all of this over what? A little sex? . . . I really overestimated you as a woman. . . . Your future is over, unless I agree to continue seeing you. You know that, don't you?"

"I know," I replied in a whisper. I really believed it.

Ellen Plasil and other patients filed a civil suit against the psychiatrist, but before the jury heard the entire case, the psychiatrist surrendered his license and left the state. Plasil's case was settled out of court.

The majority of "therapeutic" seductions consist of a male therapist abusing a female patient. However, not uncommon are sexual improprieties between a female therapist and female patient, a male therapist and male patient, and a female therapist and male patient. Research over the past several decades has shown that anywhere from 33 to 80 percent of those therapists who instigate sexual encounters with patients tend to repeat their unethical behavior with more than one patient, as illustrated by the stories of "Ruth" and "Priscilla."

"It's All Right, She's a Patient, Too"

"Ruth" had been seeing a married, male therapist for about three years. She wanted to change careers and felt that therapy might help her get the perspective needed to risk such a step. The therapist began the seduction process by setting Ruth's appointments for late in the afternoon, then asking her to join him for dinner after the session. This soon led to sex, both at her apartment and during the therapy hour.

One evening Ruth was leaving a restaurant after attending a business meeting. As she was driving away she saw her therapist assisting a young woman into his car. Curious, she followed them and parked across from the apartment building they entered, which she knew was not her therapist's home. From the light in the window, she could see the couple hugging and taking off their clothes. When Ruth confronted her therapist at the next session, he explained, "It's really all right. She's a patient, too."

Needless to say, Ruth was decimated. Not only had she wasted three years, but now she had a whole new set of problems. She felt betrayed, lied to, and so untrusting she could not talk with men.

"That's Your Problem"

"Priscilla" saw a therapist in a large downtown office complex. She often went early for her therapy hour and had coffee in the main floor coffee bar. Many times she observed one woman leaving the therapist's office, and Priscilla assumed she was the patient whose appointment preceded hers. The two began to nod to each other in recognition.

One day the other woman approached Priscilla, asking if she could join her, as she was going to get a snack before going back to work in her nearby office. This happened several times, and they soon began talking about their mutual therapist. Before long the two women discovered that their trusted therapist was sexually involved with both of them, telling each the same story: that he and his wife were divorcing (which turned out to be false) and that each was to be his true beloved, move into his house, and so on. Priscilla had even loaned him money; and at his urging she had broken off an engagement and no longer had any contact with her parents and siblings because the therapist told her they were "toxic relatives."

When confronted about the affair with the other patient, the therapist told Priscilla that her anger was not to be shown to him, that it was merely a sign of her neuroses, that it was her problem, not his. Priscilla developed many anxieties and eventually went to another therapist who informed her that sex was never a legal or legitimate part of therapy, giving her a booklet of information put out by the state. Priscilla sought and won legal redress.

What's Their Problem?

Sexually exploitative therapists have been classed into three major groupings:

1. The poorly trained (those who do not have sufficient training and are ill informed)
2. The distressed (those with emotional or drug or alcohol problems)
3. The perverse (those with characterological problems, usually the repeaters whose character defects and selfish values permit them to indulge themselves)

Based on close to four hundred interviews during the past ten years with individuals (primarily women) who were sexually exploited by their psychotherapists, coauthor Singer has identified several recurring themes in therapies that induce sexual involvement between therapist and client. The following is our condensed list of ways therapists go astray and become sexually involved. Not every therapist does each of these things, but the list conveys the characteristics of the therapist likely to become sexually involved. For simplicity, we will use the male pronoun to describe these sexual predators, but we do so with the understanding that female therapists have also been perpetrators of this type of abuse of power.

• *In general the therapist appears undertrained (has a limited set of treatment skills), has poor professional and personal boundaries, and exhibits a moderate to severe narcissism*. Some of these therapists are similar to those we have criticized for their cookie-cutter approach—the therapists described earlier who induce patients to adopt such notions as past-life regression, extraterrestrial abduction, and the value of rebirthing. But many therapists who engage in sexual acts with clients often don't have such a clever line; apparently they aren't even that sharp. Rather, they treat therapy much as if it were a social event. In many cases, their therapy sounds more like idle conversation than a program designed to aid the patient. The therapist also inappropriately reveals too much personal material to the patient.

For example, one therapist told his patient that he wanted to take her photo because she looked so much like his daughter! Numerous abused patients describe their so-called therapy as free-flowing conversation, with the therapist talking about himself, his past, his family, and other patients—all of which eventually led to sex. It's as if these men simply carry their social conversation and behavior from a bar, their dining room table, or living room into the therapy hour.

• *The therapist has a self-centered and simplistic notion that he is above the law and the ethical restraints of his profession*. These therapists tend to believe that it's those "other therapists, not me, who have to avoid dual relationships, but I don't. I know how to handle these situations and avoid trouble." And they give this justification to their patients.

For example, one female therapist had a client baby-sit for her, clean her house, do her billing, and care for her house when she was out of town. She also gave the client stock market tips, all the while telling her not to let anyone know about these things. She informed the client that in general psychologists were not to have multiple relationships with clients, but that she could because "I know how to handle these relationships."

• *The therapist often fails to secure an adequate history of the patient.* Or if a history is taken, the therapist doesn't seem to understand its implications for therapy. Along with that, he fails to make a correct diagnosis, missing or overlooking the real issues and diagnostic implications. When this is the case, the therapist generally begins to treat patients in accordance with his pet theories.

• *The therapist does not formulate a treatment plan.* The therapist either doesn't understand the value of a plan of treatment or simply isn't thoughtful enough to come up with one. Generally, then, therapy sessions degenerate into unfocused chatter, far from the atmosphere of a professional consultation. Such behavior tends to allow the therapist to fail to differentiate roles between himself and the patient; and from there, boundaries are easily crossed into acting out sexualized behavior.

• *The therapist tends to break confidentiality.* The therapist may talk about other patients in a manner that conveys to the patient that because she is "special" he can share with her. Many patients describe this as a seductive closeness that allowed them to forget why they came to treatment. Again, the ambience shifts from a professional situation to a social one. This behavior also reinforces the therapist in dropping his professional role and forgetting his ethical code and the basis of psychotherapy—namely, keeping the patient's needs foremost.

• *The therapist is poor at recognizing the transference and countertransference effects typically present in psychotherapy.* Simplistically, *transference* is usually regarded as the projecting, or transfer, of the patient's feelings or attitudes onto the therapist. *Countertransference* is usually regarded as the therapist projecting, or transferring, his feelings or attitudes onto the patient. The therapist's training should have taught him how to deal with his own feelings as well as those of the patient, and how to avoid getting into dual roles, becoming sexually involved, and acting in other harmful ways. Training should have pointed out the dependency needs of the patient and the imbalance of power between therapist and patient. The therapist should have been trained to know when to get consultation to avoid becoming sexually involved.

- *The therapist who engages in sexual activity with patients tends to be a repeater—that is, he has sex with more than one patient, either at the same time or sequentially.* Because the therapist's behavior is unbridled and unchecked, he often gets greedy. Like any other Don Juan, his patients become sex objects to be conquered and playthings for his amusement. Promiscuity is often the hallmark of the therapist who sexually exploits his patients.

Over time the therapist may become inured to the wrongness of the professional boundary violation, as well as blind to the damage it can do to the patient. The narcissism alluded to earlier comes to the foreground. The therapist sees the situation only from his own perspective.

- *The therapist tends to disregard normal standards of behavior common to a respectful relationship, often exerting a great deal of control and undue influence over the patient with whom he is sexually involved.* The abuse of power tends to go to the therapist's head. The relationship between the therapist and client often takes on cultic overtones, as the therapist controls more and more of the client's daily life and worldview.

Another outcome of these power abuses and corruptions is the development of psychotherapy cults. Unethical professionals take on self-appointed roles as superior guides and leaders; clients, and sometimes student trainees, are encouraged to turn over their decision making to the therapist. Classic cultic techniques are used to induce behavior change, not for the betterment of the client but for the benefit of the therapist.

Once the therapist crosses the boundaries into a sexual relationship, therapy ceases. The patient's needs are forgotten, and she serves only the therapist's needs.

Although at first glance this may not seem as "crazy" as some of the other therapies we've been exploring, we believe the therapist as sexual predator is as wily, as misguided, and as offbeat as some of the others we've met, if not more so. "Trust me," "submit to my authority," and "listen to my theory" are familiar approaches in all crazy therapies. Because of the sexual exploitation found here, and because of the prevalence of this violation, we rank it high among the abusive goings-on in the mental health field.

"Trust Me"

In the Western world, psychotherapy is seen as probably the most private and intimate relationship that occurs between trained professionals and their clients. Traditionally, the client is led to believe that she can place unconditional trust in the therapist. Because of the ethics of the profession and because of societal expectations, the client believes that the therapist will tap into his training, background, and experience to aid her in her search for a better mental outlook, greater ability to deal with her emotions, and solutions to life's problems.

In return for trusting the mental health professional and believing that he will keep her welfare the primary goal and focus of the therapy, the client, as a partner in this special relationship, is expected to be open and honest and to provide the therapist with a full and uncensored version of her history and feelings. In this highly confidential and charged atmosphere the patient will reveal her emotions, dreams, fears, and secrets. The general premise is that in this personally secure therapeutic environment, improved mental health is achieved as the patient becomes aware of, and adequately deals with, how past learning and experiences have molded her behavior, values, attitudes, reactions, and feelings.

The patient will, as a matter of course, project ("transfer") attitudes from her past onto the therapist. Together they will analyze how this affects her behavior now. The therapist's training should have prepared him to properly handle his role and to keep separate his own "transference" issues and not to act on them. No matter which form or school of therapy is applied, the therapist is to keep the patient's welfare primary and remain aware of these issues. The therapist should have been trained to know how to avoid falling into unprincipled behaviors. In other words, the therapist must not become the lover, hater, or neglector of his patient by acting on his own emotional or sensual needs in relation to the patient. But here are some examples of what can happen when the therapist violates the trust placed in him.

"I'd Never Treat You That Way"

"I had just moved to a new town with my husband and three young children under school age. I didn't have any close friends, and missed my family in the South terribly. I began to be visibly depressed. I had trouble getting up in the morning, was too blue to carry out my responsibilities as a mother and wife, had trouble sleeping, and was losing weight rapidly, for I had no appetite at all. I went to a psychologist who as it turned out never treated me for my depression, never even referred me for a medical evaluation. Instead, he told me I had an 'abusive' husband. It became a real propaganda campaign on his part—and it worked.

"The psychologist would say things like he'd never treat me like my husband did. He told me I'd never be better as long as I was around my 'abusive' husband. He'd point out that my husband worked long hours just to keep away from me, and that he, the psychologist, would never allow a 'beautiful, sexual creature' like me to 'languish alone' like my workaholic husband did. Those were his exact words!

"I see now how much who he was had an influence on me. I felt like a dutiful child. I believed whatever he said because he was the doctor, the authority. He had a wall full of degrees and certificates, and came highly recommended. I figured he was a professional, a scientist of a sort, and that he knew what he was doing. I totally trusted him and listened to his every word—and I obeyed.

"Then he started to cuddle me during the session, telling me it would allow me to feel what it was like to have a loving and comforting man. During one session he told me to trust him completely, and he put me on the floor and had sexual intercourse with me. I felt extremely guilty about this. Besides loving my husband very much, I felt terrible about having betrayed our marriage vows. And I wasn't the least bit attracted to the psychologist.

"But after a time, with all his badgering, I felt brainwashed into believing that my husband was a bad, unloving, workaholic. I even asked for a separation. My husband asked the psychologist for marital counseling, or a referral to someone so that we could work on our marriage and home life. But the psychologist had such a strong hold over me that I refused. I told my husband that it was over, that he'd had his chance. All this time, the psychologist was continuing the sex during our sessions. He told me that he was a widower and promised he'd marry me some time in the future.

"Then I got pregnant. I immediately told the psychologist, hoping we'd now marry. He became irate, called me a 'clumsy idiot,' and stormed out of the office. So there I was hurt, pregnant, estranged from my husband, and guilty over what had occurred. So I tried to commit suicide and lost the baby in the ordeal. I never went back to the psychologist, but he called me repeatedly, even appeared at my door threatening that he could 'prove' I was a mental case and that I'd lose my children. After that I went to a lawyer and sued. During the legal process, I learned that he was a repeat offender. Other female patients were located with whom he had had sexual liaisons during therapy. Once that came out, a settlement occurred, and he eventually lost his license."

When the therapist sexualizes the professional relationship, his behavior becomes a confusing element for the patient. The therapist's

dropping of his professional role and moving into the role of seducer, lover, and in effect, betrayer, takes a continuing toll on the patient. It is a source of stress and conflict. She has now lost her therapist and has instead to deal with an "incestuous," traumatic, and unreal relationship, which forces her into a quandary. She no longer has a therapist. She has no one to confide in. She is now truly alone.

Even when she is stirred to dreams and hopes that the therapist will be her lover forever, the aura of unreality, guilt, and conflict is so pervasive that at best there is continuing painful ambivalence and a search for guidelines about what to do, both with him and her life in general. At worst, more than one distraught, abused patient has attempted suicide.

"Submit to My Authority"

When the therapist sexualizes what goes on during the therapy hour, a type of incestuous tone is introduced into the relationship. The therapist shifts from being the benign parental figure, expected not to violate the taboos of incest, to indulging in what psychiatrist Peter Rutter aptly called "sex in the forbidden zone." Suddenly the rules are changed. The patient's needs are no longer primary. Instead, the therapist's emotional, sexual, and other needs become supreme. At this point, therapy ends and exploitation and harm begin. The patient has become an incestuous sex object.

There is a gross imbalance of power between a therapist and his client. The therapist is the authority; the client is hurting, needy, vulnerable. The therapist may cleverly disguise the unethical, and in some states illegal, nature of what's occurring, saying that having sex with him will benefit her, or that it's really okay, or that the therapy has ended so they can just be two ordinary people. Yet, what's really going on is that he is taking advantage of someone admittedly in a "lesser" position. In general, the patient will submit to the therapist's advances. The conduct of the authoritarian, seductive therapist tends to make the patient regress in a way sometimes seen with incestuous overtures.

Whatever problems the patient originally came to the therapist for are lost in this role reorientation. The therapist is no longer honoring the patient's welfare as the reason they are working together. The therapist uses his higher status, education, and expertise as a wedge to control, regress, and seduce the patient. As the authority figure in the relationship, he generally meets little overt resistance in her submission to his propositions. This is reinforced by the dependency that builds up, and which he encourages, over time.

"My Special, Secret Therapy"

"May," a recently divorced thirty-eight-year-old, sought therapy to recover from extreme loneliness precipitated by the end of her marriage. She also needed to find a job, and wanted help in assessing her skills and improving her self-image. She went to a psychiatrist who, after seeing her a few times, told her he had a program that would help her recover from her sense of aloneness. He called it his "special, secret therapy." He then proceeded to seduce her. He told her to keep her appointments at her regularly scheduled hour each week, which May did. In most sessions, the two of them had intercourse. The therapist sometimes talked about his personal life, yet always billed May for therapy for all the sessions.

In looking back, May spoke of him in this way: "He always acted like a real authority on everything. He just exuded confidence, and seemed competent and like he always knew the right thing to do and say. He sometimes seemed more like a professor instructing a class or a surgeon advising a patient about an operation. So when he spoke of his 'special, secret therapy,' I fell for it. After all, he had the knowledge, he was the authority."

May began to feel worse than ever. She felt used, yet fearful that if she complained she would have no adult companionship. She overdosed on sleeping pills, but was found by a neighbor and sent to the hospital. When May's psychiatrist was notified, he went to the hospital and took over May's care, actually preventing her from talking with anyone about their relationship and persuading her to sign out of the hospital. May said, "He was convincing, and so authoritative. Even the people at the hospital obeyed his powerful, domineering manner. He told me that no one must ever know about our special, secret therapy. I felt trapped, alone, and more hopeless than ever."

About a month later May got in her car, intending to kill herself by crashing into a cement pillar along the freeway. The highway was slick with rain, causing May's car to skid off the road into a ditch. She was taken to an emergency room, where she told the attending physician about her attempt to kill herself and about her relationship with her psychiatrist. At May's request the doctor allowed no visitors, so that her deviant psychiatrist could not come and get hold of her again. She was referred to a therapist who provided proper care and to a trained career counselor. She sued the psychiatrist, who settled out of court.

"Let Me Check Him Out First"

"Barbara" began therapy with a psychologist because she felt lonely, tired, and without energy. The psychologist did a brief interview with her; he never inquired about her medical status nor referred her for evaluation of her chronic tired state (which after she left therapy was medically diagnosed and treated). Barbara was a bit alarmed that the therapist had a photo on his desk of a man with an erection, but she thought he knew what he was doing so she put aside her doubts.

The psychologist recommended that Barbara be in group as well as individual therapy with him two times a week. With a therapy bill of $1,200 a month, she had to work three different jobs to cover it and her living expenses.

Barbara met a man named "Bruce" at one of her jobs. The psychologist told Barbara she had to get Bruce to enter therapy with him or else he would kick her out of her therapy. He also told her that he had to "check out" Bruce to see if he were sane and right for

her. Soon after Bruce began therapy, the psychologist began breaking confidentiality, telling Barbara that Bruce was a narcissist, was
never going to amount to anything, and was bisexual and prone to
violence with women. Although none of these things was true, Barbara's ardor cooled.

Meanwhile the therapist had seduced Bruce into engaging in
what Bruce later called "grope sessions" in which the therapist dark-
ened the treatment room and the two men grasped and rubbed
against each other as well as fondled each other. Bruce was told by
the therapist that he should not date Barbara or other women until
the therapist led him into a "stable bisexual orientation."

Bruce soon left therapy and got Barbara to listen to what had
happened to him. They shared stories of their independent knowledge of the therapist. They sought legal advice, threatened a lawsuit
for damages, and the therapist settled before the case went to trial.

As the corrupt therapist gets carried away with his need to control and dominate, the relationship may take on the flavor of one-
on-one cultlike abuse. In some cases, the therapist involves an
entire group in his hunger for power and self-satisfaction. Again,
patients' trust is violated as the therapist uses his power and authority over them to manipulate them into becoming cultlike followers,
as seen in the example of the Center for Feeling Therapy, introduced in Chapter Six.

The Center for Feeling Therapy, begun by two defectors from
Janov's Primal Therapy, was notorious for its scandalous behavior.
In 1985 the legal hearing to review the alleged charges against the
center was honored with being "the longest, costliest, and most
complex psychotherapy malpractice case in California history."
There was a long list of abuses and ethical violations. Former
patients testified during license revocation hearings that they were
seduced by the therapists, given sex assignments, and publicly
ridiculed and humiliated, sometimes being made to stand naked

before the group. Therapists slept with patients and ordered them to sleep with other patients. Female patients were put on extreme diets for years; at least one patient was commanded to masturbate in front of her therapist.

An ex-patient described one session in which a woman was ordered to remove her blouse and crawl on the floor, mooing like a cow. Others told of being beaten during therapy. A male patient who wanted to return to college and stop working in a business run by the therapists was made to wear diapers, sit in a crib, and eat baby food for eight weeks. Women were psychologically coerced into having abortions and giving up their children for adoption, having been told they were "too crazy" to care for children.

In *Therapy Gone Mad,* a gripping description of the rise and demise of the center, author Carol Mithers summarizes the suffering of one former participant:

> At thirty-nine, she has spent as much time trying to undo Feeling Therapy as she'd spent in it. The job might take the rest of her life. She could no longer be sure she'd ever have a real profession, ever have a chance for normal, pleasurable sex, ever get another chance to have a child. She might never have any of the things that would have been hers if, at eighteen, she'd been directed to an ordinary counselor and a very different road. And there was nothing she could do about it. That each day of her life be a tiny bit better than the last was so much less than she'd once hoped for, but now, it was all she could ask.

In general, therapy decreases clients' resistance and opens up their emotions, and sometimes clients become extremely reliant on the therapist. Therapy clients tend to be more open to suggestion, persuasion, and control in the therapy milieu than they might be in other roles in their life. In unethical situations, as described here, the therapist is no longer promoting mature decision making, autonomy, and free discussion. The power of the therapist becomes central and dominant. As a result, patients become more powerless, regressed, and obedient to the dictates of the therapist, while they are also in a state of conflict and anxiety. In such situations, women may find that they don't have the innate personal power of other women their age, nor are they able to exercise their ability to reject a sexual proposition as they would outside the therapy context. Afterward, some abused patients remember wondering at the time, "Why is this happening to me? Have I done something wrong? How am I to respond? Is this part of therapy?"

"Listen to My Theory"

Former patients of sexually abusing therapists generally say that they had to really work at participating in the therapist's sexual requests, often regarding him as fearsome, disgusting, unattractive. Most times, these victims experienced great pangs of guilt and shame. Some do speak of moments when they felt flattered, in a very child-like way, saying, "It made me think I was very special, if he was changing from therapy to this."

Some patients are told by errant therapists that having sex with them is part of therapy. The therapists justify their behavior by explaining to the patient that it will be good for her, help her grow psychologically, help her get rid of barriers and hangups. They wrap the sex act around some crackpot theory that they present as a great therapeutic truth. There appears to be an unending variety of tales told by some sexually exploitative therapists in efforts to smooth the way for sexual encounters.

Gender Bending

"Mandy," age thirty-six, was grieving over the unexpected death of her uncle who had raised her, so she went to see a psychologist listed in her health plan. Mandy, a lesbian, lived with her partner of many years and held a responsible technical job. When Mandy saw the psychologist, he only cursorily discussed Mandy's grief. Because she had never been in therapy before, she had no idea what to expect. She assumed that because the therapist had a doctoral degree, he knew what to do.

Shortly after beginning therapy, Mandy was struck by a car as she rode her bike to work and was badly injured. After this she was in desperate straits. Unable to work because of the need for prolonged physical rehabilitation therapy, she was clearly demonstrating symptoms of posttraumatic stress disorder (PTSD) and a moderately severe depression. Mandy was confined to her home, except when attending physiotherapy for her injuries and when seeing the psychotherapist. She spent hours each day crying, and becoming more and more agoraphobic. Both Mandy's own report and the therapist's notes secured during a legal action she eventually brought against him indicate that the therapist never treated Mandy's depression, her PTSD, or her growing agoraphobia. Instead, he instituted his own agenda.

The therapist put forth his theory: Mandy's depression over losing her male relative was symbolic of her grief that she was not a man. He explained to her that the accident had been her way of masochistically getting out of having to face that she was a woman, a badly damaged woman. "To be cured of this disorder, you need desensitization to males," he said confidently. He even told her that these were the latest theories in "gender psychology."

Soon after explaining these theories, the therapist began to hold, hug, and suggestively caress Mandy, while insisting that she touch and fondle his body parts. When he suggested nude bathing with him in his home swimming pool, she quit therapy with him. Mandy found a woman therapist and told her what had happened. The new therapist provided Mandy with information about professional ethics and the state laws. Because of the charges against him, the male therapist lost his license.

Suckling the Inner Child

"Jack" had never been in therapy before and wanted help with shyness. A friend recommended a local female psychologist with whom Jack began treatment. From the beginning he wondered about her facilities—an office suite with three segments: a playroom, a bedroom, and an ordinary office—but he thought that because she was highly recommended, she must be okay. The therapist told Jack that she had to regress and rebirth him so that he could overcome his shyness by relearning how to relate to people, particularly women. She explained that this theory went back to Freud and was widely recognized and used. The treatment would include acting like a baby with her in various ways, and she assured him that it was okay and he shouldn't feel embarrassed. She told him she'd be using a lot of hypnosis because then the effects of their work together would go deeper and he'd "grow up again" faster.

The therapist then had Jack put on diapers. She hypnotized him and had him crawl about on the playroom floor. Sometimes he was to drink from a bottle while lying on the bed. The therapist encouraged Jack to urinate into the diapers and then describe how this made him feel. She continued hypnosis, commenting on what a good deep trance he was able to achieve.

One day Jack awoke out of trance to find that he was suckling the therapist's breast. He was very distressed, but the therapist reassured him that this was a usual technique. She said she needed to care for his inner child. When Jack came out of trance on another occasion, he found himself lying in bed under the covers with the therapist on top of the covers beside him, patting his groin area. She explained this as a partial rebirthing process.

After that, Jack did not return to therapy but instead sought a lawyer to get his money back, as he said he really needed good therapy at this point but had no money left.

Unearthing the Past

"Roger," a twenty-year-old college student, was concerned about whether or not he was an alcoholic. He drank a bottle of beer a day and on weekends drank a six-pack. On occasion Roger had some concern about his sexual identity. He had dated some women, and from time to time had sexual intercourse with a longtime woman friend. But sometimes he felt attracted to his men friends, and this is what he wanted to talk about.

The man who answered the clinic's phone urged Roger to come immediately to the clinic, based on a brief intake and on learning of Roger's excellent insurance coverage. Soon the therapist had Roger drop out of school and come in for long treatment sessions, during which he'd be hypnotized. Roger apparently was an excellent hypnotic subject, going into deep trance almost upon being seated in the home office of the therapist. The therapist had created his own theory of what he called "the road to healthy mental life." He said this was achieved through a psychological treatment that combined deep hypnosis and a search for "long-lost memories." He also had Roger read a few books on reparenting that validated his idea that separation from family and friends at this time would reinforce a positive treatment result.

The therapist told Roger that he wouldn't remember large parts of the hypnosis sessions, explaining that Roger "was not yet up to" dealing with much of his past. Until then, Roger had no idea that he couldn't recall the large segments of his past to which the therapist alluded. The way the therapist spoke, Roger became frightened that he must have been insane or committed terrible acts. The sessions often went on for three hours daily, with seven- to nine-hour weekend sessions.

The therapist had Roger disconnect from his parents and friends, and he eventually moved Roger into his home in order to reparent him.

Roger was made to crawl about on the floor and was spanked for minor mistakes. He was fed out of a bottle and held diapered in the therapist's lap. Under hypnosis, Roger was induced to suckle the therapist's nipples and penis. The therapist would tell Roger after these sessions that he would now be comfortable with both males and females.

Roger broke off therapy for a time, but the therapist kept calling him, so he went back. Roger's behavior deteriorated: he felt he was being driven crazy but was so dependent on the therapist that he remained with him several years before seeking both better psychiatric care and a lawyer. Settlement was agreed to prior to trial, and follow-up reveals that Roger is still in therapy overcoming the effects of the bizarre treatment he encountered.

The methods of starting the sexual touching are as varied as the strange rationalizations used to seduce clients. Typically, the therapist's chair rolls closer and closer, and simple pats on the hand or shoulder eventually evolve into sensualized touching. One gets the impression that the client is being slowly desensitized to the therapist's encroaching nearness—and ultimate goal.

The dependency of the client on the therapist is also an important factor in the unfolding of this sexual adventure. How clients actually feel during the sexual activities and time with the abusive therapist is highly individual, ranging from reactions of love to covert and continuing disgust throughout the liaison. But clients abused in this way always express how much they were afraid of losing the therapist. It is as if the errant therapist almost senses how to hold off the improper touching and subsequent acts until the patient is utterly dependent on him.

Dumping the Patient

Because of his self-serving involvement, the sexualizing therapist falls below the standard of practice in most areas. He loses sight of the treatment goals and no longer monitors the patient's mental status. The therapist fails to notice the patient's confusion, conflict, and concern about the changed roles. All of this is bewildering to the patient, who feels obligated to respond to this new situation. In failing to observe, or ignoring, the patient's distress and possible deterioration, the therapist has become truly negligent.

It is almost always the sexually exploitative therapist who ends the illicit relationship, and usually in a precipitous, disastrous, and uncaring manner. Traditionally, termination of therapy is mutually planned and done in a way that is growth producing for the patient. But the sexually involved therapist tends to use his own inner urges and personal needs as the indicator for when to end the relationship. Often the woman's mental health has deteriorated to the point that she is desperate, and the therapist no longer regards her as a "fun person" to be with. The involvement with the therapist may have ruined her marriage or other significant relationships, caused her to invest money jointly with the therapist, and led her to neglect her children, job, and friends. Emotionally she is often no longer wanted and desired by the therapist because he has found another, more appealing patient. Sometimes he has fears that his wife, woman friend, or colleagues will learn of the improper relationship with the patient.

Cast aside in this way, the patient may desperately need counseling, but usually she feels so betrayed that she hesitates to seek help. "Besides, who will believe me?" she wonders. These women often feel unable to trust anyone at this point.

Covering for One Another

Sometimes when patients manage to confide in another therapist, they find that there is a kind of professional bonding, and in fact they receive little comfort or understanding from the new therapist.

He Sent Me Back—"Jacqueline's" Story

"I had two small children and a very demanding job, and had recently divorced a husband who was a real scoundrel—he was lazy, worked only occasionally at odd jobs, even though he had a college degree. He preferred to sit at home and smoke pot while I worked at a high-pressure sales job. After my suicide attempt, the hospital doctor put me on an antidepressant and I kept in touch with him for medication. He referred me to a psychoanalyst type. I began to see him because I was so depressed I could hardly function.

"The psychiatrist, 'Jim,' was much older than I. He would sit smoking a pipe, not saying much. After about six months of therapy he began to hug me at the beginning and end of each hour. I found myself physically attracted to him and became obsessed with thinking about him. I never spoke about it because I sensed if I did he would reject me, or interpret it in some way that would make me feel blamed and dumb. I thought about him all the time. One day as he hugged me he ran his hands over my whole body, kissed me, and led me back to his couch where we made love. This continued in every session for about eighteen months.

"What this was doing to me was awful. I was never really fully present and participating in anything. Much of my mind was absorbed in fantasizing about Jim. People at work commented that I seemed spacey and dreamy. My kids were neglected as I sat thinking about Jim and going over our last lovemaking and making up dreams of the future together. I never thought of dating and rarely went out with women friends.

"I realized I needed help and went to another psychiatrist. Instead of helping me—at least seeing me long enough to check for himself if the affair was really going on—after my first session with him, this other doctor called Jim, without my permission. Of course Jim covered himself by saying I was delusional, had erotomania, and other things I can't even recall. The second psychiatrist called me and told me about the conversation and sent me back to Jim. Then Jim called and said I needed an appointment the next day. I went. He was furious, but oddly enough the hour ended with us having sex on the floor of his office, and making plans for a short vacation together.

"The so-called vacation was a cruel event. We drove to a nearby resort. We went to a lovely hotel and ate the best of food, and then he told me he would never leave his wife, and that even if he did, he'd never marry me—I was too young, had two kids, and so on. I remember the trip home from the 'vacation'—I sat stupefied in Jim's car, mute, weeping. He dropped me off at my door, kissing me and rubbing my body with his hands. I almost fainted it was so awful. I felt completely alone in the world. I forgot about my kids, went in the house and swallowed every pill I had, then went to the kitchen and began gulping from a bottle of liquor. Luckily the baby-sitter, an older woman, stayed a while and called 911 when I passed out.

"I eventually got therapy from a decent, professional man, who referred me to an attorney. I sued Jim and won. I needed money to pay for good therapy since I had used up all my money and my insurance paying for all those hours with Jim. I often wonder and talk with my new therapist about it: what kind of man is Jim? How could he have done what he did, with so little feeling about the consequences to me? He knew I had severe depressions, that I had tried suicide once before, that I was vulnerable and alone in the world. How can he live with himself? And call himself a helper of people? And I'm also still angry at that second guy, who betrayed me and sent me back to Jim."

She Wouldn't Listen—"Jane's" Story

"I had been sexually molested by my psychologist and had many things I wanted to discuss in treatment afterward. I went to a female social worker, thinking a woman would be understanding. When I told the social worker that I'd begun a legal suit against my former psychologist, the woman advised me that she wouldn't see me if I continued with the legal case. She wanted me to back off, stay as her client, and not sue the other person.

"I saw the social worker three more times and then quit. I felt like I had to lie to her to keep her as my therapist, yet I needed to talk to someone about what the psychologist had done to me. She was really opposed to my doing any kind of lawsuit, saying that I would come out of it feeling very guilty. She said she couldn't take the stress of ever having to deal with lawyers about any case. I felt like I was not able to tell the truth to her about what was really happening in my life and what the psychologist had done to me. She wouldn't even listen."

The Harm Done

The self-esteem of most clients who are sexually abused by their therapist is so shattered that they feel unworthy and doubt their judgment. All are psychologically more impaired at the end of sexually exploitative therapy than when they began therapy. Whether the person had minor or major psychological problems at the start of therapy, these problems are exacerbated by the sexual exploitation. The client's preexisting conditions may be compounded by the appearance of variants of posttraumatic stress disorder, depression, anxiety, self-hatred, self-doubt, guilt, and marked ambivalence or anger toward the therapist. The psychological harm comes from several sources:

- The predator role and boundary violations perpetrated by the therapist

- The neglect of treatment

- The failure to monitor the decline in the patient's mental health, social activities, work productivity, and general welfare

- The appearance of, and concomitant neglect of, new and serious diagnosable psychological conditions

- The traumatic termination of the relationship

Thus, it is not just the sexual touching that should be studied. Also to be taken into account is the impact on the client of the many transgressions, omissions, and violations by the therapist in his role as a professional.

Warning Signs That Your Therapy May Be in Trouble

Despite the centuries of ethical taboos, some therapists are wont to blame the victim when they hear of sexual encounters between therapists and clients. Many male therapists in particular tend to think of the client as responsible for the travesty, saying that she is guilty of seductiveness.

By the late 1980s most professional associations had established ethical guidelines prohibiting such behavior, and many states have passed clear-cut laws bluntly stating that the therapists are to be held responsible. Aside from the laws meant to hold therapists accountable for their actions, we should like to think that therapists' training, knowledge, and professional ethical standards would be enough to keep them from having sexual encounters with clients. Yet the stories in this chapter, and the countless other cases of sexual victimization of client by therapist, inspire us to add some words of warning. Four clusters of conduct on the part of the therapist should alert you that your therapy may be going awry.

1. *Engaging in sexually suggestive behavior with you.* This includes giving seductive looks, telling sexual jokes and stories, discussing the therapist's sex life and experiences, and discussing details of the therapist's personal life or intimate personal behavior.

Also watch out for the therapist moving too close, hugging you in prolonged, full-body hugs, sitting next to you on the couch, lying next to you, or rolling his chair closer and closer each session until he's actually touching you.

More blatant behaviors would include showing up at your house or place of work, phoning you like a social friend, giving you gifts or soliciting presents from you, inviting you to sit in a hot tub, expecting you to accept or give massages, or asking you to go on a business trip or vacation with him.

2. *Making you a special person.* This is done by confiding in you, taking you to dinner, and seeing you in his office at the end of the day when no one else is around.

Generally this type of behavior also includes breaking the confidentiality of other patients by revealing information about them to you.

3. *Sequestering you.* Here the therapist attempts to make you more dependent on him by isolating you or trying to limit your social contact with others. This includes bad-mouthing your partner, suggesting that you should drop intimate friends, and separating you from your family by downplaying their merits—for example, labeling them toxic or dysfunctional.

The therapist will also encourage you to put increasing amounts of time into therapy, or with him, telling you that this will speed your recovery and that you are becoming the perfect companion.

4. *Putting his interests above yours.* Over time, you see that your needs and problems have been dropped. Your problems have become low-priority items or are never discussed, and sessions focus more on the therapist's needs and life.

When your therapy begins to resemble much of what was just described, we suggest that you stop seeing the therapist in question.

Some might wonder why we don't recommend asking for consultation with the therapist or for a second opinion from another therapist about what's going on. Simple: we have heard enough about the impact of these narcissistic and character-disordered therapists that we believe getting out of their way as fast as possible is the wisest solution. In general, trying to speak with these impaired professionals or asking them to consult with another therapist will usually result in the therapist's trying to make you feel guilty, telling you that you are not trusting enough, not committed to therapy, resisting change, or whatever argument he may feel will keep you in his clutches.

What to Do When Sexual Contact Has Occurred

First of all, and most important, do not blame yourself. As one state law says, "Therapists should never use the therapy relationship for their own sexual gain. This is sexual exploitation and is illegal."

Professional Therapy Never Includes Sex, a model brochure distributed by the State of California Department of Consumer Affairs, says it quite nicely:

> Therapists who encourage, ask for, or permit sexual involvement with their clients are exploiting them.

Professional therapy never includes sex. It also never includes any other kind of sexual contact or behavior. All therapists are trained and educated to know that this kind of behavior is unethical, against the law, and can be harmful to the client.

Your next step would be to speak with someone you trust and to get some personal and emotional support. Although it may seem threatening at first, consider seeing another counselor so that you can work through the psychological harm caused by the sexual victimization you experienced.

The following suggestions may lead you to helpful resources and information regarding your options.

1. Call the state licensing board in your state and inquire about the procedure for filing a complaint. It is important that the sexual violators be reported and held accountable for their actions. This may help prevent further exploitation of other clients.

2. Contact professional associations—preferably at the state and national levels—for names of local persons to contact. Also ask about filing a complaint.

3. Contact sexual assault and crisis centers for referrals and information. Numbers can usually be found in the front of your telephone directory.

4. Seek legal consultation with an attorney who specializes in therapist malpractice.

Sex with a therapist or counselor is not okay and is not going to benefit the client. If anything, as we've seen, it will cause new problems and exacerbate previous ones.

Regardless of what the sexually exploitative professional may be telling you, he is merely taking advantage of the authority bestowed on him as someone in a healer role, typically a respected function in all societies. The therapist as sexual predator is violating both societal and professional trust. Remember, as the booklet says: professional therapy *never* includes sex.

8

Alphabet Soup for the Mind and Soul
NLP, FC, NOT, EMDR

Among the myriad enthusiastic offerings asserted to be panaceas for mental and emotional problems, many techniques have been offered to consumers as fast, easy, and seemingly magical ways to provide psychological treatment. We have selected only a few to discuss here.

Fast, magical-fix techniques have attracted followers from the psychological and self-improvement communities who, from our observations, share several characteristics. Some are seemingly prone to fall prey to fads; others merely want to be in the avant-garde, and espouse one after another of the new treatment modalities. Some may dream of being a magical healer, hoping the surefire techniques will help them achieve fame and plaudits from patients and colleagues.

Yet other providers in this quick-fix milieu appear undertrained. Lacking in useful techniques to help clients, these insecure, unskilled practitioners grab onto the "cures" offered by the never-ending stream of psychotechnology gurus.

And still others seem to operate from a pure power platform: "I, the expert, will lead you, the client, to accept what *I* like and find fascinating."

Not to be overlooked in all of this are the sales tactics used by the innovators to promote their newly invented psychological cure-alls. One marketing technique that has done well in the professional world is to start a certification program soon after conjuring up a new procedure. Being able to display an award with a gold embossed seal stating that the holder is "certified" has apparently clinched the deal on many workshops and programs. The public is led to think that some higher, socially approved agency has awarded the certificate. The certifiers ride on the tails of state licensure, as well as on the aura of sanctity and credibility of state medical boards, psychological and social work boards of examiners, famous universities, or other legally sanctioned agencies whose stamp of approval typically means that some minimum standards have been met.

Meanwhile, the certificate may be homemade, coming from a small, commercial organization that is latching onto the centuries-old tradition of healers who have actually met rigorous standards of achievement and quality control. Sometimes only one man or woman is the total organization issuing the certificates. We're not saying that the multitude of organizations offering certification are all phony or illegal, but we want to call attention to the remarkable propaganda value such a piece of paper appears to carry in the public eye.

Another successful sales technique—one employed by some of the promoters of the methods discussed in this chapter—is to seduce customers with rash promises and endorsements from acolytes and sycophants.

Neuro-Linguistic Programming

Neuro-Linguistic Programming (NLP) was developed by John Grinder and Richard Bandler in the 1970s. At the time they were a linguistic professor and a computing student at the University of California, Santa Cruz. Far from passé, NLP trainings have been provided in companies such as Hewlett-Packard, IBM, McDonald's, NASA, the U.S. Army, and U.S. Olympic teams, and in countless public school systems. According to one source who runs a full-service NLP training center in the Midwest, there are approximately

38,250 certified practitioners. NLP trainings are available throughout the United States and in more than thirty-eight other countries.

NLP originators Grinder and Bandler have been called "magicians" by those who studied with them. Rumor had it that their new
discovery was creating permanent changes in people in minutes.
Lifelong phobias were no longer a problem. Allergic reactions had
vanished. Learning capacities expanded in a fraction of the time
normally expected. Performance improved a thousandfold. The
raves went on and on.

Today NLP is often called "software for the mind." Others call
it simply an overrated version of hypnosis. Founder Bandler says the
name NLP was "phrased on the fly from several book titles on the
floor of his car one night when a policeman asked his occupation."

Just what exactly is NLP, and does it work? Are the courses that
cost thousands worth it? Is even the $40 audiotape worth it? NLP
circles claim as their own such successes as motivational speaker
Tony Robbins and East/West healer of the mind and body Deepak
Chopra. Can they be wrong?

What Is It?

Much of early NLP theory was based on the work of three prominent and successful therapists of the 1970s—Virginia Satir, Milton
H. Erickson, and Fritz Perls. Bandler and Grinder concluded that
there were similar underlying patterns in the work of the three therapists, from which the two created a model for more effective communication, personal change, accelerated learning, and greater
enjoyment of life. NLP proponents call it a technology, a series of
techniques, a model, an attitude, a system, a methodology. It unlocks
secrets, they say, all the while insisting that it's not a magic pill.

Early advocates touted that NLP could be easily taught and
learned: "A client can learn enough basic skills in a weekend or
two to make his therapy much faster and more effective. . . . An
experienced NLP practitioner can deal with most phobias and
many other simple problems in a half hour or less. Probably at least

half the other symptoms that bring people into therapy can be dealt with in a one-hour session or two." Those enamored with NLP say it can be applied to learning languages, learning and enhancing sports performance, speed reading, memory improvement, business management, medical problems, and general education. It can change lifelong patterns of behavior in minutes, we're told. Yet one NLP proponent writes: "I find it works scarily well. So well that even someone with poor training in it can do a lot of damage. There was no quality control in the field."

NLP uses such influence techniques as mirroring and matching, reframing, pacing, and anchoring, which include noticing eye movements, gestures, breathing patterns, voice tone changes, pupil dilation, and skin color changes. It's a matter of noticing and interpreting subtle cues, then mirroring them back at the other person. Essentially this means that when you are with someone, you mimic that person's behavior and attitudes so that he or she feels comfortable with you. Instant bond! Instant communication! You then have the upper edge and can more easily influence that person and obtain the results you desire.

Bandler and Grinder claimed that their techniques allowed a person to look at the external behavior of another person and reliably determine that person's internal state. This in effect says you can look at the outside of a human and tell what is going on inside. You *can* judge a book by its cover. And not only that, so the claim goes: by using NLP you will also increase your influence over others.

Initially Bandler and Grinder stated that each person had a Preferred Representational System (PRS). That's fancy language for saying that each person prefers to communicate either through visual, auditory, or kinesthetic interpretations. Observing a person's eye movements allows you to know whether the person is constructing or remembering visual, auditory, or kinesthetic images. Eyes looking up are accessing visual imagery; eyes level are accessing auditory images; and eyes looking down are accessing kinesthetic or body sensations. Viewing to the left is interpreted as remembering, viewing to the right is constructing. Thus, according to NLP, if the speaker turns his eyes up and to the right he is constructing and manipulating visual images. If the speaker's eyes go up and to the left, he is accessing remembered imagery.

NLP practitioners are taught that a person using a stored visual image will use phrases such as "I see a way to . . . ," whereas a person in an auditory mode will say, "That sounds right to me." A person using a kinesthetic system will say, "I feel we should. . . ." Catching on to how a person relates allegedly reveals ways to influence her by conveying a congruence between what she says and does and what you, the therapist or influencer, says and does.

Over the years NLP has expanded to include in its "family" many training centers, certificate programs, and evolved courses. NLP and its variants may be sold under many names and at many training centers, such as Advanced Neuro Dynamics, Dynamic Learning, Trance-Action, Achievement Technologies, Anchor Point, Life Design™, Living Vision, IDHEA Seminars, and Design Human Engineering™ (DHE).

Lauded as the synthesis of the past ten years of Bandler's work, DHE™ claims to be the toolbox for housing all of NLP's tools. What does it do? "In DHE™, we install machine-like devices inside the mind that create new states (ones never experienced before) and then tie these states to visual representations," write two representatives of IDHEA Seminars.

The proponents of this latest innovation of NLP caution us: "Be warned however, it is not for whiners, rule makers, new technique searchers, or info junkies. DHE™ is for those of us who want a true brain work-out to explore the untold millions of possibilities that exist."

Does It Work?

"Does NLP really work?" "Has it been scientifically validated?" These are two questions on the Internet's NLP FAQ and Resources home page. The home page answer reveals, in our opinion, a combination of wishful thinking and passing the buck that is often characteristic of quick-fix schemes: "It's difficult to prove that something doesn't work or doesn't exist. Most of the people on this news group believe they have seen and/or created positive, often magical results from the application of NLP. Discussions of whether a particular aspect of NLP has yet been scientifically validated are probably more appropriate for sci.psychology."

According to NLP researcher, developer, and trainer Robert Dilts, NLP "is theoretically rooted in principles of neurology, psychophysiology, linguistics, cybernetics, and communication theory."

Some NLP spokespeople and practitioners shy away from the theory question: "So, now to the question of our basic theory in NLP. We don't really have one. NLP is not based on theory. It is based on the process of making models. There is a big difference. A model doesn't have to be 'true' or 'correct' or even perfectly formed. It only has to be useful when applied to what it's designed for. If it isn't, it can be discarded in any situation where it fails." How's that for a fail-safe argument?

Another practitioner describes it this way: "NLP is heavily pragmatic: if a tool works, it's included in the model, even if there's no theory to back it up. None of the current NLP developers have done research to 'prove' their models correct. The party line is 'pretend it works, try it, and notice the results you get. If you don't get the result you want, try something else.'" Even Bandler himself has said, "It wasn't my job to do theory."

Despite all these disclaimers, NLP promoters and advertisers continue to call the originators "scientists" and to use such terms as "science," "technology," and "hi-tech psychology" in describing NLP. In this maze of unintelligible words and concepts, a suspicious person might wonder if the purpose of all this gobbledygook is to lead the average person to believe that something really profound is being said. Just listen to some of the jargon: MetaPrograms, submodalities, pragmagraphics, meta-model, Advanced Calibration

System™, deep structure, surface structure, incompatible representation systems, accessing cue, non-accessing movement.

Yet, with all this fancy lingo, two top NLP/DHE™ spokespeople, Rex Steven and Carolyn Sikes, perhaps say it like it really is: "What occurs is a way of consciously creating the placebo effect." Hmm.

Sikes also wrote, "The attitude of NLP is one of wanton curiosity and wanton experimentation." But here's how several customers of NLP therapists felt about their encounters:

The Echoing Therapist

"Louise" had been assaulted during a nighttime robbery of her apartment. She was having trouble not thinking about the incident. Her family doctor referred her to a new therapist in the office building. "I never returned after my first visit," Louise said, "because the experience was just weird." She went on to say:

"The guy was in his late twenties, I guess, well dressed and sort of trendy looking. He sat facing me, watching my every move. He seemed to be doing some repeat maneuvers, for example, echoing what I had just said, or asking a series of questions about every statement I made. I felt like I was in high school English class and the teacher was prodding me to expand every sentence into a paragraph. In the end, we never connected as human beings because he was always saying things like, 'You seem to be looking at that idea,' 'You have a picture in your mind about that,' or 'Picture yourself seeing that.'

"He seemed hung up on ideas of looking, having mental pictures and visualizing things. I tried to see if he knew anything about how to get rid of my mental distress and fear at night. I told him I was having trouble studying, reading. But he never really heard what I said. Even though he picked at and parroted my words and phrases, he didn't seem to get anything and I never got an answer from him.

"He didn't seem to want to learn from me. I guess his thing was to play some kind of game with sentences. Finally the hour was over and I never went back. Luckily I eventually found a good therapist who knew what I was talking about, who related to me, and heard what I was saying in a real sense. The first guy was just plain weird."

The Miming Therapist

"Nick" had recently begun working on a master's degree. He'd been a police officer, but a leg injury from a shooting had forced him to retire from that line of work. He went to a therapist because he felt "down" and was having trouble adjusting to his new sedentary lifestyle. A friend at school said he really liked his therapist, who used a technique called NLP, so Nick thought he would give it a try.

"I only went to him once," Nick said. "I mean, give me a break! After all, at the police academy I'd been trained in interviewing and observation, you know. It didn't take me long to figure out that he was reflecting back at me everything I did. He'd adjust his body like me, cross his legs, try to speak in the same way, the same volume, with the same inflections. It was as if I were at the amusement park in front of one of those glass boxes where a pantomime artist imitates every little move you make until you just crack up in laughter. Only the therapist wasn't that good. But he was that obvious. At one point I asked him, 'Why are you doing all that?' He told me it was a great way to build rapport. I said, 'Not with me.' I never went back, and found a new therapist who's a real person."

The director of one NLP-approved training institute wrote, "NLP is really an epistemology (the study of the origin and structure of knowledge itself). Everything in NLP is based on specific evidence procedures for effectiveness and is thoroughly tested."

But not according to the National Research Council of the National Academy of Sciences.

In 1984, the U.S. Army Research Institute asked the National Academy "to examine the potential value of certain techniques that had been proposed to enhance human performance." Each of the techniques (one of which was NLP) had been developed outside the mainstream human sciences, and each was making strong claims of high effectiveness. The academy formed a committee of fourteen prominent scientists equipped to judge the various techniques.

In commenting on studies testing NLP, the committee wrote in its 1988 report: "Individually and as a group these studies fail to provide an empirical base of support for NLP assumptions . . . or NLP effectiveness. Different critics may attach different values to the quality of these studies, but the fact remains that none supports the effectiveness of NLP in improving influence or skilled motor performance."

The committee's report goes on: "The lack of evaluation is not apt to be easily remedied. For one thing, the proprietors, purveyors, and practitioners of NLP are not experimentalists and are not interested in conducting such studies. . . . In sum, then, the absence of any evaluation of the effectiveness of NLP and the lack of any scientific basis for it constitute serious reservations against using it for expert modeling purposes. . . . The committee cannot recommend the employment of such an unvalidated technique."

Yet, current advertisements by NLP practitioners state that use of NLP may cause a person to quit smoking, lose weight, gain freedom from allergies, eliminate phobias, overcome fear, replace outworn thought patterns, attract abundance, become motivated at will, enhance self-esteem, beat addictions, reduce stress, detraumatize past traumas, and heal broken relationships. Other ads tout its use in sports medicine, conflict resolution, career advancement, chiropractic work, and corporate consulting. One ad proudly announces that an early advocate is currently creating NLP models of the strategies of Albert Einstein, Walt Disney, and Jesus of Nazareth. Lord help us.

Parents of children with physical, mental, and learning disorders have been preyed on by merchants of magic since time immemorial. Among these merchants are certain therapists who have taken advantage of many parents with offspring who are autistic, retarded, cerebral palsied, or learning disabled. Certainly, being a parent of a learning-disabled child carries a great deal of responsibility—and often relentless hope for a key to understanding and improved functioning, a "cure." Willing to explore many avenues, risking failure and financial loss, families such as these are especially vulnerable to the lure of mental health miracles.

Two alleged therapies—Facilitated Communication and Neural Organization Technique—are promoted by a number of psychotherapists, educational psychologists, chiropractors, and others. An examination of both of these methods reveals why they are surrounded with controversy and heated debate.

Facilitated Communication

Facilitated Communication (FC) is an educational technique meant to bring about communication from those who previously had been unable to communicate through either speaking or signing. Centered at an institute in Syracuse, New York, FC has supporters and advocates worldwide. The institute has a home page on the Internet, and FC appears to be going strong despite critics' assertions that it is a pseudoscience. Detractors' main criticisms relate to the lack of controlled studies and to the proponents' tendencies to make light of facilitator influence over the subject's responses.

What Is It?

FC consists of a "facilitator" sitting beside a patient with the facilitator's hand over the patient's hand. Sometimes the facilitator supports the arm or wrist. The patient's hand is then "facilitated" to point to pictures or words, or to spell words, phrases, or sentences, as the hand moves over an alphabet board, typewriter, or computer keyboard. In this way, the facilitator "assists" the nonverbal person to communicate. Purportedly the facilitator's presence and touch enables the patient to communicate as never before, and supposedly the selection of keys or answers is not influenced by the facilitator. The procedure is often claimed to produce "unexpected literacy."

Although some say that FC was discovered independently in at least five nations, generally the development of FC is credited to Rosemary Crossley, a Melbourne teacher, who came upon the technique in Australia in the 1970s. Crossley became convinced that the cerebral palsied youngsters with whom she was working had unrecognized literacy and math skills—despite their having had little or no instruction and having lived most of their lives in rather impoverished institutional environments. Crossley became a heroine in the disabled movement, and use of her technique spread throughout Australia and abroad.

The theory behind FC is that autistic persons and others with severely impaired learning capabilities do not suffer from cognitive defects but rather have a motor impairment that prevents the initiation and control of vocal expression. Because of the neuromotor impairment, the person needs someone else to stabilize hand functions. The facilitator—as opposed to a family member or some other non-FC-trained individual—offers both a special touch and emotional support, and is therefore crucial to the procedure.

After observing Crossley work in Australia, a Syracuse University special education professor, Douglas Biklen, introduced FC into the United States as a method of working with autistic nonverbal persons. Biklen established the Facilitated Communication Institute, and the American movement took off. Satellite programs were set up to train facilitators. Thousands of professionals are said to have tried this technique on patients, and millions of tax dollars have been invested in promoting the adoption of FC. Yet, a fifteen-week study that evaluated FC's utility and validity concluded that students were unable to correctly respond to questions for which the facilitator lacked answers.

Much of the enthusiasm for FC was aided by glowing media reports. From 1990 to the present, a series of articles appeared in non-peer-reviewed literature. Additionally, proponents of FC have been quoted in popular magazines, newspapers, and professional newsletters, and have been interviewed on television and radio.

An interesting twist with FC was its evolution into what some have called "another therapy leading to a witch hunt." Suddenly, allegations of sexual abuse were being made against parents, family members, teachers, social workers, and others. What a legal dilemma these cases posed! When the only evidence is a "facilitated" allegation, how is the court to evaluate its veracity?

Because of the seriousness of these situations—both for the alleged victim and the accused—controlled testing was instituted in some courts and investigative bodies in the United States, Canada, and Australia. Legal actions were to be terminated if, under the controlled circumstances, the FC user did not convey information accurately and reliably and there was no other solid evidence.

According to Gina Green, director of research at the New England Center for Autism, who carefully follows this issue, termination of the legal action was the outcome of testing in every case of which she was aware. Unfortunately, by then both patient and accused were traumatized by the incident, and thousands of dollars were spent on related legal fees. On the other hand, Douglas Biklen says that some courts have accepted testimony given through facilitation and some cases have led to convictions and/or confessions by the accused.

Does It Work?

From the start, disputes arose over the extent of influence by the facilitator, and a large body of reports—pro and con—evolved. As with other fads, there was little objective evaluation of FC's validity or efficacy. Some of those who hopped on the FC bandwagon completely ignored or ridiculed a 1989 investigation sponsored by the Australian government, which showed that the effects of FC were facilitator influenced. And some scholars believe that some FC proponents continue to regard as trivial the ongoing research that has resulted in negative findings on FC.

Although facilitators may not be aware and may not be openly deceiving the parent or the patient, numerous research studies have shown that facilitators are inadvertently producing movements by which the hand of the nonverbal person is pushed to spell out messages. One illustration was the case of a mute young girl. Known to be without knowledge or awareness of the meaning of money or the significance of holidays and presents, the girl "allegedly typed out that she didn't like Christmas because she didn't have the money to buy her mother a present."

Another study compared FC to channeling, automatic writing, and the use of a Ouija board, proposing that in all cases people using these techniques fail to perceive their active role. Regarding FC, the report concluded: "Facilitator influence has been found to be endemic, although there was no indication that facilitators were knowingly or intentionally influencing what was typed." Even staunch proponent Biklen admits that "influence can definitely occur."

In late 1993 PBS's *Frontline* aired the results of its critical investigation, a telling presentation. Viewers watched double-blind demonstrations in which the patient and the facilitator were shown different photographs. In every instance, the photo seen by the facilitator was the one identified, not the one seen by the autistic patient. In another example, the patient was "facilitated" to add up two presented numbers; the addition, as assisted by the facilitator, was done correctly, yet it was obvious the patient was looking away and not paying any attention to what was going on. Despite these revelatory demonstrations, an FC advocate interviewed on the program blatantly disregarded the negative findings and defended FC as though the criticisms were so minor as to merit being ignored.

The combination of wishful thinking, emotional appeal, and pseudoscience is apparent in this mother's account:

"Tad" Can't Type for Mom

"Tad" was nine when a teacher at the special classes told us of a psychologist-facilitator who worked with a new method from Australia. I contacted her, Ms. "Liz," and paid her to work with Tad an hour every day after he finished the special classes at his school. He's been autistic since the early months of his life. We've taken him to everyone to get help.

Ms. Liz had a large alphabet board in her office. She had Tad put his hand on a little wooden arrow that slid easily around the board, and she and Tad sat side by side. She put her hand over Tad's and talked with him about how she was going to facilitate his communication as he slid his hand over the letters. I was asked to wait outside. In a week or so she asked me to sit in on part of a session. She was terribly enthused about Tad's progress, saying she wanted me to see the hidden communicative skills that had lain dormant in Tad. She always had her hand over his to help his motions. In that session Tad "typed" out such things as, "Hi, Mom. I love you. I love these lessons. I can write about anything I want." I was surprised to see him sitting there spelling out words. I didn't even know he understood some of the words.

I got an alphabet board and a little block of smooth wood and tried sitting by him and being a facilitator at home. He would cry and pull away and seemed very distressed when I held his hand lightly and asked him questions like, "What is your name?" He couldn't spell out any words with me. Each time we tried he cried and sobbed and made motions indicating he had "failed." I brought this up with Ms. Liz, and she got very angry with me, saying that I was contributing to Tad's sense of failure. She really fussed at me. When I talked with some other parents months later, I learned they had had the same sad experience: their children could only "type" when the facilitator was doing the hand guiding. Then I began to contact some other scholars in the international autism groups and learned that FC was all a fantasy. I heard of test trials in which the teachers and psychologists were probably, without really meaning to cheat or trick the child or parents, pushing the hand of the handicapped young person and influencing the answers. Without that facilitator, the person hadn't learned to communicate at all.

Then I heard that some of the facilitators had had children writing out what turned out to be false sexual accusations against parents and staff. Not long after, I saw a TV program exposing it all. What a tragedy. I wonder what Tad really experienced with Ms. Liz. She left the area and opened a school in another state.

Even though Biklen asserts that there are controlled studies providing evidence that FC works, a 1994 statement by the American Psychological Association warned that "scientifically based studies have repeatedly demonstrated that this is not a valid technique for individuals with profound developmental disabilities." Similarly, the American Speech-Language Hearing Association has drafted a position statement declaring that "facilitated communication has no scientific validity or reliability."

Allegations charging parents, teachers, and program staff with abuse have been made in at least sixty FC-related cases in the United States. With two exceptions, the cases stopped before extended prosecution or trials went forward. Nevertheless, the stigma of having been accused, the cost of legal defense, the resultant unemployment and alienation produced should cause FC users to heed the havoc they can cause by typing messages that may tend to reflect their own fantasies and thoughts more than any other reality.

Despite the controversies, the research results, the suits and countersuits, those who believe in FC continue to hold and attend national conferences and promote its use. As recently as late 1995, an FC-related book was published that received quite a bit of media attention. In it, the mother of an autistic child claims that through facilitated communication her daughter is able to describe past lives. The nine-year-old is now accepted as the "spiritual master" of the family.

The use of FC requires careful consideration. One must take into account not only the potential for abuse of patients' rights but also the possibility of harm and damage to families. Some critics recently wrote: "The uncritical acceptance and dissemination of FC by erstwhile prestigious universities, and by some practitioners, once again underscores the dangers inherent in promoting a scientific theory to further a social and epistemologic agenda, particularly when there are derivative clinical practices with the potential to negatively impact vulnerable people. . . . Fad treatments are not benign. . . . Practitioners must offer both appropriate treatment and protection from inappropriate care. They need the skills to know the difference."

Neural Organization Technique

Treatment or torture? That's how one critic, a University of California professor and chairperson of a fraud task force of the National Council Against Health Fraud, spoke of Neural Organization Technique (NOT). Devised by a chiropractor, but soon advocated by psychologists and educators as a method for treating dyslexic and learning-disabled children, NOT is supposed to correct blocked "neural pathways" by means of painful and stressful "adjustments" of the bones of the skull. This is done by pressing on various parts of the head in attempts to move the skull bones. Techniques include compression of the skull with viselike hand pressure, thumb pressure on the roof of the mouth, and finger pressure against the eyes.

As of 1990 the founder of this technique claimed to have trained more than six hundred practitioners and treated more than thirty-five hundred patients from around the world. By calling the NOT Center you can receive a list of practitioners around the country, many of whom will happily send a packet of brochures— all saying the same thing, all presumably from the NOT Center, with a space to stamp in each practitioner's name, address, and phone number. Fees for this therapy can average more than $3,500 per patient.

What Is It?

The origin of NOT is attributed to Carl Ferreri, a New York chiropractor. He promoted his version of applied kinesiology (a form of chiropractic treatment) and NOT procedures for numerous conditions, including various forms of learning and neurological disorders. Boasting that his cure is "simple, inexpensive, uses no drugs and is almost instant," Ferreri has been successful in spreading the NOT procedures far and wide, having conducted NOT seminars throughout the United States and Europe.

Asserting that the bones of the skull move with respiration, Ferreri states that those with dyslexia and learning disabilities suffer from the faulty motion of certain skull bones. He theorizes that these bone misalignments may be corrected by manipulation that includes specific cranial bone adjustments and special eye muscle correction. Further treatment is required as the bones slip back out of position. These follow-up treatments are called "catch up." One critic comments that these corrective catch-ups serve to let Ferreri and his cronies off the hook when the treatment doesn't work.

Ferreri does not offer a logical working model or explanation of any behavioral characteristics seen in learning-disordered, retarded, or dyslexic populations. His theories are not backed up by any peer-reviewed research. In fact, there appear to be no independent studies or data at all to support Ferreri's work, only unfounded claims of success and quotes from his own articles. Standard textbooks in medicine and dentistry state that cranial bones do not move, making Ferreri's claims inconsistent with generally accepted knowledge in physiology and anatomy.

Does It Work?

In spite of the nonscientific status of this procedure, a school district in northern California was persuaded to embark on a study to apply the NOT techniques to elementary school children with learning disabilities. This came about after a psychologist from the school district attended a Ferreri seminar and became a NOT enthusiast. After several presentations, the project was approved by the Del Norte Unified School District.

Ferreri came to California to make a special presentation to the Crescent City community and the school staff in May 1986—the very month in which a hearing panel in New York recommended that Ferreri be placed on probation for two years and fined $4,000. Meanwhile, at the meeting in California Ferreri apparently claimed that NOT could be used to treat dyslexia, bedwetting, cerebral palsy, Down's syndrome, color blindness, nightmares, bowel problems, and a host of other conditions.

Those who objected to the study were given little consideration, and in January 1987 parents were encouraged to enroll their learning-disabled and developmentally disabled children in the study. Forty-eight children ages four to sixteen were signed up as subjects for the experiment.

Early in the year, district parents of learning-disabled children received a letter on school district stationery encouraging them to enroll their children. The letter explained that the procedure involved manipulation of soft and hard tissue. It assured parents that the treatment was nonintrusive, that nothing would be ingested by the children, and that they would not have to remove any clothing. The letter also stated that the treatment was being used "throughout the United States and Europe with exceptional results."

That summer, a kindergarten teacher on vacation learned of a court action restraining some Utah chiropractors from promoting the NOT techniques for the treatment of dyslexia. The teacher expressed her concerns both to the school superintendent and the school board when she returned home, but to no avail, as by this time the study was well underway.

A mother who had two children in the study vividly described the goings-on: "The doctor would press so hard on the roof of [my daughter's] mouth that you could see him just shaking. One time she began vomiting and the doctor didn't even stop. He just kept applying pressure, like this was commonplace. I jumped over and had to grab her away." The woman's son told her: "If you try to make us go back to that doctor, I'll lock us in the car and we won't let you in."

A mother of a six-year-old boy with delayed speech said, "Two doctors worked on him very intently as I sat across his legs to help hold him down. They focused their attention on his head and mouth areas. They were applying such tremendous pressure to [my son's] skull and the roof of his mouth that they would break into a sweat and their bodies would just shake with the force of their exertion. All during this so-called treatment [my son] was screaming and struggling to get away from these doctors."

One mother wrote the California Board of Chiropractic Examiners: "My heart is ripped into pieces. . . . [The doctor] was pushing in [my son's] eye sockets when suddenly my son (who had never had a seizure before) had some type of seizure. His right arm went out of control up into the air and in a circular type motion fell limply hanging off the table. At the same instant, his eyes rolled up and back into their sockets."

Although parents had been reassured that their children would remain clothed, it seems that the school's letter failed to tell them that the children would also be tortured with an unproven technique.

Parents and teachers eventually filed seventeen formal complaints with the California Board of Chiropractic Examiners, stating that some children had suffered physical and emotional harm. The State Department of Consumer Affairs investigated, and the Del Norte district attorney filed civil and criminal suits, with charges including false representation, consumer fraud, battery, malpractice, and practicing without a state license. The school district superintendent and three of the five school board members were recalled in a special election. In 1991, Ferreri was ordered by the court to pay $565,000 in damages to seven children and their parents, and two other chiropractors involved in the case settled out of court for $207,000.

Once again, parents of children with special problems were lured into trusting professionals presenting a cure-all. This particular cure-all turned out to be a painful, unproven method.

Our opinion: NOT is not a good idea; do NOT try it. If you want to check out alternative theories and therapies, evaluate them carefully, request verifiable research data, speak to critics and objective examiners. Don't take the pied piper's word for it; he's usually marching to a different drum.

Eye Movement Desensitization and Reprocessing

Eye movement desensitization and reprocessing (EMDR), a popular therapeutic technique in the mid-1990s, was originated by Francine Shapiro, a California psychologist. Its stated aim is to activate the client's information-processing system so that negative thoughts, memories, or self-images can be transformed into positive ones, thereby relieving anxiety and the aftereffects of all sorts of trauma.

Shapiro recounts that she came across this technique while walking through a park one day in May 1987. During her stroll, Shapiro apparently "discovered" that rapid flickering eye movements reduced her anxiety as she pondered unpleasant thoughts. She described the phenomenon in her 1995 book: "I noticed that when disturbing thoughts came into my mind, my eyes spontaneously started moving very rapidly back and forth in an upward diagonal . . . I started making the eye movements deliberately while concentrating on a variety of disturbing thoughts and memories, and I found that these thoughts also disappeared and lost their charge."

Believing that she had, as she puts it, "stumbled on some mind process that worked with thoughts," the discoverer then began to try it out on her clients. After working with seventy people in a six-month period, Shapiro developed a standard procedure that, according to her, "consistently succeeded in alleviating their complaints." Soon thereafter, EMDR became the new wonder technique, the "miracle" therapy latched onto by many hopeful practitioners. Originally offered as a treatment for posttraumatic stress disorder (PTSD), EMDR has been applied to a plethora of situations.

By mid-1995, fourteen thousand clinicians had been licensed to perform EMDR in the United States and other countries. Shapiro's bio sheet on the EMDR Institute's Internet home page says she has "used the method in thousands of treatment sessions with patients evincing a considerable range of presenting complaints, including having suffered rape, sexual molestation, Vietnam combat and natural disaster."

EMDR is now touted by many as the preferred therapy for a vast array of problems and for a wide age range of clients. According to Shapiro's book and related literature, EMDR could be used for pain control, grief, delusions, ritual abuse, phobias, generalized anxiety, paranoid schizophrenia, learning disabilities, eating disorders, substance abuse, pathological jealousy, rage, guilt, multiple personality disorder, cancer, AIDS, somatic disorders, couples therapy, and for children as young as two.

What Is It?

Originally called eye movement desensitization (EMD), the "reprocessing" was added several years later, so it is now EMDR. Over time the procedure has changed from the original hand waving or wand waving in front of the client's eyes to a more complex eight-phase process. The revised version of the therapy includes repeated sets of hand waving along with more traditional talk therapy.

Even though Shapiro says she came upon this technique quite spontaneously during a stroll, when asked by a journalist why Shapiro (or another person) is needed to direct the process, Shapiro replied that people's eyes were not able to move that way naturally or by instinct; a therapist's hands were needed to guide the movements.

Shapiro began by having clients track her two upright fingers, palm facing the client, as the fingers swept rhythmically from right to left in sets of twelve to twenty-four strokes, alternating at a speed of two strokes per second, about twelve to fourteen inches from the person's face—not unlike a hypnotist swinging a watch. The client, meanwhile, was to conjure up an image of a traumatic memory or think about a negative self-statement and the accompanying phys-ical anxiety response. "This results in (1) a lasting reduction of anx-iety, (2) changes in the cognitive assessment of the memory, and (3) cessation of flashbacks, intrusive thoughts, and sleep distur-bances," claimed Shapiro in 1989. "This procedure can be extremely effective in only one session."

Shapiro wrote in 1991 that "thousands of additional clients and subjects have been treated. . . . While successful treatment without training may be achieved perhaps 50 percent of the time, in the other cases, untrained clinicians place the client at risk, e.g., expe-riencing ocular problems, re-traumatization, suicidal reactions, etc. EMDR is neither a simple technique nor a 'cookie cutter.'"

Shapiro has maintained tight control over who can use her tech-nique. During a 20/20 news program, viewers were told that they would not be allowed to see the wand waving or hand movements for fear that some untrained persons would mimic the technique and cause harm. While Shapiro argues for quality control and patient protection, others comment that "this policy interferes with efforts by unbiased outside investigators to replicate her results." Partici-pants in her workshops must agree not to audiotape any portion of

the workshop, train others in the techniques without formal approval, or disseminate EMDR training information to colleagues.

Warnings are made that "EMDR has the potential to evoke very powerful emotional reactions. . . . Abreactions may occur during the process. . . . If EMDR is not used appropriately, the client may be retraumatized and may become immobilized in the process." An appendix in Shapiro's book advises that a second-level training be taken by those who use EMDR "with more highly disturbed clients of any diagnosis." Shapiro presents a client-safety section in her book, noting eleven situations, or types of symptoms or diagnoses, that argue against the use of EMDR.

Does It Work?

Explanations of how EMDR works tend to be vague and anecdotal. Shapiro has never been able to clearly explain the theoretical basis for EMDR and its purported successes. For example, in referring to PTSD, Shapiro writes: "Information is stored in the same form in which it was initially experienced, because the information-processing system has, *for some reason,* been blocked" (emphasis ours). On television interviews, she has said, "It seems to open up blocked processing." From a scientific standpoint, such statements don't carry much weight.

Scott Lilienfeld of the Department of Psychology at Emory University is one notable critic of the technique. He has criticized Shapiro's efforts at explaining how EMDR works by saying that her elaborations "may mystify even those familiar with the technique." Lilienfeld offered this example from a 1994 article by Shapiro: "The system may become unbalanced due to a trauma or through stress engendered during a developmental window, but once appropriately catalyzed and maintained in a dynamic state by EMDR, it transmutes information to a state of therapeutically appropriate resolution." Huh?

Equally unsettling, in her book Shapiro says, "EMDR has undergone a number of modifications, rendering the original articles obsolete." That's one way to get around things. And she also says that "theories that explain why EMDR works have arisen after the fact and have not yet been confirmed. However, the lack of definitive explanation of the underlying mechanisms of EMDR in no way detracts from the demonstrated effectiveness of the method."

Gerald Rosen of the University of Washington conducted a limited study with six psychologists and graduate students who volunteered to spend fifteen to twenty minutes at home thinking positive and negative thoughts while trying to notice rapid saccadic eye movements. The results: "Nobody experienced eye movements either during the purposeful induction of positive and negative thoughts, or during the transition periods."

Rosen had the same persons walk in the woods, with no earth-shattering results. Rosen concluded that Shapiro "serendipitously discovered this technique by experiencing spontaneous saccadic eye movements in response to disturbing thoughts during a walk in the woods. This explanation is difficult to accept because normal saccadic eye movements appear to be physiologically undetectable and are typically triggered by external stimuli. In the present limited study, all subjects failed to elicit any experience of eye movements, thus calling into question how best to interpret Dr. Shapiro's experience and the origin of EMD."

Further questions arise about the technical details when Shapiro reports having done EMDR on blind clients, and other EMDR users report similar successes with taps on the knee. This makes little sense: technically the procedure requires the use of eye movements, because Shapiro has implied that its success "may be linked to the mechanisms (and subsequent benefits) inherent in REM sleep."

Several researchers have done "dismantling" studies in which EMDR was compared with otherwise identical procedures minus the eye movements. In all cases, EMDR was not consistently more effective than the other methods. Other types of studies have had similar results, but Shapiro claims that EMDR is supported by controlled research.

For now the most cautious attitude may be that expressed by Drs. James Herbert and Kim Mueser in the *Harvard Mental Health Letter*, who write: "EMDR may seem innocuous, but it is not. There are well-established, validated treatments for many of the conditions for which EMDR is being recommended. Patients should not be induced to forgo established treatments for the sake of an unproven therapy—in effect participating in a research project—when they cannot give informed consent because they are not told about the alternatives. Furthermore, public trust in the mental health professions is eroded when faddish treatments make exaggerated claims that inevitably fall under the weight of scientific evidence and the disillusionment of practitioners."

When therapists who are dedicated EMDR users, trained under the developer, were interviewed, they commented on how fast the work went, that it allowed them to plan and structure every case and to train their clients to "understand" how they had become stuck in their unprocessed memories. They liked the directive, high-control approach.

On the other hand, a sample of experienced therapists who took the approved training and then did not practice the method offered a range of responses when interviewed. For example:

"I have not elected to use it. It goes against everything I have found important in therapy, such as building a good relationship."

"It is too mechanistic."

"When we practiced on each other in the training course, it did nothing for me. It didn't shift anything for me."

"I wouldn't want to be sitting there not knowing and not being able to monitor what was going on for the patient."

"There is too little contact."

"It is for therapists who do not want to follow the process the client is going through in therapy. Some do not want to have their own feelings stirred up."

"It was never made clear how the finger movements related to proven knowledge about saccadic movements. It was presented as the one-way-to-do-therapy."

"I think of myself as tailoring each treatment to the needs of each client and this was production-line work."

"It probably has remarkable placebo effects."

"I was concerned about patients who, like I did, would notice nothing happening at all, and yet because of the enthusiasm of the therapist could not tell this dedicated person that nothing, but nothing, was going on inside."

"I am waiting to see what clean-cut research finds."

Interviews with a series of persons who had been treated with EMDR and left after one or more sessions revealed that they felt that the therapist was going to focus continuously on negative experiences and images from the past and did not want to do full-range therapy with counseling about career, marital issues, and present and future decision-making issues. Some also complained about the impersonal, technique-oriented, programmatic way the therapists proceeded. All said their former therapists would consider them a cure, as the clients had reported feeling better just to terminate the repetitive process. In her book, Dr. Shapiro warns against such limited and narrow use of the EMDR technique.

Despite the widespread use of EMDR, despite its claims of success, despite the fervor with which its practitioners push the technique, EMDR remains controversial, as was recently highlighted in the APA Monitor, a publication of the American Psychological Association. Some proponents feed this controversy when they say EMDR dramatically reduces traumatic memories, and in the same breath say they're not sure how. Whether positive results come from the placebo effect, patient expectancy, posthypnotic suggestion, or just plain luck, the fact remains that EMDR is regarded by some in the scientific community as an unfounded, unproven technique.

In her concern about an APA task force in the process of making a list of scientifically validated methods of therapy, Shapiro, addressing her fellow therapists, wrote in a widely circulated professional journal:

> Do you know how your favored treatment modality was experimentally tested? Do you know if the technique was practiced adequately by experienced clinicians during the study (or even if such a study took place)? The pending legislation could threaten your right to be reimbursed for the treatment and your clients' ability to benefit from it. According to the APA task force, if a method has not had a sufficient number of controlled studies supporting it, the clinician will have to inform the client that it is experimental. As we know, insurance companies do not reimburse for experimental procedures.

Although some may agree with Shapiro's concern that the APA-approved list may be too short, our position remains that consumers have a right to be told whether or not a procedure has been sufficiently tested.

It's Fast, It's Easy, It's Magical and NEW!

The four therapies described in this chapter represent but a smidgen of the offerings available to the consumer today. Over the years a variety of mental health "miracles" have been concocted, based on everything from Jung's archetypes to the enneagram to exotic decks of cards with flamboyant images on them. Flowers, herbs, drugs, homeopathic potions, ancient Oriental remedies, whispered mantras, and high-pitched tones zapped into your ears—nothing has bypassed the innovator who wishes to bring humankind a cure.

Using the results of a phone survey on alternative medical treatments, two researchers estimated that "in 1990, Americans made 425 million visits to providers of unconventional therapy at a cost of approximately $13.7 billion."

Some therapeutic practices disappear as rapidly as they hit the scene. Others have been with us for years. How quickly a new therapy becomes a fad is usually indicated by the increasing registration in workshops offering the technique, the number of certificates printed, and the amount of media coverage. And how well it takes hold may be monitored by counting the number of practitioners mentioning it in their ads in related magazines and New Age directories, the number of books published on the subject, and the number of presenters at professional conferences.

But bear in mind, just because something becomes the hottest technique on the block doesn't necessarily mean it's going to help you. If your therapist is saying, "I don't understand it, but it sure does work," you're possibly in for trouble. Or if he's answering your questions with a lot of jargon you don't understand, insist on straightforward explanations. Or if she's telling you that it's tried and true, do some independent research and find out what the critics are saying.

In many cases, fad therapies are promoted by people who are (1) imposing an agenda that may not fit your needs and (2) abandoning testing and science. Well-meaning as they may be, remember: it's your mind, your emotions, and your pocketbook that are being played with.

9

How Did This Happen?
And What Can You Do?

This book was written to help consumers—those who are contemplating choosing a therapist, those already in therapy that they may be questioning, and those who are looking back on some therapy that they feel may have harmed rather than helped them. We hope it is also useful for that occasion when a family member, friend, or coworker may ask for help in choosing a therapist or a treatment. Going to see a therapist or counselor can be a weighty decision, especially now that therapies and treatments are being offered in such diversity.

We believe in good therapy, and much good psychotherapy is provided by thousands of mental health professionals to many more thousands of patients. A recently published study showed that in 1987 nearly eighty million psychotherapy visits were made at a total cost of $4.2 billion. And according to a 1994 survey, a great portion of clients are satisfied with their psychotherapy.

The difficulty for the consumer is that the therapy smorgasbord is offered as if all treatment methods were equal and all were beneficial and free of harm. But we have shown they are not. We hope that from reading this book you will have understood not only the vast array of therapies available but also the possible risks involved in getting into a crazy therapy.

In the preceding chapters we have illustrated some pretty wild therapies, each being sold as the one ideal way to seek mental health, harmony, peace, emotional stability, a career change, better relationships, or whatever is sought by the consumer. Selecting which ones to present was indeed a struggle for us, and we ended up choosing those we felt were among the most widespread, the most popular, and the most representative.

If a particular therapy wasn't mentioned, that doesn't mean we think it's okay. For example, we barely touched on the wealth of what we sometimes call "nonprofessional" offerings, in which totally untrained persons or sheer venal hucksters see a gap in the market and fill it. They see how many people want spiritual or psychological guidance and how easy people are to manipulate. These so-called healers ride the tide, offering psychic powers, angels who will come back from the great beyond, warriors to walk unseen beside you, inner children for you to hold, auras to be adjusted, and more.

You might be encouraged to loll naked in hot tubs with others, sweat out your juices in a tepee, dangle from a rope high above a deep crevice, run naked between a row of people swatting your behind, dance barefoot across hot coals, or stand before a group to be humiliated and demeaned.

You might be asked to take massive doses of vitamins, or drink foul-tasting potions of algae, seaweed, herbs, or flowers, or remain on a bizarre diet regime, or rub yourself with strange-smelling oils.

Be an avatar. Be a shaman. Be a goddess. Be your body. Be your mind. Be your self. Lose your self. Go on a spiritual journey. Unlock the psychology of your past, your future. Clean out your internal waste. Replenish your inner fluids. Try natural healing. Try ayurvedic remedies. Try alchemical hypnotherapy. Try bodywork, eyework, breathwork, brainwork. You can even have happy gums with harmonious dentistry. There seems to be no end to the creative concoctions.

In this chapter, we present our understanding of how and why crazy therapies have been allowed to proliferate, we review the characteristics of some of these therapies, and we offer guidelines for selecting and evaluating a therapy or a therapist so you can avoid wasting your time and money or risking psychological harm.

How Did This Happen?

There is no one simple answer to the question of how and why we find ourselves in a society riddled with bizarre mental health offerings. Nevertheless we can identify three factors that have had a crucial influence: (1) the special nature of the relationship between client and therapist, (2) the emergence of the blame-and-change approach in the field of psychotherapy, and (3) the flight from rational thought in our society as a whole.

The Therapeutic Relationship

The relationship between patient and therapist is unique in important ways when compared to relationships between clients and other professionals, such as physicians, dentists, attorneys, and accountants. The key difference is present from first contact: *it is not clearly understood exactly what will transpire*. There is no other professional relationship in which consumers are more in the dark than when they first go to see a therapist.

In other fields, the public is fairly well informed about what the professional does. Tradition, the media, and general experience have provided consumers with a baseline by which to judge what transpires. If you break your arm, the orthopedist explains that she will take an X ray and set the bone; she tells you something about how long the healing will take if all goes well and gives you an estimate of the cost. When you go to a dentist, you expect him to look at your teeth, take a history, explain what was noted, and recommend a course of treatment with an estimate of time and cost. Your accountant will focus on bookkeeping, tax reports, and finances, and help you deal with regulatory agencies.

Consumers enter these relationships expecting that the training, expertise, and ethical obligations of the professional will keep the client's best interests foremost. Both the consumer and the professional are aware of each person's role, and it is generally expected that the professional will stick to doing what he or she is trained to do. The consumer does not expect his accountant to lure him into accepting a new cosmology of how the world works or to "channel" financial information from "entities" who lived thousands of years ago; or for his dentist to induce him to believe that the status of his teeth was affected by an extraterrestrial experimenting on him. Nor does the patient expect the orthopedist to lead him to think the reason he fell and broke his arm was because he was under the influence of a secret Satanic cult.

But seeing a therapist is a far different situation for the consumer. In the field of psychotherapy there is no relatively agreed upon body of knowledge, no standard procedures that a client can expect. There are no national regulatory bodies, and not every state has governing boards or licensing agencies. There are many types and levels of practitioners. Often the client knows little or nothing at all about what type of therapy a particular therapist "believes in" or what the therapist is really going to be doing in the relationship with the client.

In meeting a therapist for the first time, most consumers are almost as blind as a bat about what will transpire between the two of them. At most, they might think they will talk to the therapist and perhaps get some feedback or suggestions for treatment. What clients might not be aware of is the gamut of training, the idiosyncratic notions, and the odd practices they may be exposed to by certain practitioners.

Consumers are a vulnerable and trusting lot. And because of the special, unpredictable nature of the therapeutic relationship, it is easy for them to be taken advantage of. This makes it all the more incumbent on therapists to be especially ethical and aware of the power their role carries in our society. The misuse and abuse of power is one of the central factors in what goes wrong, as was

illustrated in many of the personal accounts in the preceding chapters. This destructive thread will be described in more detail later
in this chapter.

Blame and Change

In previous chapters we mentioned parent bashing as a main theme
that has permeated psychotherapy since Freud's day. This development has for the most part gone unchallenged as a core feature of
much psychotherapy. Underlying this approach is a heavy reliance
on one of two notions: one, that getting insight will automatically
change conduct; the other, that emotional catharsis will make you
a more perfect being. The perpetuation of these three ideas has
helped bring us to where we are today.

The attack on the family began with Freud, and was mounted
in earnest after World War II when psychotherapy became available and popular in the United States. Eventually, a full onslaught
against parents took hold within mental health circles. With this
emphasis on parent blaming, most therapists were trained to teach
their clients to "blame" as a way of finding change. Clients are led
to inspect their childhood and blame their parents or those who
cared for them as the causes of their present-day distress, lack of
comfort, and so forth.

Using a blame-and-change approach, the therapist never has to
have cognitive, behavioral, or psychoeducational methods to assist
clients to learn new behaviors. Essentially, blame-and-change therapies imply to the client that if you find whom to blame for your
miseries, you will automatically get well and feel better.

Best of all, blame-and-change therapists rarely or never have to
confront clients about their characterological problems. These therapists are spared from hearing stories of conduct that might suggest a
real lack of sympathy on the clients' part toward their partner, family, and fellow humans. Traits such as a sense of entitlement, self-
centeredness, lack of compassion, greediness, lack of responsibility,

and lying require real skill on the part of therapists to handle and help. But if the therapist is just doing blame and change, she doesn't have to worry about these other sticky wickets.

Not to be left unmentioned, many therapists feel economically dependent. Therapists may shy away from even subtly bringing up how a client's behavior elicits the responses it does from others, out of fear that the client will get mad and not come back.

Looking for someone, or something, to blame became a big part of therapy. The philosophy seeped into the thinking of many mental health professionals and other types of counselors. Interwoven were the other two main threads we have discussed: (1) search your soul or memory for that one key insight that will suddenly make everything clear and better, or (2) enact, reenact, and feel and emote to purge yourself of the bad feelings, and that will suddenly make everything clear and better. Each of these three points of view presumes that there is one way and one answer: single cause–single cure.

Gone unchecked, these therapeutic trends—blame and change, insight, and catharsis—have had a direct influence on the development of most of the therapies discussed in this book. The result has been that certain therapists tend to skip over the reality of the client's problems, because they do not have methods for realistically helping and can only apply one method of therapy. One size fits all.

Flight from Rational Thought

For the past several decades there has been a trend in our society away from science and rational thought and toward magical thinking. Much of this is a result of trends that began in the 1960s with antiestablishment and antiauthoritarian movements and came to be known as the New Age. Concurrently there has been a growing interest in self-improvement and self-awareness. Much of this took shape during the 1960s and 1970s and came to be known as the human potential movement. Combined, we have the potential for both expanded awareness and disaster.

A cursory glance at today's best-seller lists or television program guides alerts us to the prevalence of New Age thinking, usually couched in psychological or spiritual jargon. For prime-time viewing we have angels on baseball fields, alien autopsies, and mystical messages from everyone from Jesus and Mary to a hodgepodge of self-styled philosophers and soothsayers. *The Celestine Prophecy,* a fable about one man's search for a mysterious manuscript holding the keys to life, has been at the top of the book sales charts for more than two years. Considered by many to be a New Age healer, Deepak Chopra, M.D., currently has two books on the best-seller lists. There are also *Women Who Run with Wolves* and *Men from Mars* and *Chicken Soup for the Soul. Bringers of the Dawn,* a popular book "channeled" to the author by a mass of collective energy from the star cluster Pleiades, has sold more than 200,000 copies. Academic John Mack may have studied ET encounters for his hit book *Abduction,* but academic Hank Wesselman went one step further. *Spiritwalker* describes the anthropologist's personal shamanic journey in the spirit world via twelve episodes while in an altered state.

Happy-go-lucky Trekkies have been superseded by *X-Files* aficionados. Currently one of the most popular shows on TV—on Friday night, no less—its two main characters get involved in frightening paranormal mysteries: we've had "firestarters, alien threats to mankind, UFOs, genetically warped serial killers who ate human livers, evil clone children, and alien abduction galore." Documentary versions of similar subject matter can be found on *Sightings* and *Encounters.* Another show, *Mysteries, Magic and Miracles,* was rated number one on the SciFi cable channel. Commenting on this trend, a writer for Omni magazine said, "Not since the advent of spiritualism and H. P. Blavatsky in the nineteenth century have so many Americans been so interested in the possibility that the bizarre is real." During hard times in his tenure, even President Clinton met with firewalker and self-development guru Anthony Robbins.

As lighthearted and good-natured as much of this may be, there is a lurking danger. With the popularity of these ideas, we have been nurtured over the years to reduce our thinking to the lowest common denominator. We are expected to accept the most outlandish claims on blind faith. Bubbling enthusiasm has replaced serious thought processes. Convoluted gibberish has often been substituted for logic and reason.

In June 1995, the New York Academy of Sciences held a meeting of two hundred doctors, scientists, philosophers, and thinkers from around the country who expressed great concern over this very matter of the "flight from science and reason," as they called it. These worried scientists were hoping to organize a call to arms, urging all to defend scientific methodologies and to "counterattack faith healing, astrology, religious fundamentalism, and paranormal charlatanism." They also called attention to the current trend of exploiting scientific ideas to enhance magical thinking. Some New Age critics of science will, for example, distort the physics of relativity and quantum mechanics to argue that nothing in science is certain, or that mystery and magic are as valid as science.

Riding on this wave of interest in the self and this thrust toward magical thinking, some inadequately trained and unmonitored therapists and "healers"—reinforced by praise from colleagues, celebratory media appearances, and mass-market book sales—are influencing their clients, their students, and the general public. The odd and sometimes harmful techniques used by some of these practitioners tend to perpetuate unhealthy, irrational, and in some cases unethical ways of living, working, and relating socially—to which the rest of us are reluctantly subjected.

Consumer Guidelines

In this final section, we offer four sets of guidelines to help consumers wend their way through the mental health maze and avoid crazy therapies. These guidelines will cover questions to ask a new therapist, ways to evaluate your current therapy, the "Procrustean Bed Test," and common traits of bad therapy.

Questions to Ask Your Prospective Therapist

Ultimately, a therapist is a service provider who sells a service. A prospective client should feel free to ask enough questions to be able to make an informed decision about whether to hire a particular therapist.

We have provided a general list of questions to ask a prospective therapist, but feel free to ask whatever you need to know in order to make a proper evaluation. Consider interviewing several therapists before settling on one, just as you might in purchasing any product.

Draw up your list of questions before phoning or going in for your first appointment. We recommend that you ask these questions in a phone interview first, so that you can weed out unlikely candidates and save yourself the time and expense of initial visits that don't go anywhere.

If during this process a therapist continues to ask you, "Why do you ask?" or acts as though your questioning reflects some defect in you, think carefully before signing up. Those types of responses tell you a lot about the entire attitude this person will express toward you—that is, that you are one down and he is one up, and that furthermore you are quaint to even ask the "great one" to explain himself.

If you are treated with disdain for asking about what you are buying, think ahead: how could this person lead you to feel better, plan better, or have more self-esteem if he begins by putting you down for being an alert consumer? Remember, you may be feeling bad and even desperate, but there are thousands of mental health professionals, so if this one is not right, keep on phoning and searching.

1. How long is the therapy session?

2. How often should I see you?

3. How much do you charge? Do you have a sliding scale?

4. Do you accept insurance?

5. If I have to miss an appointment, will I be billed?

6. If I am late, or if you are late, what happens?

7. Tell me something about your educational background, your degrees. Are you licensed?

8. Tell me about your experience, and your theoretical orientation. What types of clients have you seen? Are there areas you specialize in?

9. Do you use hypnosis or other types of trance-inducing techniques?

10. Do you have a strong belief in the supernatural? Do you believe in UFOs, past lives, or paranormal events? Do you have any kind of personal philosophy that guides your work with all your clients?

11. Do you value scientific research? How do you keep up with research and developments in your field?

12. Do you believe that it's okay to touch your clients or be intimate with them?

13. Do you usually set treatment goals with a client? How are these determined? How long do you think I will need therapy?

14. Will you see my partner, spouse, or child with me if necessary in the future?

15. Are you reachable in a crisis? How are such consultations billed?

After the interview, ask yourself:

1. Overall, does this person appear to be a competent, ethical professional?

2. Do I feel comfortable with this person?

3. Am I satisfied with the answers I got to my questions?

4. Are there areas I'm still uncertain about that make me wonder whether this is the right therapist for me?

Remember, you are about to allow this person to meddle with your mind, your emotional well-being, and your life. You will be telling her very personal things, and entrusting her with intimate information about yourself and other people in your life. Take seriously the decision to select a therapist, and if you feel you made a mistake, stop working with that one and try someone else.

How to Evaluate Your Current Therapy

What if you have been in treatment a while? What do you ask or consider in order to help evaluate what is going on? The issues discussed here may assist you.

1. *Do you feel worse and more worried and discouraged than when you began the therapy?* Sometimes having to assess one's current life can be a bit of a downer, but remember, you went for help. You may feel you are not getting what you need. Most important, watch out if you call this to your therapist's attention and he says, "You have to get worse in order to get better." That's an old saw used as an exculpatory excuse. Instead of discussing the real issues, which a competent therapist would, this response puts all the blame on you, the client. The therapist one-ups you, telling you he knows the path you have to travel. It's an evasion that allows the therapist to avoid discussing how troubled you are and that his treatment or lack of skill may be causing or, at the very least, contributing to your state.

2. *Is your therapist professional? Does she seem to know what she is doing?* Or do features such as the following characterize your therapy:

The therapist arrives late, takes phone calls, forgets appointments, looks harassed and unkempt, smells of alcohol, has two clients arrive at one time, or otherwise appears not to have her act together at a basic level.

The therapist seems to lack overall direction, has no plans about what you two are doing.

The therapist seems as puzzled or at sea as you do about your problems.

The therapist repeats and seems to rely on sympathetic platitudes such as "Trust me," or "Things will get better. Just keep coming in."

The therapy hour is without direction and seems more like amiable chitchat with a friend.

The therapy hour just rambles on. Does the therapist provide direction or simply respond to what you say? Does she rarely connect one session with another, just starting anew each time?

The therapist implies that just seeing her is what is going to cure you.

The therapist tells you about herself, her feelings, her history, implying that hers is the proper way to live.

The therapist avoids confronting you, always sides with you, tries to stay your friend, or seems fearful that you will leave therapy if she questions or challenges behavior that you describe. Do you think the fact that you pay her causes her to avoid challenging you because she doesn't want to lose a customer?

3.   *Does your therapist seem to be controlling you, sequestering you from family, friends, and other advisers?*

Does the therapist insist that you not talk about anything from your therapy with anyone else, thus cutting off the help that such talk normally brings to an individual, and making you seem secretive and weird about your therapy?

Does the therapist insist that your therapy is much more important in your life than it really is?

Does the therapist make himself a major figure in your life, keeping you focusing on your relationship with him?

Does the therapist insist that you postpone decisions such as changing jobs, becoming engaged, getting married, having a child, or moving, implying or openly stating that your condition has to be cured and his imprimatur given before you act on your own?

Does the therapist mainly interpret your behavior as sick, immature, unstable? Does he fail to tell you that many of your reactions are normal, everyday responses to situations?

Does the therapist keep you looking only at the bad side of your life?

Does the therapist tell you that your family is the sole cause of any distress you have in your life?

Does the therapist attribute malevolent motives to others in your life—your family, friends, spouse, children, fellow workers—and, in the end, seem to cause you to be even more dependent on him as he alienates you from them?

Do you feel torn between what your therapist wants or supports and what someone else very close suggests might be beneficial for you? Do you feel unable to talk with the therapist about this apparent conflict of interests?

Do most of the therapist's interpretations of your behavior make you feel that he does not trust you or regards you as inadequate, incompetent, and pathological? Does he tell you that you appear to be sabotaging yourself, driven to ruining yourself, when you don't get that kind of feedback elsewhere in your life?

4.   *Does your therapist try to touch you?* Handshakes at the beginning and end of a session can be routine. Anything beyond that is

not acceptable. Some clients do allow their therapist to hug them when they leave, but this should be done only after you've been asked and have given your approval. If you are getting the impression that the touching is becoming or is blatantly sexualized, quit the therapy immediately.

Are you noticing what we call "the rolling chair syndrome"? Some therapists who begin to touch and encroach on the bodies of their clients have chairs that roll, and as time goes by they roll closer and closer. Before you realize what's happened, your therapist might have rolled his chair over and clasped your knees between his opened legs. He may at first fake this as a comforting gesture. Don't buy it!

Remember: *sex is never part of therapy.* Thus no matter how flattering it may seem at first that an older, professional person finds you attractive, when that happens, therapy has gone out the window. You are merely being used by a law-violating, impaired, self-gratifying, incompetent, and narcissistic therapist. Both male and female therapists violate personal boundaries with improper touching and by sexualizing the therapy. For more guidelines on how to handle improper touching or sexual advances, review Chapter Seven.

5.   *Does your therapist seem to have only one interpretation for everything? Does she lead you to the same conclusion about your troubles no matter what you tell her?* You might have sought help with a crisis in your family, a seemingly irresolvable dilemma at your job, some personal situation, a mild depressed state after a death of a loved one, or any number of reasons. But before you were able to give sufficient history so that the therapist could grasp why you were there and what you wanted to work on, the therapist began to fit you into a mold. You find that, for example, the therapist insists on focusing on your childhood, telling you your present demeanor suggests that you were ritually abused or subjected to incest, or that you may be a multiple personality—currently three very faddish diag-

noses. If the therapist has her agenda and set belief about what is bothering you, it is unlikely that what you brought in to work on will ever get dealt with.

The Procrustean Bed Test—One Size Fits All

As you may recall, Procrustes was the villain in Greek mythology who forced travelers to fit into his bed by stretching their bodies or cutting off their legs. The term is now used to characterize someone who has ruthless disregard for individual differences or special circumstances. For our purposes, this refers to a therapist who believes in single cause–single cure or who imposes his agenda on you, rather than taking into consideration your concerns and needs as a client.

From the nearly four hundred interviews done by coauthor Singer in the past decade and from other studies of individuals who had bad results from therapy, we can summarize some general patterns found in therapists who have been inadequately and poorly trained, who are considered to be "impaired professionals," and who harm, control, or apply untested, unscientific methods, some of which are personally devised theories and techniques. Being able to recognize these therapist behaviors will allow you, the client, to check whether or not you are being put in a Procrustean bed—that is, whether you are the subject of one-size-fits-all therapy. Notice whether the following are occurring or have happened:

1. *The therapist teaches you a mythology about human behavior.* It might be any one of the following, which is by no means meant to be an all-inclusive list of the possible theories or belief systems thrust upon clients:

- Humans have lived past lives, and so have you.

- Space aliens are kidnapping people, and you are one of those who've been abducted.

- A symptom checklist will reveal whether you were molested as an infant.

- There is a massive secret conspiracy of worldwide Satanic cults, and your parents were or are part of it.

- All those conflicting feelings you have are actually a sign that you have multiple personality disorder.

- Reexperiencing the birth trauma will rid you of your troubling symptoms.

- Through hypnosis you can retrieve memories of everything that ever happened to you.

2. *You are taught and encouraged to use the language and jargon the therapist uses as part of this mythology or pet theory.* Much as a cult leader teaches followers to use certain jargon and accept the myths he wants them to accept, so do many therapists. Jargon is adopted in order to reinforce the myth, and you find that you are speaking a kind of code language in your sessions and elsewhere. For example:

- You have to learn what a primal is, how to locate and cuddle your inner child, how to fall into trance and create a past life, how to assume the warrior role, how to become a survivor, how to become an "experiencer," or how to "let it all out."

- You refer to your feelings, vexations, or moments of poor behavior as examples of your "alters" or explain them by saying, "The children are acting up."

- You must learn such expressions as "I am in resistance," "I am in denial," "I am a survivor," "I came from a dysfunctional family," and so on.

3.   *The therapist arrived at your diagnosis all too swiftly and seems unwilling to consider any interpretations and meanings other than the ones he assigns.* He turns everything back on you if you don't accept his point of view. He abuses his power by making you feel that you just don't understand or are not working hard enough. For example:

- If you say you don't agree with the therapist's conclusions, he tells you that you are "resisting" and that you will never get well until you fully accept his reasoning.

- If you disagree with the therapist's interpretation of what's going on with you, you are told you are "in denial."

- If you protest that something was nice and good about your family, the therapist again insists you are "in denial."

4.   *The therapist tries to get you to believe that she can tell what happened to you in your past even if you have no memory of it at all.* For example:

- Because you have come to be dependent on the therapist and are feeling very needy, and because you've been indoctrinated into being "a good patient," you begin to revise your past.

- You no longer trust your own memory and you find that you fill in what the therapist is asking about with what she seems to want to hear.

5.   *The therapist is taking control over more and more of your life.* For example:

- He may tell you not to have children because "multiples abandon their children." The therapist of course has no factual or scientific support for this; it is just a myth of the trade that he may have heard at the last weekend seminar, or something he made up in his head.

- You are told not to see your family anymore. The therapist tells you that your family is the cause of all your problems, and being around them is dangerous to your mental health.

- The therapist starts limiting your friendships and tells you to socialize only with other people in groups run by the therapist or groups where his particular belief system is promoted.

Why are these practices frowned on by well-trained, conscientious therapists who practice within the ethical bounds of their profession? Because therapists are trained to promote autonomy in patients, to help patients become more independent, make their own decisions, and be responsible to themselves and to society. Inducing dependency and forcing you to fit into the therapist's Procrustean bed is doing you no good.

Common Traits of Bad Therapy

1. Inadequate history taken at the outset
2. No diagnosis or ill-formed, incorrect diagnosis
3. Lack of formulation or conceptualization of the problem and how to proceed
4. No goals, no treatment plan, or inappropriate treatment plan

5. Unclear roles or boundaries, including self-revelations and seductive or sexual remarks

6. No appreciation of discrepancy in power

7. Dependency and regression fostered

8. Therapeutic techniques mismanaged or inappropriate techniques used, including placing client in group too soon, misuse or overuse of hypnosis and/or medications

9. Overriding adherence to paranormal theories or New Age philosophies that cannot be rationally or scientifically proven and that are covertly or overtly foisted on clients, requiring them to make tremendous leaps of faith in order to go along with the therapist's interpretations and treatment

10. No rational theoretical connection between the practices and the goal of rehabilitation

11. Transference mismanaged, including failure to recognize, interpret, and understand its impact on the therapeutic relationship

12. Confidentiality violated, including telling client about others and/or telling others about client

13. Objectivity and professionalism lost, including becoming sexually or otherwise involved

14. Failure to monitor progress

15. Failure to treat or deal with presenting problems

16. Precipitous abandonment of client

Avoiding Myths and Mayhem

Engaging in therapy with a practitioner who upholds unfounded theories or glorifies bizarre techniques involves too many risks. We see that all too often basic human and social instincts for a better life and a better world are being corrupted by lazy theories and cockeyed procedures by which some persons are making a name and fortune while their patients are being used, abused, and made to feel worse instead of better.

Crazy therapies promulgate myths and perpetuate mayhem. Keeping this in mind, consumers would do well to heed the advice of writer Charlotte Brontë, "Look twice before you leap."

Notes

Introduction

p. xvi, Over the years . . .: S. J. Kingsbury, "Where Does Research on the Effectiveness of Psychotherapy Stand Today?" *Harvard Mental Health Letter*, Sept. 1995, p. 8.

Chapter One

p. 3, "the psychological society": M. L. Gross, *The Psychological Society: A Critical Analysis of Psychiatry, Psychotherapy, Psychoanalysis and the Psychological Revolution* (New York: Random House, 1978).

p. 3, According to one researcher . . .: K. Butler, "Caught in the Cross Fire," *Family Therapy Networker*, Mar./Apr. 1995, p. 28.

p. 3, A book published in 1980 . . .: R. Herink, (ed.) *The Psychotherapy Handbook: The A to Z Guide to More Than 250 Different Therapies in Use Today* (New York: NAL/Dutton, 1980).

p. 6, out-and-out quackery: L. J. West and M. T. Singer, "Cults, Quacks, and Nonprofessional Therapies," in H. I. Kaplan, A. M. Freedman, and B. J. Sadock (eds.), *Comprehensive Textbook of Psychiatry/III*, Vol. 3. (Baltimore: Williams & Wilkins, 1980), pp. 3245–3257.

p. 14, the founding of Gestalt Therapy: F. Perls, *The Gestalt Approach and Eyewitness to Therapy* (New York: Bantam Books, 1973); A. W. Clare with S. Thompson, *Let's Talk About Me: A Critical Examination of the New Psychotherapies* (London: British Broadcasting Corp., 1981), pp. 61–62.

p. 14, Fliess believed . . .: W. Fliess, *Die Nasale Reflexneurose Verhandlungen des Kongresses fur Innere Medizin* (Weisbaden, Germany: Bergmann, 1893), pp. 384–394, cited in Clare with Thompson, *Let's Talk About Me,* p. 62.

p. 15, Emma Eckstein, nearly died: J. M. Masson, *The Assault on Truth* (New York: Farrar, Straus & Giroux, 1984), pp. 62–64.

p. 15, "Teutonic Crackpottery": M. Gardner, "Freud's Friend Wilhelm Fliess and His Theory of Male and Female Life Cycles," *Scientific American,* 1966, *251,* 108–112.

p. 15, Perls went on . . .: Perls, *The Gestalt Approach and Eyewitness to Therapy.*

p. 15, Psychotherapist Jacob Moreno . . .: Clare with Thompson, *Let's Talk About Me,* pp. 100–101.

p. 15, Privation Therapy: J. Erdheim, "Privation Psychotherapeutic Technique," in R. Herink (ed.), *Psychotherapy Handbook,* pp. 496–498.

p. 16, Gosciewski developed Photo Counseling: F. W. Gosciewski, "Photo Counseling," in R. Herink (ed.), *Psychotherapy Handbook,* pp. 478–480.

p. 16, Philosophical Psychotherapy: W. S. Sahakian, "Philosophical Psychotherapy," in R. Herink (ed.), *Psychotherapy Handbook,* pp. 473–476.

p. 21, One writer noted . . .: A. E. Begin, "The Effects of Psychotherapy: Negative Results Revisited," *Journal of Counseling Psychology,* 1963, *10,* 244–250; "Some Implications of Psychotherapy for Therapeutic Practice," *Journal of Abnormal Psychology,* 1966, *71,* 235–246.

Chapter Two

p. 25, As of 1992 . . .: A. Meacham, "Call Me Mom," *Changes,* Aug. 1992, pp. 56–63.

p. 25, Leonard Orr . . .: L. Orr, excerpt from *The Conscious Connection,* 1(4), posted on Rebirth International Online on the World Wide Web, at http://www.jla.com/htms/rebirth1.htm.

p. 25, Energy breathing is. . .: Orr, *Conscious Connection.*

p. 25, *Information from her organization. . . .*: From mailing received in October 1995 from The LRT (Loving Relationships Training), P.O. Box 1465, Washington, CT 06793.

p. 26, *"Rebirthers consider . . ."*: S. Ray and B. Mandel, *Birth and Relationships: How Your Birth Affects Your Relationships* (Berkeley, Calif.: Celestial Arts, 1987), p. 94.

p. 26, *a blatant abuse and misuse*: A. Jacobs, "Theory as Ideology: Reparenting and Thought Reform," *Transactional Analysis Journal*, Jan. 1994, 24(1), 39–55.

p. 29, *She developed a method . . . .*: S. Arieti, *Interpretation of Schizophrenia* (New York: Brunner/Mazel, 1955), p. 450; K. R. Eissler, "Remarks on the Psycho-analysis of Schizophrenia," in E. B. Brody and F. C. Redlich (eds.), *Psychotherapy with Schizophrenics* (Madison, Conn.: International Universities Press, 1952), p. 146; M. Sechehaye, *Symbolic Realization: A New Method of Psychotherapy Applied to a Case of Schizophrenia* (Madison, Conn.: International Universities Press, 1951).

p. 29, *Sechehaye had concluded . . . .*: M. Sechehaye, *Autobiography of a Schizophrenic Girl* (Philadelphia: Grune & Stratton, 1951), p. 146.

p. 29, *Holding an apple . . . to eat*: Sechehaye, *Autobiography of a Schizophrenic Girl*, p. 81.

p. 29, *Sechehaye's treatment . . . .*: P.R.A. May and G. M. Simpson, "Schizophrenia: Overview of Treatment Methods," in Kaplan, Freedman, and Sadock (eds.), *Comprehensive Textbook of Psychiatry/III*, Vol. 2, p. 1200.

p. 30, *"direct analysis"*: J. N. Rosen, *Direct Analysis: Selected Papers* (Philadelphia: Grune & Stratton, 1953).

p. 30, *extreme violence and torture*: J. M. Masson, *Against Therapy: Emotional Tyranny and the Myth of Psychological Healing* (New York: Atheneum, 1988), pp. 124–152. The authors want to acknowledge an intellectual indebtedness to Jeffrey Masson for his work in *Against Therapy*, for calling attention to the type and severity of deviance found in some therapies.

p. 30, *He wrote, "Sometimes . . ."*: Rosen, *Direct Analysis*, p. 151.

p. 31, In 1971 he even won . . .: Masson, *Against Therapy*, p. 126.

p. 31, An article by Rosen . . .: J. N. Rosen, "The Treatment of Schizophrenic Psychosis by Direct Analytic Therapy," *Psychiatric Quarterly*, Jan. 1947, *21*, 117–119.

p. 31, Rosen reported . . .: Rosen, *Direct Analysis*, p. 96.

p. 31, in a follow-up study . . .: W. Horwitz, P. Polatin, L. Kolb, and P. Hoch, "A Study of Cases of Schizophrenia Treated by 'Direct Analysis,'" *American Journal of Psychiatry*, 1958, *114*, 780–783.

p. 31, "the claim that . . .": Horwitz and others, "A Study of Cases of Schizophrenia," p. 783.

p. 32, "sixty-seven violations . . .": J. M. Masson, *Against Therapy*, pp. 145–146.

p. 32, as far back as 1960 . . .: Hammer v. Rosen (7 N.Y. 2d 376; 165 N.E. 2d 756; 198 N.Y.S. 2d 65), cited in Masson, *Against Therapy*, p. 125.

p. 32, the kind of care . . . with other patients: Masson, *Against Therapy*, pp. 124–152.

p. 32, "physical methods that . . .": Masson, *Against Therapy*, p. 167.

p. 33, "he would use something . . .": Masson, *Against Therapy*, p. 167.

p. 33, "Without another word . . .": J. L. Schiff and B. Day, *All My Children* (New York: Pyramid Books, 1972), p. 38.

p. 33, She wrote, . . .: Schiff and Day, *All My Children*, p. 219.

p. 33, Virginia authorities . . .: T. Jackman, "History of 'Reparenting' Marked by Controversy, Dissension," *Kansas City Times* (Missouri), Oct. 8, 1988.

p. 33, in 1972 an eighteen-year-old: Jackman, "History of 'Reparenting'"; A.M. Meacham, "Reparenting Founder Never Far From Controversy," *Changes*, Aug. 1992, p. 59.

p. 34, Schiff's adopted son . . .: *California* v. *A. Schiff*, No. 15904 (Sup. Ct. Contra Costa County, CA), convicted, involuntary manslaughter (Sept. 14, 1973), withdrawal of former plea, new plea of guilty to child abuse, a lesser offense (Nov. 27, 1974).

p. 34, "They let me . . .": *California* v. *A. Schiff.*

p. 34, Jacqui Schiff . . . incorporated into TA training: P. Crossman, interviews with the authors, July and August 1995. We would like to thank Ms. Patricia Crossman for her invaluable aid in providing documentation and books about Cathexis and the history of reparenting. Information for this section also came from J. L. Schiff, *Cathexis Reader: Transactional Analysis Treatment of Psychosis* (New York: HarperCollins, 1975).

p. 34, According to Alan Jacobs . . .: Jacobs, "Theory as Ideology," p. 48.

p. 34, all did not flow . . . the association: Jackman, "History of 'Reparenting.'"

p. 34, The local paper in Birmingham reported . . .: R. Jones, "The Strange 'Babies' of Small Heath, *Evening Mail* (Birmingham, England), Aug. 15, 1991; "Mum Sucked Thumb," *Evening Mail* (Birmingham, England), Aug. 13, 1991.

p. 35, As recently as July 1995 . . .: A. Wagner, letter to the editor, *The Script*, Nov. 1995, p. 3.

p. 35, some rather startling results . . .: S. Smith, "A Study of Clinicians Who Use Regressive Work," *Transactional Analysis Journal*, 1989, *19*(2), 75–79; Meacham, "Call Me Mom," p. 59.

p. 35, the clinic had a supply . . .: Meacham, "Call Me Mom," p. 60.

pp. 35–36, He described . . . were treated there: T. Jackman, "History of 'Reparenting'"; "'Reparenting' Clinic: Some Claim It Helps, Others Say It Destroys," *Kansas City Times* (Missouri), Oct. 8, 1988; "Many Therapists Have No License to Practice," *Kansas City Times* (Missouri), Oct. 8, 1988.

p. 36, The cases and the allegations against the Matrix . . .: All information cited was alleged in each petition filed in the related case. They are listed here in the order in which they appear in the chapter. *McCuistion v. Wakefield et al.*, Case No. CV94–20948 Civil E; *Flanders, Flanders, Flanders, Flanders, and Belner v. Mid-America Treatment and Training Institute, Inc. (aka Matrix, Inc.) et al.*, Case No. CV89–21860 Civil B; *Jester and Jester v. Leymaster et al.*, Case No. CV89–29236 Civil B; *Staggs v. Leymaster et al.*, Case No. CV86–20779 Civil I. *Michaelle v. Mid-America Treatment & Training Institute, Inc., et al.*, Case No. CV91–4113 Civil C, included for reference. All in the Circuit Court of Jackson County, Missouri, at Kansas City.

p. 40, "*My lawsuits have shown* . . .": S. Willens, Esq., letter to the authors, Jul. 31, 1995.

p. 40, "*We invented* . . .": E. McNamara, *Breakdown: Sex, Suicide, and the Harvard Psychiatrist* (New York: Pocket Books, 1994), p. 41.

p. 40, "*as a means of* . . .": P. McHugh, "Psychotherapy Awry," *American Scholar*, Winter 1994, 63, 25.

p. 41, "*describing the most* . . .": G. S. Chafetz and M. E. Chafetz, *Obsession: The Bizarre Relationship Between a Prominent Harvard Psychiatrist and Her Suicidal Patient* (New York: Crown, 1994), p. 179; McNamara, *Breakdown*, pp. 158–159.

p. 41, "*Neither of us* . . .": McNamara, *Breakdown*, p. 154.

p. 41, *Gault wrote* . . .: McNamara, *Breakdown*, pp. 158–159.

p. 42, *developed his theories:* Lark, "Rebirthing," in R. Herink (ed.), *Psychotherapy Handbook*, pp. 560–561.

p. 42, *A number of them said* . . .: L. Orr and S. Ray, *Rebirthing in the New Age* (Berkeley, Calif.: Celestial Arts, 1977); Lark, "Rebirthing."

p. 43, *Initially* . . . *allergy attacks:* Lark, "Rebirthing," p. 561.

p. 43, *One certified hypnotherapist* . . .: R. Kitchen, "Hypnotherapy," posted on the World Wide Web at http://www.he.tdl.com/~kitchen/index.html.

p. 44, *Their organization* . . . "*current life*": Informational mailing received from LRT (in the authors' possession).

p. 44, describes her own birth: Ray and Mandel, *Birth and Relationships*, pp. 4–9.

p. 44, Bob Mandel, Ray's coauthor, describes his birth: Ray and Mandel, *Birth and Relationships*, pp. 14–17.

p. 44, For example, in the chapter . . . : Ray and Mandel, *Birth and Relationships*, p. 52.

Chapter Three

p. 47, When asked . . . : E. Rafaelson, "This Doctor Brings You Back to Your Previous Lives," an interview with Dr. Glenn Williston, Dec. 1989, posted on the World Wide Web at http://www.wholarts.com/psychic/oslo/html.

p. 47, A national professional association . . . : Telephone query to Association for Past Life Research and Therapies, Inc.; also see D. Goldner, "Remembrances of Lives Past," *New Age Journal*, Nov./Dec. 1994, pp. 73–77, 135.

p. 47, The more popular . . . : "Back in Time," *PrimeTime Live*, ABC-TV, Nov. 15, 1995.

p. 47, Responding to a question . . . : Rafaelson, "This Doctor Brings You Back to Your Previous Lives."

p. 47, Between 1977 and 1990 . . . : D. Sutphen, *Earthly Purpose: The Incredible True Story of a Group Reincarnation* (New York: Pocket Books, 1990), frontispiece.

p. 48, "nationwide metaphysical network . . . ": Sutphen, *Earthly Purpose*, p. x.

p. 48, "whether you are . . . ": Sutphen, *Earthly Purpose*, front cover text.

p. 48, He has conducted . . . and attorneys: B. Goldberg, *The Search for Grace: A Documented Case of Murder and Reincarnation* (Sedona, Ariz.: In Print Publishing, 1994), p. 274.

p. 48, a client waiting list . . . : Goldner, "Remembrances of Lives Past," p. 74.

p. 48, Weiss's first book . . . : B. L. Weiss, *Many Lives, Many Masters* (New York: Fireside/Simon & Schuster, 1988).

p. 48, MacLaine's best-seller: S. MacLaine, *Out on a Limb* (New York: Bantam Books, 1983).

p. 49, One financial writer . . . : H. Gordon, *Channeling into the New Age: The "Teachings" of Shirley MacLaine and Other Such Gurus* (Amherst, N.Y.: Prometheus, 1988), p. 122.

p. 49, "My wife . . .": Gordon, *Channeling into the New Age,* p. 128.

p. 49, "This is, I think . . .": "Back in Time."

p. 51, "Subjects are so open . . .": H. TenDam, *Exploring Reincarnation* (Harmondsworth, England: Penguin Books, 1990), p. 123.

p. 51, research of Dr. Ian Stevenson: I. Stevenson, "The Evidence for Survival from Claimed Memories of Former Incarnations," *Journal of the American Society for Psychical Research,* 1858, *54,* 51–71, 95–117; *Twenty Cases Suggestive of Reincarnation* (Charlottesville: University of Virginia Press, 1974); *Cases of the Reincarnation Type: vol. 1, Ten Cases in India,* 1975; *vol. 2, Ten Cases in Sri Lanka,* 1977; *vol. 3, Twelve Cases in Lebanon and Turkey,* 1980; *vol. 4, Twelve Cases in Thailand and Burma,* 1983 (Charlottesville: University of Virginia Press, 1975–1983).

p. 51, What's not often mentioned . . . : Gordon, *Channeling into the New Age,* pp. 58–59; Wilson, I. *The After Death Experience: The Physics of the Non-Physical* (New York: Morrow, 1987), pp. 29–34.

p. 51, Her hypnotist wrote: M. Bernstein, *The Search for Bridey Murphy* (New York: Doubleday, 1956).

p. 51, Later it was discovered: K. Davidson, "Are Picasso and Money for the Birds?" *San Francisco Examiner,* Aug. 18, 1995; L. Ludlow, "Bridey Murphy," *San Francisco Examiner,* Jul. 23, 1995.

p. 52, "In the final analysis . . .": J. F. Kihlstrom, "Past-Life Hypnotic Regression," posted on the sci.psychology Internet newsgroup, Dec. 17, 1994.

p. 53, There are no . . . courses in hypnosis: "Spellbound," *Eye to Eye with Connie Chung,* CBS-TV, Dec. 1994.

p. 53, Inadequately trained people . . . hypnosis: "Spellbound."

p. 53, A recent investigative report: "Back in Time."

p. 54, "You wouldn't go . . .": "Back in Time."

p. 54, Here are some startling examples: Goldberg, *The Search for Grace,* pp. 14–15, 15–17.

p. 54, "the only one . . .": Goldberg, *The Search for Grace,* p. 248.

p. 55, the APA spokesperson . . .: Telephone interview with public relations spokesperson at the American Psychological Association, Washington, D.C., Oct. 30, 1995.

p. 57, "The way to recall . . .": TenDam, *Exploring Reincarnation,* p. 123.

p. 57, "We all have . . .": TenDam, *Exploring Reincarnation,* p. 127.

p. 57, "Even without . . ." T. Andrews, *How to Uncover Your Past Lives* (St. Paul, Minn.: Llewellyn, 1994), p. 1.

p. 57, "Actually, whether . . .": E. Fiore, *You Have Been Here Before: A Psychologist Looks at Past Lives* (New York: Ballantine, 1978), p. 6.

p. 57, "Disproving hypotheses . . .": TenDam, *Exploring Reincarnation,* p. 374.

p. 57, He taught the attendees . . .: C. Hollingsworth, "Altered Fate: Is This Life Giving You Trouble? Let Psychiatrist Brian Weiss Take You Back to Another One," *Chicago Tribune,* June 21, 1995, p. 1.

p. 58, "You can't go . . .": Goldner, "Remembrances of Lives Past," pp. 74–75.

p. 58, "there is absolutely . . .": Kihlstrom, "Past-Life Hypnotic Regression."

p. 58, Weiss includes instructions on . . .: B. L. Weiss, *Through Time into Healing* (New York: Fireside/Simon & Schuster, 1992), p. 171.

p. 58, Weiss offers a script: Weiss, *Through Time into Healing,* pp. 179–180.

p. 58, "Sometimes it takes . . .": Fiore, *You Have Been Here Before*, p. 13.

p. 58, Bruce Goldberg explains: B. Goldberg, *Past Lives, Future Lives* (New York: Ballantine, 1982), p. 2.

p. 58, The conclusion was: N. P. Spanos, E. Menary, N. J. Gabora, S. C. DuBreuil, and B. Dewhirst, "Secondary Identity Enactments During Hypnotic Past-Life Regression: A Sociocognitive Perspective," *Journal of Personality and Social Psychology*, 1991, *61*(2), 318.

p. 59, Some practitioners caution: Unarius Academy of Science, "Reincarnation: Past-Life Therapy—The New Psychiatry," posted on the World Wide Web, at http://zeta.cs.adfa.oz.au/spirit/past-life-unarius.html.

p. 59, "In my experience . . .": G. Williston and J. Johnstone, *Discovering Your Past Lives* (Northamptonshire, England: Aquarian Press, 1983), p. 19.

p. 59, by 1978 she had done . . . : H. Wambach, *Reliving Past Lives: The Evidence Under Hypnosis* (New York: HarperCollins, 1978), p. 147.

p. 59, "I have performed . . .": E. Fiore, *The Unquiet Dead: A Psychologist Treats Spirit Possession* (New York: Ballantine, 1987), p. 160.

p. 60, "programmed reactions . . .": Williston and Johnstone, *Discovering Your Past Lives*, p. 248.

p. 60, Others—like psychic researcher Brad Steiger, mystic Frances Steiger,: B. Steiger and F. Steiger, *Discover Your Past Lives* (West Chester, Penn.: Whitford Press, 1987); Andrews, *How to Uncover Your Past Lives.*

p. 60, "this is not . . ." scary places: Goldner, "Remembrances of Lives Past," p. 135.

p. 60, One person who claims: D. Showen, "Re: Past Lives, Future Lives," posted on the talk.religion.newage, alt.alien.visitors, and alt.paranormal Internet newsgroups, June 26, 1995.

p. 60, panoply of symptoms: TenDam, *Exploring Reincarnation*, p. 375.

p. 61, *Netherton cautions* . . .: M. Netherton and N. Shiffrin, "Past Lives Therapy," in R. Herink (ed.), *Psychotherapy Handbook*, pp. 460–461; *Past Lives Therapy* (New York: Morrow, 1978).

p. 61, *Fiore mentions curing* . . .: Fiore, *You Have Been Here Before*, pp. 4–8.

p. 61, *"chronic headaches, including* . . .": Fiore, *You Have Been Here Before*, pp. 7–8.

p. 61, *"There is not* . . .": Fiore, *You Have Been Here Before*, p. 8.

p. 61, *"The American Psychiatric Association believes* . . .": Telephone interview, June 4 and 5, 1996.

p. 64, *"our future selves* . . .": Williston and Johnstone, *Discovering Your Past Lives*, p. 234.

p. 64, *"no other therapist* . . .": Goldberg, *Past Lives, Future Lives*, p. 134.

p. 64, *"Yet," he writes, "if* . . .": Goldberg, *Past Lives, Future Lives*, p. 135.

p. 64, *predictions for the future*: Goldberg, *Past Lives, Future Lives*, pp. 135–136.

p. 65, *Goldberg assures clients*: Goldberg, *Past Lives, Future Lives*, p. 64.

p. 65, *"imagine a pure* . . ." *negativity*: Goldberg, *Past Lives, Future Lives*, p. 63.

Chapter Four

p. 71, *Simply put, entities therapists* . . .: M. Eliade, *Shamanism: The Archaic Techniques of Ecstasy* (New York: Pantheon Books, 1964); L. Pankratz and R. Mackenberg, "Crusader Against Spiritualist Fraud," *Skeptical Inquirer*, Jul./Aug. 1995, pp. 28–29; G. Stein, "Mediumship: Is It Mixed or Just Mixed Up?" *Skeptical Inquirer*, May-June 1995, 19(3), 30–32.

p. 71, *surveys show*: B. Larson, *Larson's New Book of Cults* (Wheaton, Ill.: Tyndale House, 1989), p. 419; J. Klimo, *Channeling: Investigations on Receiving Information from Paranormal Sources* (Los Angeles: Tarcher, 1987), p. 3.

p. 71, Two famous mediums . . . part of the time: Gordon, *Channeling into the New Age*, pp. 77–85; Klimo, *Channeling*, pp. 95–108; T. Schultz (ed.), *The Fringes of Reason* (New York: Harmony Books, 1989), pp. 58–59.

p. 72, Use of the word channeling. . .: M. T. Singer with J. Lalich, *Cults in Our Midst: The Hidden Menace in Our Everyday Lives* (San Francisco: Jossey-Bass, 1995) p. 45.

p. 72, "rush hour of the entities": B. Alexander, *Spirit Channeling: Evaluating the Latest in New Age Spiritism* (Downers Grove, Ill.: InterVarsity Press, 1988), p. 7.

p. 73, Some researchers say: Klimo, *Channeling*, p. 24.

p. 73, A recent estimate: R. A. Baker, *Hidden Memories: Voices and Visions from Within* (Amherst, N.Y.: Prometheus, 1992), p. 88.

p. 73, "the process . . .": Klimo, *Channeling*, p. 4, citing A. Hastings, "Investigating the Phenomenon of Channeling," *Noetic Sciences Review*, Winter 1986.

p. 73, "a phenomenon in which . . .": Klimo, *Channeling*, p. 1.

p. 74, one entity—Michael—is . . .: "Michael Speaks," a publication of the Michael Education Foundation, Fall 1995, p. 16; Klimo, *Channeling*, p. 50.

p. 74, One person advertises: "Open Exchange," Oct.–Dec. 1995, p. 88.

p. 74, the appearance in 1970: J. Roberts, *The Seth Material* (Englewood Cliffs, N.J.: Prentice Hall, 1970).

p. 74, Seth described himself . . .: Klimo, *Channeling*, p. 30, quoting *The Seth Material*, pp. 4–5.

p. 74, That same year . . .: R. Bach, *Jonathan Livingston Seagull* (New York: Macmillan, 1970).

p. 74, Another remarkable publication: H. Schucman, *A Course in Miracles* (Roscoe, N.Y.: Foundation for a Course in Miracles, 1976).

p. 74, According to Schucman: Baker, *Hidden Memories,* p. 235; R. Chandler, *Understanding the New Age* (Grand Rapids, Mich.: Zondervan, 1993), pp. 196–199; Klimo, *Channeling,* pp. 37–42.

p. 74, Yet in discussions . . .: T. Schultz, "Voices from Beyond: The Age-Old Mystery of Channeling." In T. Schultz (ed.), *The Fringes of Reason* (New York: Harmony Books, 1989), p. 62.

p. 75, Lazaris says: Lazaris, *Lazaris Interviews, Books I and II* (Beverly Hills, Calif.: Concept: Synergy, 1988); Klimo, *Channeling,* pp. 49–50.

p. 75, Ramtha came to prominence: H. Gordon, *Channeling into the New Age,* pp. 95–101; R. Chandler, *Understanding the New Age,* pp. 52–54.

p. 75, in her best-selling: S. MacLaine, *Dancing in the Light* (New York: Bantam Books, 1985).

p. 75, Mafu, a "highly . . .": Alexander, *Spirit Channeling,* p. 5.

p. 76, "We are starting . . .": "L.A. Trance Channeling Group Forming," posted on the sci.psychology Internet newsgroup, July 8, 1995.

p. 76, "They are so cuddly . . .": H. Cox, "For Personal Insights, Some Try Channels out of This World," *Wall Street Journal,* Apr. 1, 1987, p. 1, quoted in Klimo, p. 12.

p. 77, Brooks Alexander asked that question: Alexander, *Spirit Channeling,* p. 16.

p. 77, "the communications of . . .": C. J. Jung cited in T. Schultz, "Voices from Beyond: The Age-Old Mystery of Channeling," p. 65.

p. 77, As for Carl Raschke: Larson, *Larson's New Book of Cults,* pp. 417–418.

p. 77, "And how come the sources . . .": M. Shippey, "Are Newagers Kinder and Gentler Fascists?" Posted on the talk.religion.newage newsgroup, Nov. 19, 1995.

p. 78, Fiore's ten signs: Fiore, *The Unquiet Dead,* flyleaf.

p. 78, *Fiore commented:* Fiore, *The Unquiet Dead,* p. 3.

p. 78, *She writes . . .:* Fiore, *The Unquiet Dead,* p. 5.

p. 78, *instantaneous cures:* Fiore, *The Unquiet Dead,* pp. 7–8.

p. 79, *She came to this realization:* Fiore, *The Unquiet Dead,* p. 9.

p. 79, *"My therapeutic goal . . .":* Fiore, *The Unquiet Dead,* p. 12.

Chapter Five

p. 87, *John Mack's book:* J. E. Mack, *Abduction: Human Encounters with Aliens* (New York: Scribner, 1994a).

p. 87, *In 1992, a conference:* A. Pritchard, D. E. Pritchard, J. E. Mack, P. Kasey, and C. Yapp (eds.), *Alien Discussions: Proceedings of the Abduction Study Conference* (Cambridge, Mass.: North Cambridge Press, 1994).

p. 87, *a 478-page book:* C.D.B. Bryan, *Close Encounters of the Fourth Kind: Alien Abduction, UFOs, and the Conference at M.I.T.* (New York: Knopf, 1995).

p. 88, *Pritchard told him . . .:* Bryan, *Close Encounters of the Fourth Kind,* p. 12.

p. 88, *Edith Fiore's 1989 book:* E. Fiore, *Encounters: A Psychologist Reveals Case Studies of Abductions by Extraterrestrials* (New York: Ballantine, 1989), pp. 272–273.

p. 88, *In his 1994 book, Richard Boylan:* R. J. Boylan and L. K. Boylan, *Close Extraterrestrial Encounters: Positive Experiences with Mysterious Visitors* (Tigard, Oreg.: Wild Flower Press, 1994), pp. 187–190.

p. 88, *"'Space alien' shrink . . .:* "'Space Alien' Shrink Loses His License," *San Francisco Examiner,* Aug. 13, 1995, p. C4.

p. 88, *According to the State Board of Psychology:* "'Space Alien' Shrink Loses His License."

p. 88, *"I have my MA . . .":* L. Brown, ad posted on Internet alt.paranet.abduct newsgroup, summer 1995.

p. 88, "Abduction Experience? . . .": D. Nicolaou, "Abduction Experience," posted on the Internet at alt.paranet.abduct newsgroup, Nov. 4, 1995.

p. 89, "We can estimate . . .": Boylan and Boylan, *Close Extraterrestrial Encounters,* p. 13.

p. 89, "Confessed killer . . .": "Confessed Killer Says UFOs Made Him Do It, Will Defend Self at Trial," *Arizona Republic* (Phoenix), Jul. 15, 1995, p. B1.

p. 94, Sometimes patients are primed: J. Willwerth, "The Man from Outer Space," *Time,* Apr. 25, 1994, p. 75.

p. 94, "I stumbled onto . . .": Fiore, *Encounters,* p. xvi.

p. 94, "To this day . . .": Fiore, *Encounters,* p. xix.

p. 94, "I travel long distances . . .": Fiore, *Encounters,* p. 177.

p. 95, "You can discover . . .": Fiore, *Encounters,* p. 258.

p. 95, The reader is instructed: Fiore, *Encounters,* p. 260.

p. 95, Fiore warns: Fiore, *Encounters,* pp. 260–261.

p. 96, the demand characteristics: M. Orne, "On the Social Psychology of the Psychological Experiment: With Particular Reference to Demand Characteristics and Their Implications," *American Psychologist,* 1962, *17,* 776–783.

p. 96, Orne writes: M. Orne, "On the Simulating Subject as a Quasi-Control Group in Hypnosis Research: What, Why, and How," in E. Fromm and R. Shor (eds.), *Hypnosis: Developments in Research and New Perspectives* (Hawthorne, N.Y.: Aldine de Gruyter, 1979), p. 523.

p. 97, Fiore said, "I have no desire . . .": Fiore, *Encounters,* p. 7.

p. 97, Throughout history . . .: M. Eliade, *Myths, Dreams, and Mysteries* (New York: HarperCollins, 1957).

p. 98, The first publication . . . what happened: J. Fuller, *The Interrupted Journey* (New York: Dial, 1966); Mack, *Abduction*, 1994a, pp. 12–14; Boylan and Boylan, *Close Extraterrestrial Encounters*, p. 8.

p. 98, The conclusion . . . : Mack, *Abduction*, 1994a, p. 14.

p. 98, There was a growing interest: See for example the popular books by J. Vallee, *Dimensions: A Casebook of Alien Contact* (New York: Ballantine, 1988), and *Revelations: Alien Contact and Human Deception* (New York: Ballantine, 1991); and D. M. Jacobs, *Secret Life: Firsthand Documented Accounts of UFO Abductions* (New York: Fireside/Simon & Schuster, 1992).

p. 98, "a physical visit . . .": Boylan and Boylan, *Close Extraterrestrial Encounters*, p. 13.

p. 98, UFOlogist Budd Hopkins . . . : *Unusual Personal Experiences: An Analysis of the Data from Three National Surveys* (Las Vegas, Nev.: Bigelow Holding, 1992), p. 15.

p. 99, performed more than . . . : Bryan, *Close Encounters of the Fourth Kind*, p. 17.

p. 99, Hopkins and Jacobs made calculations . . . : *Unusual Personal Experiences*, p. 15.

p. 99, a sixty-four-page booklet: *Unusual Personal Experiences*.

p. 99, "Following Hopkins's . . . unvalidated poll data": Bryan, *Close Encounters of the Fourth Kind*, pp. 46–47.

p. 100, In it he urged: *Unusual Personal Experiences*, p. 8.

p. 100, later in a letter: Boylan and Boylan, *Close Extraterrestrial Encounters*, p. 193.

p. 100, He devised a checklist: Boylan and Boylan, *Close Extraterrestrial Encounters*, pp. 172–173.

p. 101, "There was nothing . . .": Mack, *Abduction*, 1994a, p. 2.

p. 101, "I am not . . .": J. E. Mack, *Abduction: Human Encounters with Aliens,* rev. ed. (New York: Ballantine, 1994b), p. 1.

p. 101, Mack gives us: Mack, *Abduction,* 1994b, pp. 14–16.

p. 102, Of those included: Mack, *Abduction,* 1994b, p. 5.

p. 102, Those who describe: N. P. Spanos, C. A. Burgess, and M. F. Burgess, "Past-Life Identities, UFO Abductions, and Satanic Ritual Abuse: The Social Reconstruction of Memories," *International Journal of Clinical and Experimental Hypnosis,* Oct. 1994, *17*(4), 433–446.

p. 102, In one study: N. P. Spanos, P. Cross, K. Dickson, and S. C. DuBreuil, "Close Encounters: An Examination of UFO Experiences," *Journal of Abnormal Psychology,* 1993, *102,* 624–632.

p. 102, "Before you become . . .": Baker, *Hidden Memories,* p. 305.

p. 103, Even Mack says: Mack, *Abduction,* 1994b, p. 434.

p. 104, sinister theories such as: Bryan, *Close Encounters of the Fourth Kind,* p. 4.

p. 104, Others, like Boylan: Boylan and Boylan: *Close Extraterrestrial Encounters,* p. 53.

Chapter Six

p. 109, One historian noted: F. FitzGerald, *Cities on a Hill: A Journey Through Contemporary American Cultures* (New York: Simon & Schuster, 1986), pp. 22, 265.

p. 109, The Marin therapist . . .: P. Liberatore, "Laugh, Cry and Try to Be Healthy," *Marin Independent Journal,* Jan. 30, 1996, p. C3.

p. 109, Amada said, "It sometimes . . .": Liberatore, "Laugh, Cry and Try to Be Healthy," p. C3.

p. 112, The cathartic method . . . to the patient: T. Karasu, "Psychoanalysis and Psychoanalytic Therapy," in H. I. Kaplan and B. J. Sadock (eds.), *Comprehensive Textbook of Psychiatry,* 5th ed., p. 1442 (Baltimore: Williams & Wilkins, 1989).

p. 114, As one critic put it: H. M. Ruitenbeek, *The New Group Therapies* (New York: Avon, 1970), pp. 91–92.

p. 114, commercially sold large group awareness training programs: Singer with Lalich, *Cults in Our Midst,* pp. 42–43, 85, 182–212.

p. 114, they typically use . . . : Singer with Lalich, *Cults in Our Midst,* pp. 91–92, 191–212.

p. 120, singer and songwriter John Lennon: R. D. Rosen, *Psychobabble* (New York: Avon, 1977), p. 155.

p. 120, professing that: A. Janov, *The Primal Revolution* (New York: Simon & Schuster, 1972), p. 19.

p. 120, "as the product of . . .": A. Janov, *The Primal Scream* (New York: Putnam, 1970), p. 11.

p. 121, "poor student, withdrawn, sensitive, and quiet": Janov, *Primal Scream,* p. 9.

p. 121, but Janov writes: Janov, *Primal Scream,* pp. 9–10.

p. 121, Gary called for his . . . : Janov, *Primal Scream,* p. 10.

p. 121, as one critic remarked: J. Kovel, *A Complete Guide to Therapy* (New York: Pantheon Books, 1976), p. 139.

p. 121, "not all birth is traumatic . . .": Janov, *The Primal Revolution,* p. 34.

p. 121, "Primal Therapy purports . . .": Janov, *Primal Revolution,* p. 19.

p. 122, he writes: "Primal Therapy methods are . . .": Janov, *Primal Revolution,* pp. 28–29.

p. 122, Yet Janov's World Wide Web home page warns: Opening page of Dr. Arthur Janov's International Primal Center, on the World Wide Web at http://www.directnet.com/welcome.

p. 122, A colleague of Janov's claims . . . "profoundly calm": E. M. Holden, "Primal Therapy," in R. Herink (ed.), *Psychotherapy Handbook,* p. 494.

p. 122, New Identity Process: D. Casriel, A Scream Away from Happiness (New York: Grosset and Dunlap, 1972); see also D. Casriel, "New Identity Process," in R. Herink (ed.), Psychotherapy Handbook, pp. 428–431.

p. 122, "totally new psychiatric delivery system . . .": D. Casriel, "New Identity Process," in R. Herink (ed.), Psychotherapy Handbook, p. 429.

p. 123, Bio Scream Psychotherapy: N. Saltzman, "Bio Scream Psychotherapy," in R. Herink (ed.), Psychotherapy Handbook, pp. 66–68.

p. 123, called the Center for Feeling Therapy: C. L. Mithers, Therapy Gone Mad: The True Story of Hundreds of Patients and a Generation Betrayed (Reading, Mass.: Addison-Wesley, 1994); Singer with Lalich, Cults in Our Midst, pp. 14, 175–177.

p. 123, "When we left Janov . . .": M. L. Gross, The Psychological Society (New York: Random House, 1978), p. 281.

p. 124, stay in a secluded motel . . . anxious state: Mithers, Therapy Gone Mad, pp. 65–69.

p. 125, promotional flyers promise: Flyer from S. Khamsi, summer 1995 workshops, received in the mail.

p. 128, "The therapist or group . . .": L. Berkowitz, "The Case for Bottling up Rage," Psychology Today, July 1973, p. 24; see also L. Berkowitz, "Experimental Investigations of Hostility Catharsis," Journal of Consulting and Clinical Psychology, 1970, 35, 1–7.

p. 128, "otherwise run amok . . .": As discussed in C. Tavris, Anger: The Misunderstood Emotion (New York: Touchstone/Simon & Schuster, 1989), p. 136.

p. 129, The human organism learns . . . in the first place: For a thorough and excellent treatment of these issues, see Anger by Carol Tavris.

p. 130, Social psychology is filled . . .: For an excellent discussion of this issue, see R. B. Cialdini, Influence: The New Psychology of Modern Persuasion (New York: Quill, 1984).

Chapter Seven

p. 135, annotated bibliography: H. Lerman, *Sexual Intimacies Between Psychotherapists and Patients: An Annotated Bibliography of Mental Health, Legal and Public Media Literature and Relevant Legal Cases* (Washington, D.C.: American Psychological Association, with the assistance of the Association for Women in Psychology, 1990).

p. 135, another huge book of 837 pages: G. R. Schoener, J. H. Milgrom, J. C. Gonsiorek, E. T. Leupker, and R. M. Conroe, *Psychotherapist Sexual Involvement with Clients: Intervention and Prevention* (Minneapolis, Minn.: Walk-In Counseling Center, 1990).

p. 135, the results of nineteen of the largest studies: Schoener and others, *Psychotherapist Sexual Involvement with Clients*, pp. 39–40.

p. 135, In another study on the subject: P. Rutter, *Sex in the Forbidden Zone: When Men in Power—Therapists, Doctors, Clergy, Teachers, and Others—Betray Women's Trust* (Los Angeles: Tarcher, 1989), p. 36.

p. 135, Rutter wrote: "If we . . .": Rutter, *Sex in the Forbidden Zone*, p. 36.

p. 135, complaints filed with the California psychology licensing board: "Overview of Enforcement Activity 1990–95," *Board of Psychology Update* (California Department of Consumer Affairs, Board of Psychology), Oct. 1995, no. 2, p. 12.

p. 135, a recent study of trends in health care: B. Shenker and J. Fisher, *Trends in Health Care Provider Liability* (Horsham, Penn.: LRP Publications, 1994), pp. 57–59.

p. 136, "'You're scum,' he muttered . . .": E. Plasil, *Therapist: The Shocking Autobiography of a Woman Sexually Exploited by Her Analyst* (New York: St. Martin's/Marek, 1985), pp. 1–2.

p. 137, Research over the past . . .: N. Gartrell, J. Herman, S. Olarte, M. Feldstein, and R. Localio, "Prevalence of Psychiatrist-Patient Sexual Contact," in G. O. Gabbard (ed.), *Sexual Exploitation in Professional Relationships* (Washington, D.C.: American Psychiatric Press, 1989), pp. 3–14; A. M. Brodsky, "Sex Between Patient and Therapist: Psychology's Data and Response," in Gabbard (ed.), *Sexual Exploitation in Professional Relationships*, p. 18; J. Holroyd and A. Brodsky, "Psychologists' Attitudes and Practices Regarding Erotic and Nonerotic Physical Contact with Patients," *American Psychologist*, 1977, *32*, 843–849.

p. 139, *three major groupings* . . .: K. S. Pope and J. Bouhoutsos, *Sexual Intimacy Between Therapists and Patients* (New York: Praeger, 1986), pp. 33–45.

p. 150, *"the longest, costliest,* . . .*"*: Singer with Lalich, *Cults in Our Midst*, p. 176.

p. 150, *There was a long list* . . .: Mithers, *Therapy Gone Mad*; Singer with Lalich, *Cults in Our Midst*, pp. 175–177.

p. 151, *An ex-patient described* . . .: Mithers, *Therapy Gone Mad*; Singer with Lalich, *Cults in Our Midst*, pp. 175–177.

p. 151, *"At thirty-nine, she* . . .*"*: Mithers, *Therapy Gone Mad*, p. 400.

p. 161, *Many male therapists in particular*: D. Tennov, *Psychotherapy: The Hazardous Cure* (New York: Anchor Books, 1976), p. 46.

p. 161, *countless other cases*: See, for example, C. M. Bates and A. M. Brodsky, *Sex in the Therapy Hour: A Case of Professional Incest* (New York: Guilford Press, 1989); J. Bouhoutsos, J. Holroyd, H. Lerman, and others, "Sexual Intimacy Between Psychotherapists and Patients," *Professional Psychology, Research and Practice*, 1983, *14*, 185–196; A. W. Burgess and C. R. Hartman (eds.), *Sexual Exploitation of Patients by Health Professionals* (New York: Praeger, 1986); L. Freeman and J. Roy, *Betrayal: The True Story of the First Woman to Successfully Sue Her Psychiatrist for Using Sex in the Guise of Therapy* (New York: Stein and Day, 1976); Gabbard (ed.), *Sexual Exploitation in Professional Relationships*; B. Noël with K. Watterson, *You Must Be Dreaming* (New York: Poseidon, 1992); Plasil, *Therapist*; E. Walker and T. D. Young, *A Killing Cure* (Austin, Tex.: Holt, Rinehart and Winston, 1986).

p. 163, *As one state law* . . .: taken from State of California booklet, *Professional Therapy Never Includes Sex* (Sacramento: State of California Department of Consumer Affairs, 1990), p. 4. Available from Department of Consumer Affairs, 1020 N Street, Sacramento, CA 95814.

p. 163, "Therapists who encourage . . .": State of California, *Professional Therapy Never Includes Sex,* p. 1.

p. 165, the authority bestowed: T. Sarbin, "One Body May Be Host to Two or More Personalities," *International Journal of Clinical and Experimental Hypnosis,* 1995, *18*(2), 163–183.

Chapter Eight

p. 168, NLP trainings have been . . .: C. K. Bruha, letter to the editor, *Esquire,* April 7, 1994.

p. 168, According to one source: Bruha, letter to the editor.

p. 169, Today NLP is often called . . .: From direct-mail solicitations from Nightengale-Conant Corporation selling NLP audiocassettes and manual.

p. 169, the name NLP . . .: NLP FAQ and Resources home page alt.psychology.NLP newsgroup! on the World Wide Web.

p. 169, NLP circles claim . . .: C. K. Sikes, *What Is NLP?* (Milwaukee, Wis.: IDHEA Seminars, n.d.); C. K. Sikes, *Dispelling Myths and Misconceptions about NLP* (Milwaukee, Wis.: IDHEA Seminars, n.d.).

p. 169, Much of early NLP . . . enjoyment of life: E. Campbell and J. H. Brennan, *Body Mind & Spirit: A Dictionary of New Age Ideas, People, Places, and Terms* (Rutland, Vt.: Tuttle, 1994), p. 160.

p. 169, "A client can learn . . .": J. O. Stevens, "NeuroLinguistic Programming," in R. Herink (ed.), *Psychotherapy Handbook,* pp. 423, 424.

p. 170, "I find it works . . .": S. Robbins, *Neuro-Linguistic Programming: A Definition.* Posted on the NLP World Wide Web home page.

p. 170, Bandler and Grinder claimed . . .: R. Bandler and J. Grinder, *The Structure of Magic I* (Palo Alto, Calif.: Science and Behavior Books, 1975); R. Bandler and J. Grinder, *The Patterns of the Hypnotic Techniques of Milton H. Erickson, M.D.* (Palo Alto, Calif.: Science and Behavior Books, 1975); R. Bandler and J. Grinder, *Frogs into Princes: Neuro-Linguistic Programming* (Moab, Utah: Real People Press, 1979); J. Grinder and R. Bandler, *The Structure of Magic II* (Palo Alto, Calif.: Science and Behavior Books, 1976).

p. 171, *"In DHE™, we install . . ."*: R. Steven and C. Sikes, *What is DHE™?* (Milwaukee, Wisc.: IDHEA Seminars, n.d.).

p. 171, *"Be warned however . . ."*: Steven and Sikes, *What is DHE™?*

p. 172, *"It's difficult to prove . . ."*: NLP FAQ and Resources home page, alt.psychology.NLP newsgroup on the Internet.

p. 172, NLP *"is theoretically . . ."*: R. B. Dilts, *Neuro-Linguistic Programming: Part I: Roots of Neuro-Linguistic Programming, 1976; Part II: EEG and Representational Systems, 1977; Part III: Applications of Neuro-Linguistic Programming to Therapy* (Cupertino, Calif.: Meta Publications, 1978), p. 3.

p. 172, *"So, now to the . . ."*: S. Jacobson, *Sid Jacobson's History of NLP.* Posted on the Internet NLP home page, said to be adapted from "Neuro-Linguistic Programming," *INFO-LINE,* American Society for Training and Development, April 1994.

p. 172, *"NLP is heavily . . ."*: Robbins, *Neuro-Linguistic Programming.*

p. 172, *Even Bandler himself . . .*: C. K. Sikes, *Excerpts from an Interview with Dr. Richard Bandler, Developer of NLP and DHE™* (Milwaukee, Wis.: IDHEA Seminars, n.d.).

p. 173, *"What occurs is . . ."*: Steven and Sikes, *What is DHE™?*

p. 173, *Sikes also wrote . . .*: Sikes, *Dispelling Myths.*

p. 174, *"NLP is really . . ."*: S. Jacobson, *Sid Jacobson's History of NLP.*

p. 175, *In 1984*: D. Druckman and J. A. Swets (eds.), *Enhancing Human Performance: Issues, Theories, and Techniques* (Washington, D.C.: National Academy Press, 1988), p. vii.

p. 175, *"Individually and as a group . . ."*: Druckman and Swets, *Enhancing Human Performance*, pp. 142–144.

p. 175, "The lack of evaluation . . .": Druckman and Swets, *Enhancing Human Performance*, pp. 145, 148.

p. 177, "unexpected literacy": D. Biklen, "Communication Unbound: Autism and Praxis," *Harvard Educational Review*, 1990, 60, 291–315; D. Biklen, "Autism Orthodoxy Versus Free Speech: A Reply to Cummins and Prior," *Harvard Educational Review*, 1992a, 62, 242–256; D. Biklen, "Facilitated Communication: Biklen Responds," *American Journal of Speech and Language Pathology*, 1992b, 1(2), 21–22.

p. 177, in at least five nations: D. Biklen, *Common Myths and Misunderstandings About Facilitated Communication*, posted on the World Wide Web at ftp://ftp.syr.edu/information/autism/common_myths_and_misunderstandings_FC.

p. 177, FC is credited to . . .: R. Crossley, *Facilitated Communication Training* (New York: Teacher's College, Columbia University, 1994).

p. 177, despite their having had . . .: G. Green, "Facilitated Communication: Mental Miracle or Sleight of Hand?" *Skeptic*, 1994, 2(3), 68–76.

p. 177, Thousands of professionals . . .: Green, "Facilitated Communication: Mental Miracle or Sleight of Hand?"

p. 178, Yet, a fifteen-week study . . .: R. L. Simpson and B. S. Myles, "Effectiveness of Facilitated Communication with Children and Youth with Autism," *Journal of Special Education*, 1995, 28(4), 424–439, reported by K. Frazier in *Skeptical Inquirer*, 1995, 19(5), 52.

p. 178, "another therapy leading to a witch hunt": R. T. Carroll, "Facilitated Communication," *The Skeptic's Dictionary*, on the World Wide Web at http://wheel.ucdavis/edu/~btcarrol/skeptic/facilcom.html.

p. 178, According to Gina Green . . .: Green, "Facilitated Communication: Mental Miracle or Sleight of Hand?"

p. 178, Douglas Biklen says . . .: Biklen, *Common Myths*.

p. 179, regard as trivial . . .: Green, "Facilitated Communication: Mental Miracle or Sleight of Hand?"; Carroll, "Facilitated Communication."

p. 179, numerous research studies . . .: J. W. Jacobson, J. A. Mulick, and A. A. Schwartz, "A History of Facilitated Communication: Science, Pseudoscience and Antiscience," American Psychologist, 1995, 50(9), 750–765; K. M. Dillon, "Facilitated Communication, Autism, and Ouija," Skeptical Inquirer, 1993, 17(3), 281–287.

p. 179, "allegedly typed . . .": Dillon, "Facilitated Communication, Autism, and Ouija," pp. 281–282.

p. 179, "Facilitator influence . . .": G. A. Hall, "Facilitator Control as Automatic Behavior: A Verbal Behavior Analysis," Analysis of Verbal Behavior, 1993, 11, 89–97, cited in Jacobson, Mulick, and Schwartz, "A History of Facilitated Communication," p. 753.

p. 179, Biklen admits . . .: Biklen, Common Myths.

p. 179, In late 1993 . . . merit being ignored.: K. Frazier, "Media Notes," Skeptical Inquirer, 1994, 18(2), 122.

p. 181, there are controlled studies . . .: Biklen, Common Myths.

p. 181, "scientifically based studies . . .": "Facilitated Communication Scientifically Invalid, APA Says in Statement," Skeptical Inquirer, 1995, 19(1), 6.

p. 181, "facilitated communication . . .": "Facilitated Communication Scientifically Invalid," p. 7.

p. 181, Allegations charging . . .: K. Levine, H. C. Shane, and R. H. Wharton, "What If . . . A Plea to Professionals to Consider the Risk-Benefit Ratio of Facilitated Communication," Mental Retardation, 1994, 32, 300–304; K. N. Margolin, "How Shall Facilitated Communication Be Judged? Facilitated Communication and the Legal System," in H. C. Shane (ed.), Facilitated Communication: The Clinical and Social Phenomenon (San Diego, Calif.: Singular Press, 1994), pp. 227–258; B. Rimland, "Facilitated Communication: Now the Bad News," Autism Research Review International, 1992, 6(1), 3, cited in Jacobson, Mulick, and Schwartz, "A History of Facilitated Communication," p. 756.

p. 182, an FC-related book . . .: A. Madrigal, "Autistic Girl Becomes Her Mother's Spirit Guide," review of A Child of Eternity: An Extraordinary Young

Girl's Message from the World Beyond, by Adriana Rocha and Kristi Jorde, *San Francisco Examiner and Chronicle*, book review section, Oct. 15, 1995, p. 4.

p. 182, *"The uncritical . . ."*: Jacobson, Mulick, and Schwartz, "A History of Facilitated Communication," p. 762.

p. 182, *Treatment or torture?*: R. S. Worrall, "Neural Organization Technique: Treatment or Torture?" *Skeptical Inquirer*, 1990, *15*(1), 40–49.

p. 182, *Techniques include . . .*: S. Barrett, "The Mental Health Maze," in S. Barrett and W. T. Jarvis (eds.), *The Health Robbers: A Close Look at Quackery in America* (Amherst, N.Y.: Prometheus, 1993), pp. 438–439.

p. 183, *As of 1990 . . .*: Worrall, "Treatment or Torture?" p. 41.

p. 183, *Fees for this . . .*: Worrall, "Treatment or Torture?" p. 41; *State of Utah* v. *Wayman et al.*, Civil No. C87–2868, Third Judicial District Court in and for Salt Lake County, temporary restraining order, April 28, 1987.

p. 183, *He promoted his version . . .*: C. A. Ferreri, "Dyslexia and Learning Disabilities Cured," *Health Freedom News*, Oct. 1983, pp. 38, 39; C. A. Ferreri, "Dyslexia and Learning Disabilities Cured," *Digest of Chiropractic Economics*, 1984, *25*, 74–75; C. A. Ferreri and W. B. Wainwright, *Breakthrough for Dyslexia and Learning Disabilities* (Pompano Beach, Fla.: Exposition Press, 1985).

p. 183, *Ferreri has been successful . . .*: Ferreri, "Dyslexia and Learning Disabilities Cured," Oct. 1983, p. 39; Ferreri and Wainwright, *Breakthrough for Dyslexia*, p. 51; *Breakthrough for Dyslexia and Learning Disabilities*, promotional brochure (Brooklyn, N.Y.: Neural Organization Technique Centers, n.d.); Neural Organization Technique Seminar brochure, from the New York Chiropractic College, Glen Head, N.Y., 1987.

p. 183, *One critic comments that these . . .*: L. B. Silver, "The 'Magic Cure': A Review of the Current Controversial Approaches for Treating Learning Disabilities," *Journal of Learning Disabilities*, Oct. 1987, *20*(8), 502.

p. 183, *Ferreri does not offer . . .*: Worrall, "Treatment or Torture?" p. 44.

p. 184, *inconsistent with . . .*: Silver, "The 'Magic Cure,'" p. 501; Worrall, "Treatment or Torture?" p. 44.

p. 184, a hearing panel . . .: In the Matter of Carl A. Ferreri, Original Order No. 4134, report of the Regents Review Committee of the University of the State of New York, July 7, 1986.

p. 184, Ferreri apparently claimed . . . .: "AK Takes Heat as 'NOT' Draws Fire," *Chiropractic Journal*, Dec. 1988, p. 3; Worrall, "Treatment or Torture?" p. 42.

p. 184, Early in the year . . . "exceptional results": Letter to parents on Del Norte County Unified School District letterhead, n.d., in *Harrah and Skaggs* v. *Del Norte Unified School District*, C88–5121-RHS, U.S. District Court, Northern District of California.

p. 185, restraining some Utah chiropractors . . . .: State of Utah v. Wayman et al.

p. 185, "The doctor would press so hard . . .": "AK Takes Heat," p. 3.

p. 185, "If you try . . .": "AK Takes Heat," p. 3.

p. 185, "Two doctors worked . . .": Worrall, "Treatment or Torture?" p. 46.

p. 185, "My heart is ripped . . .": Worrall, "Treatment or Torture?" p. 49.

p. 186, with charges including . . .: Del Norte Judicial District, Justice Court of California County of Del Norte, Case Number 63–77; "AK Takes Heat," p. 3; Worrall, "Treatment or Torture?" p. 43.

p. 186, In 1991 . . .: Barrett, "The Mental Health Maze," p. 439.

p. 186, "I noticed . . .": F. Shapiro, *Eye Movement Desensitization and Reprocessing* (New York: Guilford Press, 1995), p. 2.

p. 187, "stumbled on some . . .": ABC News, "The Healing of a Troubled Mind," *20/20* transcript, 1995.

p. 187, "consistently succeeded . . .": Shapiro, *Eye Movement Desensitization and Reprocessing*, p. 3.

p. 187, By mid-1995 . . .: B. Bower, "Promise and Dissent," *Science News*, 1995, *148*, 270–271, cited in S. O. Lilienfeld, "EMDR Treatment: Less Than Meets the Eye?" *Skeptical Inquirer*, 1996, *20*(1), 25–31.

p. 187, *Shapiro's bio sheet:* "Francine Shapiro," biographical data sheet posted on EMDR Institute home page on the World Wide Web at http://www.octave.com/emdr/shapiro.html.

p. 187, *children as young as two:* Shapiro, *Eye Movement Desensitization and Reprocessing,* p. 280.

p. 188, *when asked by a journalist . . . :* ABC News, "The Healing of a Troubled Mind."

p. 188, *"This results in . . . only one session":* F. Shapiro, "Eye Movement Desensitization: A New Treatment for Posttraumatic Stress Disorder," *Journal of Behavior Therapy and Experimental Psychiatry,* 1989, 20, 211.

p. 188, *"thousands of additional clients . . .":* F. Shapiro, "Eye Movement Desensitization and Reprocessing: A Cautionary Note," *Behavior Therapist,* 1991, 14(8).

p. 188, *During a 20/20 news program . . . :* ABC News, "The Healing of a Troubled Mind."

p. 188, *others comment that . . . :* J. D. Herbert and K. T. Mueser, "What Is EMDR?" *Harvard Mental Health Letter,* 1995, 12(9) p. 8; J. D. Herbert and K. T. Mueser, "Eye Movement Desensitization: A Critique of the Evidence," *Journal of Behavior Therapy and Experimental Psychiatry,* 1992, 23, 173; R. M. Acierno, M. Hersen, V. B. Van Hasselt, G. Tremont, and K. T. Mueser, "Review of the Validation and Dissemination of Eye-Movement Desensitization and Reprocessing: A Scientific and Ethical Dilemma," *Clinical Psychology Review,* 1994, 14, 287–299.

p. 188, *Participants in her workshops . . . :* G. M. Rosen, "A Note to EMDR Critics: What You Didn't See Is Only Part of What You Don't Get," *Behavior Therapist,* 1993, 16, 216; cited in Lilienfeld, "EMDR Treatment: Less Than Meets the Eye?" p. 30.

p. 190, *"EMDR has the potential . . .":* Shapiro, *Eye Movement Desensitization and Reprocessing,* p. 370.

p. 190, *"with more highly . . .":* Shapiro, *Eye Movement Desensitization and Reprocessing,* p. 372.

p. 190, *noting eleven situations:* Shapiro, *Eye Movement Desensitization and Reprocessing,* p. 367.

p. 190, *"Information is stored . . .":* Shapiro, *Eye Movement Desensitization and Reprocessing,* p. 40.

p. 190, *"It seems to . . .":* ABC News, "The Healing of a Troubled Mind."

p. 190, *"may mystify even . . .":* Lilienfeld, "EMDR Treatment: Less Than Meets the Eye?" p. 27.

p. 190, *"The system may . . .":* F. Shapiro, "EMDR: In the Eye of a Paradigm Shift," *Behavior Therapist,* 1994, *17,* 153.

p. 190, *"EMDR has undergone . . .":* Shapiro, *Eye Movement Desensitization and Reprocessing,* p. 370.

p. 191, *"theories that explain why . . .":* Shapiro, *Eye Movement Desensitization and Reprocessing,* p. 309.

p. 191, *"Nobody experienced . . .":* G. M. Rosen, "On the Origin of Eye Movement Desensitization," *Journal of Behavior Therapy and Experimental Psychiatry,* 1995, *26*(2), 122.

p. 191, *Rosen concluded . . . :* G. M. Rosen, "On the Origin of Eye Movement Desensitization," p. 121.

p. 191, *its success "may be . . .":* "Eye Movement Desensitization and Reprocessing (EMDR)." Description on the World Wide Web home page of Mental Research Institute of Palo Alto, Calif., where Shapiro is senior research fellow, found at http://www.webcom/~smartbiz/mri/emdr.html.

p. 191, *"dismantling" studies:* See Lilienfeld, "EMDR Treatment: Less Than Meets the Eye?" p. 29; G. Renfrey and C. R. Spates, "Eye Movement Desensitization: A Partial Dismantling Study," *Journal of Behavior Therapy and Experimental Psychiatry,* 1994, *25,* 231–239.

p. 192, *"EMDR may seem . . .":* Herbert and Mueser, *Harvard Mental Health Letter,* p. 8.

p. 193, as was recently highlighted: F. Cavaliere, "EMDR Remains Controversial," *APA Monitor,* Aug. 1995.

p. 193, they're not sure how: F. Cavaliere, "Team Works to Quell Stress in Bosnia," *APA Monitor,* Aug. 1995.

p. 194, "Do you know . . .": F. Shapiro, "Doing Our Homework," *Networker,* Sept./Oct. 1995, p. 50.

p. 195, "in 1990, Americans made . . .": S. Barrett, "Quackery and the Media," in Barrett and Jarvis (eds.), *The Health Robbers,* p. 450.

Chapter Nine

p. 197, A recently published study showed . . .: M. Olfson and H. A. Pincus, "Outpatient Psychotherapy in the United States, I. Volume, Costs, and User Characteristics. II. Patterns of Utilization," *American Journal of Psychiatry,* Sept. 1994, *151*(9), 1281–1288, 1289–1294.

p. 197, according to a 1994 survey . . .: M.E.P. Seligman, "The Effectiveness of Psychotherapy," *American Psychologist,* Dec. 1995, pp. 965–974.

p. 203, "firestarters, alien . . .": D. Bischoff, "X-Files: Behind the Scenes of TV's Hottest Show," *Omni,* Dec. 1994, p. 44.

p. 203, "Not since the advent . . .": Bischoff, "X-Files," p. 44.

p. 203, President Clinton met with . . .: A. Devroy, "Seeking Answers, Clinton Consults New Age Gurus," *San Francisco Chronicle,* Jan. 4, 1995, p. A3.

p. 204, the New York Academy of Sciences . . . as valid as science: New York Times article reprinted as "Scientists Fear Flight from Rational Thought," *San Francisco Chronicle,* June 6, 1995, p. A11.

Further Reading

Against Therapy, by Jeffrey M. Masson. Monroe, Maine: Common Courage Press, 1994.

Anger: The Misunderstood Emotion, by Carol Tavris. New York: Touchstone, 1989.

Beware the Talking Cure, by Terence W. Campbell. Boca Raton, Fla.: Upton Books, 1994.

Captive Hearts, Captive Minds: Freedom and Recovery from Cults and Abusive Relationships, by Madeleine Tobias and Janja Lalich. Alameda, Calif.: Hunter House, 1994.

Channeling into the New Age: The "Teachings" of Shirley MacLaine and Other Such Gurus, by Henry Gordon. Amherst, N.Y.: Prometheus, 1988.

Cults in Our Midst: The Hidden Menace in Our Everyday Lives, by Margaret Thaler Singer with Janja Lalich. San Francisco: Jossey-Bass, 1995.

The Demon-Haunted World: Science as a Candle in the Dark, by Carl Sagan. New York: Random House, 1995.

Flim-Flam: Psychics, ESP, Unicorns and Other Delusions, by James Randi. Amherst, N.Y.: Prometheus, 1986.

The Fringes of Reason: A Field Guide to New Age Frontiers, Unusual Beliefs and Eccentric Sciences, edited by Ted Schultz. New York: Harmony Books, 1989.

Hidden Memories: Voices and Visions from Within, by Robert A. Baker. Amherst, N.Y.: Prometheus, 1992.

House of Cards: Psychology and Psychotherapy Built on Myth, by Robyn M. Dawes. New York: Free Press, 1994.

Influence: The New Psychology of Modern Persuasion, by Robert B. Cialdini. New York: Quill, 1984.

Making Monsters: False Memories, Psychotherapy, and Sexual Hysteria, by Richard Ofshe and Ethan Watters. New York: Scribner, 1994.

The Memory Wars: Freud's Legacy in Dispute, by Frederick Crews and His Critics. New York: New York Review of Books, 1995.

The Myth of Repressed Memory: False Memory and Allegations of Sexual Abuse, by Elizabeth Loftus and Katherine Ketcham. New York: St. Martin's Press, 1994.

Psychobabble, by R. D. Rosen. New York: Avon, 1977.

The Psychological Society: A Critical Analysis of Psychiatry, Psychotherapy, Psychoanalysis and the Psychological Revolution, by Martin L. Gross. New York: Random House, 1978.

Psychotherapy: The Hazardous Cure, by Dorothy Tennov. Garden City, N.Y.: Anchor Books, 1976.

Satanic Panic: The Creation of a Contemporary Legend, by Jeffrey S. Victor. Chicago: Open Court, 1993.

Satan's Silence: Ritual Abuse and the Making of a Modern American Witch Hunt, by Debbie Nathan and Michael Snedeker. New York: Basic Books, 1995.

Sex in the Forbidden Zone: When Men in Power—Therapists, Doctors, Clergy, Teachers, and Others—Betray Women's Trust, by Peter Rutter. Los Angeles: Tarcher, 1989.

Suggestions of Abuse: True and False Memories of Childhood Sexual Trauma, by Michael D. Yapko. New York: Simon & Schuster, 1994.

Therapist: The Shocking Autobiography of a Woman Sexually Exploited by Her Analyst, by Ellen Plasil. New York: St. Martin's/Marek, 1985.

Therapy Gone Mad: The True Story of Hundreds of Patients and a Generation of Betrayal, by Carol Lynn Mithers. Reading, Mass.: Addison-Wesley, 1994.

Understanding the New Age, by Russell Chandler. Grand Rapids, Mich.: Zondervan, 1993.

Victims of Memory: Incest Accusations and Shattered Lives, by Mark Pendergrast. Hinesburg, Vt.: Upper Access Books, 1995.

You Must Be Dreaming, by Barbara Noël with Kathryn Watterson. New York: Poseidon, 1992.

The Authors

Margaret Thaler Singer is a clinical psychologist and emeritus adjunct professor of the Department of Psychology, University of California, Berkeley. She received her doctoral degree in clinical psychology from the University of Denver, and has been a practicing clinician, researcher, and teacher for more than fifty years. She has taught diagnosis and therapy to countless psychologists, psychiatrists, social workers, and counselors, and has been a consultant to many agencies.

Singer is coauthor (with Janja Lalich) of *Cults in Our Midst: The Hidden Menace in Our Everyday Lives* (Jossey-Bass, 1995) and has written more than one hundred articles and chapters published in professional journals and anthologies. Over the past two decades, Singer has been an active consultant and expert witness in many legal cases and has appeared frequently on television and radio discussing influence, persuasion, therapy, and general psychological issues of the day. She has done research on the relation of stress to health, on schizophrenics and their families, on the influence process in psychotherapy, and on the extreme stresses experienced by prisoners of war, hostages, civilians, and military personnel.

Singer has received numerous national awards for her research work, including awards from the American Psychiatric Association, the Society for Clinical and Experimental Hypnosis, the American College of Psychiatrists, the National Mental Health Association, the American Association for Marriage and Family Therapy, and the American Family Therapy Association. She received the Leo J. Ryan Memorial Award for her work with former cult members, and was a Lubin Memorial Lecturer at the Naval Health Research Center. She also held a Research Scientist Award from the National Institute of Mental Health. She was the first woman and first clinical psychologist elected president of the American Psychosomatic Society.

Singer lives in Berkeley, California, with her husband, Jay, a physicist whose special contributions have been in the development of magnetic resonance imaging. Her son is a public relations and political consultant, and her daughter is a resident in orthopedic surgery. Singer is the happy grandmother of twin boys, James and Nicholas.

Janja Lalich is an educator and consultant in the field of cults and psychological persuasion. She specializes in helping people who have been psychologically exploited or abused in either a group or a one-on-one situation. She received her B.A. degree in French from the University of Wisconsin, Madison, and spent the following year in Aix-en-Provence, France, doing postgraduate research as a Fulbright scholar.

Author, lecturer, and recognized cult information specialist, Lalich has lectured widely and been interviewed nationally and internationally about the prevalence of cultic groups and psychological con artists in our society, the risks of involvement with them, and the aftereffects of these experiences. She has also written about her personal experience of more than ten years as a member of a political cult. She has given numerous public seminars and has led or participated in many preventive-education workshops for civic, professional, religious, and campus organizations. She has also served as a consultant to attorneys and mediators in cult-related and undue-influence litigation. Lalich is the coordinator and co-facilitator of a local support group for people coming out of cultic or psychologically abusive situations.

Lalich is coauthor of two books: *Cults in Our Midst: The Hidden Menace in Our Everyday Lives* (with Margaret Singer, Jossey-Bass, 1995), and *Captive Hearts, Captive Minds: Freedom and Recovery from Cults and Abusive Relationships* (with Madeleine Tobias, Hunter House, 1994). She wrote a chapter in *Recovery from Cults: Help for Victims of Psychological and Spiritual Abuse* (Norton, 1993), and has been published in *Women and Therapy, Creation Spirituality,* and the *Cultic Studies Journal,* among others. For her numerous contributions exposing the exploitative nature of cults, Lalich received the 1995 Media Award from the Cult Awareness Network.

Lalich lives in Alameda, California, with her partner, Kim, and their dogs, Lucy and Rikki.

About the Cartoonist

Jim Coughenour is an artist and writer living in San Francisco. His cartoons, fiction, and reviews have appeared in publications ranging from academic journals to scabrous zines. He is the creator of Daimonix Raw Art Cards and the author of the itty-bitty book *Instant Noir: Savage Tales for Short Attentions.* Some of his more ludic work may be viewed on the Internet at http://www.daimonix.com.

Index